## What They Say about Us

*"One organization with a long record of success in helping people find jobs is The Five O'Clock Club."*

FORTUNE

*"Many managers left to fend for themselves are turning to the camaraderie offered by [The Five O'Clock Club]. Members share tips and advice, and hear experts."*

The Wall Street Journal

*"If you have been out of work for some time . . . consider The Five O'Clock Club."*

The New York Times

*"Wendleton has reinvented the historic gentlemen's fraternal oasis and built it into a chain of strategy clubs for job seekers."*

The Philadelphia Inquirer

*"Organizations such as The Five O'Clock Club are building . . . an extended professional family."*

Jessica Lipnack, author, *Professional Teams*

*"[The Five O'Clock Club] will ask not what you do, but 'What do you want to do?' . . . [And] don't expect to get any great happy hour drink specials at this joint. The seminars are all business."*

The Washington Times

*"The Five O'Clock Club's proven philosophy is that job hunting is a learned skill like any other. The Five O'Clock Club becomes the engine that drives [your] search."*

Black Enterprise

*"Job hunting is a science at The Five O'Clock Club. [Members] find the discipline, direction and much-needed support that keeps a job search on track."*

Modern Maturity

*"Wendleton tells you how to beat the odds—even in an economy where pink slips are more common than perks. Her savvy and practical guide[s] are chockablock with sample résumés, cover letters, worksheets, negotiating tips, networking suggestions and inspirational quotes from such far-flung achievers as Abraham Lincoln, Malcolm Forbes, and Lily Tomlin."*

Working Woman

*"On behalf of eight million New Yorkers, I commend and thank The Five O'Clock Club. Keep the faith and keep America working!"*

David N. Dinkins, former mayor, City of New York

## What Job Hunters Say

*"During the time I was looking for a job I kept Kate's books by my bed. I read a little every night, a little every morning. Her common-sense advice, methodical approach, and hints for keeping the spirits up were extremely useful."*

Harold Levine, coordinator, Yale Alumni Career Resource Network

*"I've just been going over the books with my daughter, who is 23 and finally starting to think she ought to have a career. She won't listen to anything I say, but you she believes."*

Newspaper columnist

*"Thank you, Kate, for all your help. I ended up with four offers and at least 15 compliments in two months. Thanks!"*

President and CEO, large banking organization

*"I have doubled my salary during the past five years by using The Five O'Clock Club techniques. Now I earn what I deserve. I think everyone needs The Five O'Clock Club."*

M. S., attorney, entertainment industry

*"I dragged myself to my first meeting, totally demoralized. Ten weeks later, I chose from among job offers and started a new life. Bless you!*

Senior editor, not-for-profit

*"I'm an artistic person, and I don't think about business. Kate provided the disciplined business approach so I could practice my art. After adopting her system, I landed a role on Broadway in* Hamlet."

Bruce Faulk, actor

*"I've referred at least a dozen people to The Five O'Clock Club since I was there. The Club was a major factor in getting my dream job, which I am now in."*

B. R., research head

*"My Five O'Clock Club coach was a God-send!!! She is truly one of the most dynamic and qualified people I've ever met. Without her understanding and guidance, I wouldn't have made the steps I've made toward my goals."*

Operating room nurse

*"The Five O'Clock Club has been a fantastic experience for my job search. I couldn't have done it without you. Keep up the good work."*

Former restaurant owner, who found his dream job with an organization that advises small businesses

## What Human Resources Executives Say about The Five O'Clock Club Outplacement

*"**This thing works.** I saw a structured, yet nurturing, environment where individuals searching for jobs positioned themselves for success. I saw 'accountability' in a nonintimidating environment. I was struck by the support and willingness to encourage those who had just started the process by the group members who had been there for a while."*

Employee relations officer, financial services organization

*"**Wow! I was immediately struck by the electric atmosphere** and people's commitment to following the program. Job hunters reported on where they were in their searches and what they had accomplished the previous week. The overall environment fosters sharing and mutual learning."*

Head of human resources, major law firm

*"The Five O'Clock Club program is **far more effective** than conventional outplacement. Excellent materials, effective coaching and nanosecond responsiveness combine to get people focused on the central tasks of the job search. Selecting The Five O'Clock Outplacement Program was one of my best decisions this year."*

Senior. vice president, human resources, manufacturing company

*"**You have made me look like a real genius** in recommending The Five O'Clock Club [to our divisions around the country]!"*

Senior. vice president, human resources, major publishing firm

The Five O'Clock Club®

Advising Professionals, Managers, and Executives for Over 25 Years

# LAUNCHING THE RIGHT CAREER

KATE WENDLETON

THOMSON™
DELMAR LEARNING

Australia Canada Mexico Singapore Spain United Kingdom United States

**Launching the Right Career**
Kate Wendleton

**Vice President, Career Education SBU:**
Dawn Gerrain

**Director of Editorial:**
Sherry Gomoll

**Acquisitions Editor:**
Martine Edwards

**Developmental Editor:**
Kristen Shenfield

**Editorial Assistant:**
Jennifer Anderson

**Director of Production:**
Wendy A. Troeger

**Production Manager:**
J.P. Henkel

**Production Editor:**
Rebecca Goldthwaite

**Director of Marketing:**
Wendy E. Mapstone

**Marketing Specialist:**
Gerard McAvey

**Marketing Coordinator:**
Erica Conley

**Cover Design:**
TDB Publishing Services



Printed in Canada
1 2 3 4 5 XXX 09 08 07 06 05

Thomson Delmar Learning is a part of The Thomson Corporation. Thomson, the Star logo, and Delmar Learning are trademarks used herein under license.

For more information contact Thomson Delmar Learning, Executive Woods, 5 Maxwell Drive, Clifton Park, NY 12065-2919.

Or find us on the World Wide Web at
www.thomsonlearning.com, www.delmarlearning.com, or www.careersuccess.delmar.com



Library of Congress Cataloging-in-Publication Data

Wendleton, Kate.
Launching the right career / Kate Wendleton.
p. cm.
"The Five O'Clock Club."
Includes index.
ISBN 1–4180–1505–9
1. Vocational guidance." 2. Career development. I. Five O'Clock Club (New York, N.Y.) II. Title.

HF5381.W437 2006
650.1–dc22 2005050689

**NOTICE TO THE READER**

For college students, recent grads, and
those who now want a career instead of a job.

*For I know the plans I have for you,*
*declares the Lord, plans to prosper you*
*and not to harm you, plans to give you*
*hope and a future.*

Jeremiah 29:11

# Preface

Dear Member or Prospective Member of The Five O'Clock Club:

This book is for students, recent grads, and those who now want a career instead of a job. Students typically don't have time to search, don't know how to search, and don't plan for the long term. You (or your mom and dad) paid tens of thousands of dollars for college, and now you don't want to drop the ball when it comes to using that education in the best way possible. Not only do most colleges fail to help young adults face the job market—where is Career Planning 101?—most résumés of new grads look exactly alike!

Recent grads are often busy working. I know you're busy. That's why we have this one book, based on 14 years of research, to help you along.

Then there are those poor folks who perhaps got started on the wrong foot, took a job that led to one job after another—and never got started on a *career.* There's hope. It's not too late to have a career instead of a job, and the stories in this book should inspire you.

A small amount of time with a career counselor or doing the exercises in this book can help anyone decide on at least a tentative career direction. You can develop a résumé that differentiates you from the thousands of other grads competing in the job market. And small-group strategy sessions (especially those offered at The Five O'Clock Club) can help immeasurably.

For starters, I suggest you look at Julie's before and after résumés in Part 4, "Building a Great Résumé." I'm sure you will be stunned when you see them and be convinced that this is no ordinary job-search book. The "before" résumé shows how college students, recent grads, and those with no career path typically do their résumés. Then we show you The Five O'Clock Club way. Make no mistake about it: The way you present yourself in your résumé will affect your ability to get interviews and even guide the interviewing process.

You probably think there is only one best way to get interviews in your target market. You may personally believe ads are best for you, or search firms or networking. You are probably incorrect. Chances are, the technique that helped you get your last job or internship will not be the best technique for you this time around. The situation has changed. You have more (or at least different experience) to offer, the kind of job you want next may have changed, and the job market has certainly changed.

Luckily, we have spent the over 25-plus years researching and keeping up-to-date on the job-search techniques that work. You can benefit from our efforts on your behalf. It is very difficult for job searchers themselves to know which techniques will work best this time around. Therefore, we suggest you take an organized, methodical, *research* approach to your own search. Observe what is working for you and what is not—and do more of whatever is working. We'll show you how.

There are four basic techniques for getting meetings in your target market: search firms, ads (in print, online, and through your school), networking, and contacting companies directly. We urge you to consider all four techniques—and their variations—for your search. The best searches rely on two or more techniques for getting meetings.

Chances are, you are going after published job *openings* rather than unpublished job *possibilities.* If you chase advertised openings, you will automatically have competition for those openings. We suggest that you develop more *possibilities.* This means contacting hiring managers who do not happen to have an opening right now but would *love to* have someone like you on board. Then we'll want you to keep in touch with those managers (we'll tell you how) and develop 6 to 10 similar contacts.

This may sound like a lot of work, but it's a lot less work than applying for openings and continually being rejected (or, worse yet, taking the wrong job and ending up on the wrong path). As a matter of course, Five O'Clock Clubbers regularly develop 6 to 10 leads—and more. We want them to wind up with 3 concurrent job offers so they will have a choice. You can do this, too.

We found that there is no one job-hunting technique that always works. Job-hunting formulas hold true in the aggregate, but may not for a specific situation. The techniques that work depend, to a large extent, on the industry being pursued, the kind of job you want within that industry, and your own style and personality.

This book gives you guidelines, but also offers flexibility in deciding which job-hunting approach is right for you. When you understand what is happening and why, you will be in a better position to plan your own job-hunting campaign and rely less on chance or on what a specific expert tells you.

Job hunting can be thought of as a project—much like any project you might handle in school or in your regular job. Most of the approaches in this book are businesslike rather than intensely psychological. Thinking of job hunting in a business type of way allows you to use the problem-solving skills you might use at work.

I feel duty-bound to address the issue of career planning. Most people are interested in job-hunting techniques but don't want to give much thought to what they should do with their *lives.* So be sure to do the Seven Stories Exercise and the Forty-Year Vision to make sure your career is heading in the right direction. When you uncover what it is you want to do long term, then you can look for a job that will take you in that direction.

This book is the result of years of research into how successful job hunters land the best jobs at the best pay, and provides the most detailed explanation of the search process.

We want to stay with you throughout your career. As you grow in experience and education, you will work with Five O'Clock Club consultants and fellow members who are right for you. After all, no matter how young or old you are, this is the *beginning* for you. You don't want just any old job. This is the start of your *career.* We'll be there with you every step of the way.

Cheers, God bless, and good luck!

Kate Wendleton
New York City, 2005
*www.fiveoclockclub.com*

# Contents

## PART SIX Getting What You Want:

*(THE FIVE O'CLOCK CLUB APPROACH TO INTERVIEWING AND NEGOTIATING)*

# PART ONE

# The Changing Job Market

## HOW IT WORKS TODAY

# You and the Job Market

*I'm going to fight hard.*
*I'm going to give them hell.*

Harry S Truman
Remark on the presidential campaign, August 1948

## Bad Market for Career Starters? Oh, It's Not Horrible

Just a few years ago, young people expected to earn millions in Internet jobs and retire by 30. They snubbed their noses at the brick-and-mortar folks, who seemed *hopelessly lost*. There was a labor shortage—fueled in part by the dot-com hiring.

Young people were in demand—and they were demanding: "Challenge me." "Meet my spiritual needs." Some showed up for interviews in sandals or with pierced tongues. Others did not show up at all.

Because of the labor shortage, companies were forced to hire anyone they could. Young people got lots of offers, and they attributed this to their own brilliance. Of course, it was"the economy, stupid."

Ah, the market comes and goes. Sometimes young people are in demand. Other times, companies decide to cut back younger workers (last in, first out) or not hire them at all.

## What Can a Young Person Do?

Young people need to search the way the rest of us do: Be more expansive. Julie, whose story you can read about in this book, contacted 205 architectural firms, landing four terrific offers. Of the firms she contacted, 75 percent were in a major metropolitan area and 25 percent in the burbs. Interestingly, all nine responses and four offers were from firms in remote areas. Young people need to contact firms that are off the beaten path. Here are a few other tips:

- Don't just go after just the companies of your dreams. Make an A list, a B list, a C list. Get offers from all of them. This increases your chance of getting a dream job.
- Follow up using letters and phone calls. Let employers know you are really interested.
- Get real work experience throughout your college years. Anyone who works at summer camps for four years is unlikely to get a good job after graduation.
- Look for paid work if you need it. Some students can take unpaid internships, but most have to work at real jobs for real money because college tuition has skyrocketed.
- Look and dress seriously. Ties for young men; female equivalent for young women: no bare midriffs.
- Don't just chase the money. Pay your dues; think long term; build a career. Don't go into investment banking just because your parents want you to or all your friends are.
- Don't use your age (young or old) as an excuse. Maybe the problem is something else. Try to figure out what it is. At The Five O'Clock

Club, younger people who work the system are finding good work.

## Things Aren't All That Bad

It's no longer enough to talk to four companies and then expect four offers. What about people who earned great money and got laid off? How can they make what they were making before?

That's the wrong question. Instead, they should hope to get paid at market rates. If you get paid above market, you're likely to get fired quickly. Many were paid extraordinary sums at dot-coms: Companies were spending investor money, and there was a labor shortage. Now, everyone has to come down to earth. It's really not a bad place to be.

## More Competition

A higher percentage of the population is graduating from college than ever before. *Simply having a college degree does not separate you from your competition.* **You have to be sharper**. In today's ever-changing economy, job hunters face greater competition for the jobs that are available. Your prospective employers have to be more serious about every position they fill. You, too, must take your job hunt more seriously.

---

*Security is mostly a superstition. It does not exist in nature, nor do the children of men as a whole experience it. Avoiding danger is no safer in the long run than outright exposure. Life is either a daring adventure or nothing.*

Helen Keller

## Don't Be Scared by the Headlines

*Labor is the superior of capital, and deserves much the higher consideration.*

Abraham Lincoln

Job hunters are starting to realize that a large number of people may be laid off in one part of an organization, while different kinds of people are hired in other parts of the same organization. You will hear about the layoffs in the news, but you will not hear about the hiring—the organization would be deluged with résumés.

Get used to the headlines. Organizations must react quickly to changing world circumstances, and they no longer have time to figure out where the laid-off people could fit into other parts of the same organization. Some organizations now allow laid-off employees to job-hunt both inside and outside the organization. It can be an efficient way for the organization to change direction and save perhaps 10 percent of the laid off employees who can fit into the new direction.

The laid-off employee is usually able to find a position outside more quickly because, by definition, there are more positions outside. No matter how big the old organization is, it is smaller than the outside world. Smart employees would devote 10 percent of their efforts to an inside search, and 90 percent outside.

## A Changing Economy

Today, we know that doing a good job is not enough. Our career prospects can now change for reasons that have nothing to do with our personal job performance but with the performance of our employers. It's a new economy—a world economy—and the changes are not going to slow down. Not only will things not return to the way they were, the amount of change will increase.

Government statistics show the impact of change on job hunters.

### The Average American Has Been in His or Her Job Only Four Years

The average American getting out of college today can expect to have five careers during his or her lifetime—that's not five jobs, but five separate careers!

You will probably have 12 to 15 jobs in the course of your 5 careers.

## Ten Years from Now, Half the Working Population Will Be in Jobs That Have Not Yet Been Invented

Let's make that more personal: Ten years from now, half the people reading this book will be in jobs that do not exist today. That's okay. We'll tell you where some of the new jobs are, but you'll have to do research as well.

A few smart organizations have wisely embraced a process of helping employees take charge of their own careers. Most of us, however, will have to develop career plans on our own, and this book can help you do just that.

## Continual Career Development: An Enlightened Approach

All of this fits in with what we have taught at The Five O'Clock Club since 1978: It is best for both the employee and the employer if *job hunting* is seen as a continual process—and not just something that happens when a person wants to change jobs. **Continual job search means continually being aware of market conditions both inside and outside our present organizations and continually learning what we have to offer—to both markets.**

With this approach, workers are safer because they are more likely to keep their present jobs longer: They learn to change and grow as the organization and industry do. And if they have to go elsewhere, they will be more marketable. Organizations are better off because employees who know what is going on outside their insular halls are smarter, more sophisticated, and more proactive, and they make the organization more competitive.

The economy is changing too fast for you to use the same old career planning techniques or the same old attitudes about job hunting.

## The Good Old Days: People Were Stuck

I remember the *good old days*—the days of one employer and one career. It used to be that when you found a job, you had found a home. You expected to get in there, do what the organization wanted, learn to play the game, rise through the ranks, and eventually retire. People had secure jobs with large, stable employers.

People may have had job security, but the downside is that they were often stuck. Changing jobs was frowned upon. For every satisfied person, there was someone stifled, who knew he or she had made a dreadful mistake.

Today, many of us might fear losing our jobs, even from week to week, but *no one—absolutely* no one—needs to feel stifled, deadened, or stuck in a career they no longer find satisfying. *Everyone has an opportunity to do something that is better.*

*People are always blaming their circumstances for what they are. I don't believe in circumstances. The people who get on in this world are the people who get up and look for the circumstances they want, and if they can't find them, make them.*

George Bernard Shaw

## Understanding How the Job-Hunting Market Works

Knowing why things work the way they do will give you flexibility and control over your job hunt. Knowing how the hiring system works will help you understand why things go right and why they go wrong—why certain things work and others don't. Then you can modify the system to fit your own needs, temperament, and the workings of the job market you are interested in.

It is overly simplistic to say that only one job-hunting system works. The job-selection process is more complicated than that. Employers can do what they want. You need to understand the process from their point of view. Then you can plan your own job hunt, in your own industry. You will learn how to compete in this market.

Always remember, **the best jobs don't necessarily go to the most qualified people, but to the people who are the best job hunters**. You'll increase your chances of finding the job you want by using a methodical job-hunting approach.

## The Only Port in This Storm: You

"They" cannot offer you job security or even a career direction. The rules have changed very quickly, and they expect you to adapt very quickly.

**If you don't plan your own path through all of this, you will continue to be thrown around by the turbulence**. The better you understand yourself—your motivations, skills, and interests—the more solid your foundation will be.

If you have done the exercises in this book—especially the Seven Stories—you will understand your own value, and your self-esteem is more likely to remain intact. You will keep yourself on course and continue to follow your plan. Otherwise, in our world of revolving bosses—whether you are on payroll or not—you will come across a shallow, rough person who does not understand your value.

The better you are at plotting out your own future, the more you will get out of each of your jobs or assignments. Each one will fit in with your long-term vision, and you will not get so ruffled by corporate politics and pettiness. You will be following your own vision.

## Changes Mean New Opportunities

The world is changing. What's hot today is not tomorrow. You can use these changes to your advantage. You can choose to head your career in the direction that's right for you.

You can impose your own terms upon life. You don't have to accept the terms it offers you. Read on, and see what others have done.

---

*Alice said nothing: she had sat down with her face in her hands, wondering if anything would ever happen in a natural way again.*

Lewis Carroll, *Alice in Wonderland*

# Job Hunting versus Career Planning

*Most people say their main fault is a lack of discipline. On deeper thought, I believe that is not the case. The basic problem is that their priorities have not become deeply planted in their hearts and minds.*

Stephen R. Covey,
*The Seven Habits of Highly Effective People*

*For most of us, it is easier to think about how to get what we want than to know what exactly we should want.*

Robert N. Bellah et al.,
*Habits of the Heart*

You are probably reading this because you want a job. But you will most likely have to find another job after that one, and maybe after that. After all, the average American has been in his or her job only four years. To make smoother transitions, learn to plan ahead.

If you have a vision and keep it in mind, you can continually *position* yourself for your long-range goal by taking jobs and assignments that lead you there. Then your next job will be more than just a job. It will be a stepping-stone on the way to something bigger and better.

When faced with a choice, **select the job that fits best with your Forty-Year Vision—the job that positions you best for the long term**.

It takes less than an hour to make up a rudimentary Forty-Year Vision. But it is perhaps the single most important criterion for selecting jobs. Do the exercise quickly. Later, you can refine it and test it against reality. Do the Forty-Year Vision using the worksheet in this book. This is exactly what helped the people in the following case studies. **All of the people described are real people, and what happened to them is true**.

## CASE STUDY *Harry*

### Stuck in a Lower Level Job

Harry was a window washer for the casinos, earning an excellent hourly salary. The pay was high because the building was slanted, making the job more dangerous.

Harry did a great job; he was responsible and well-liked. He was offered a supervisory position, which could lead to other casino jobs. But the base pay was less than his current pay including overtime, and it allowed for no overtime pay. Harry decided he could not afford to make the move and stayed as a window washer paid by the hour. Today, several years later, he still cleans windows.

There's nothing wrong with washing windows or any other occupation. But if you make choices based on short-term gain, be aware that you may be closing off certain options for your future.

**Sometimes we have to make short-term sacrifices to get ahead—if indeed we *want* to get ahead**.

## Selecting the Right Offer

Doing the exercises will give you some perspective when choosing among job offers. I hope that you will attempt to get 6 to 10 job possibilities in the works (knowing that 5 will fall away through no fault of your own). Then, most likely you will wind up with 3 offers at approximately the same time.

If you have three offers, the one to choose is the one that positions you best for the long run.

## People Who Have Goals Do Better

Money is not the only measure of success. When you have a clear, long-term goal, it can affect everything: your hobbies and interests, what you read, the people to whom you are attracted. Those who have a vision do better at reaching their goals, no matter what those goals are. A vision gives you hope and direction. It lets you see that you have plenty of time—no matter how young or how old you are.

---

*The psychic task which a person can and must set for himself is not to feel secure, but to be able to tolerate insecurity, without panic and undue fear.*

Erich Fromm, *The Sane Society*

## CASE STUDY *Bill Clinton*

### A Clear Vision

Bill Clinton is a good example of the power of having a vision. A small-town boy, Bill decided in his teens that he wanted to become president. He developed his vision and worked his entire life to make that dream come true.

## CASE STUDY *Bruce*

### Plenty of Time

Bruce—"young, gifted, and black"—was doing little to advance his career. Like many aspiring actors, he worked at odd jobs to survive and auditioned for parts when he could.

But, in fact, Bruce spent little time auditioning or improving his craft because he was too busy trying to make ends meet. What's more, he had recently been devastated by a girlfriend.

Using The Five O'Clock Club assessment, Bruce realized he was going nowhere. His first reaction was to attempt to do everything at once: quit his part-time jobs, become a film and stage director, and patch things up with his girlfriend. With the help of the Forty-Year Vision, Bruce discovered that his current girlfriend was not right for him in the long run and that he had plenty of time left in his life to act, direct, and raise a family.

Because of his vision, Bruce knew what to do next to get ahead. He was prompted to look for a good agent (just like a job hunt) and take other steps for his career. Six months later, Bruce landed a role in *Hamlet* on Broadway. He is on tour with another play now.

---

*A man may not achieve everything he has dreamed, but he will never achieve anything great without having dreamed it first.*

William James

## CASE STUDY *Sophie*

### Making *Life* Changes First

Sophie, age 22, had a low-level office job, wanted a better one, and did the assessment.

She did her Forty-Year Vision but was depressed by it. Like many who feel stuck, Sophie imagined the same uninspiring situation from year to year. It seemed her life would never change.

With encouragement and help, she did the exercise again and let her dreams come out, no matter how implausible they seemed. She saw herself eventually in a different kind of life. Although she initially did the exercise because she wanted to change jobs, she saw she needed to change other things first.

She moved away from a bad situation at home, got her own apartment, broke up with the destructive boyfriend she had been seeing for eight years, and enrolled in night school. It took her two years to take these first steps.

She is now working toward her long-term goal of becoming a teacher and educational filmmaker. She says that she is off the treadmill and effortlessly making progress.

---

*It's time to move from a consumer mentality to a producer mentality. In school, you were the consumer; in the labor force, you are the producer.*

Dr. Richard Bayer

## Thinking Big; Thinking Small

A Forty-Year Vision gives you perspective. Without one, you may think too small or too big. Writing it down makes you more reasonable, more thoughtful, and more serious. **Having a vision also makes you less concerned about the progress of others because you know where *you* are going**.

**Consider Objective and Subjective Information**

**If you tend to pay too much attention to subjective information, balance it by asking: "What is the logical thing for me to do regardless of how I feel?"**
**If you tend to be too objective, ask: "I know the logical thing to do, but how do I really feel about it?"**

CASE STUDY *Dean*

## Expect to Be Paid Fairly

Dean had been making $40,000. He lost his job and uncovered two choices: one at $45,000 and one at $60,000. He asked to meet with me.

Dean was not worth $60,000 at this stage in his career, and I told him so. In addition, that organization was not a good fit for him.

The $45,000 job seemed just right for Dean. He had an engineering degree, and the work dealt with high-tech products.

Yet he took the $60,000 position. Within four months, he was fired.

Dean met with me again to discuss two more possibilities: another position for $60,000 and one at a much lower salary. Since he had most recently been making $60,000, interviewers thought perhaps he was worth it. Again, he opted for the $60,000 position—he liked making that kind of money. Again he could not live up to that salary, and again he was fired.

## Life Skills, Not Just Job-Hunting Skills

A vision helps people see ahead and realize that they can not only advance in their careers but also change their life circumstances—such as who their friends are and where they live.

Your career is not separate from your life. If you dream of living in a better place, you have to earn more money. If you would like to be with better types of people, you need to **become a better type of person yourself**.

The Forty-Year Vision cannot be done in a vacuum. **Research is the key to *achieving* your vision. Without research, it is difficult to imagine what might be out there, or to imagine dream situations**. Be sure to read the two chapters on research in this book.

## Optimism Emerges as Best Predictor to Success in Life

"Hope has proven a powerful predictor of outcome in every study we've done so far," said Dr. Charles R. Snyder, a psychologist at the University of Kansas. . . . "Having hope means believing you have both the will and the way to accomplish your goals, whatever they may be. . . . It's not enough to just have the wish for something. You need the means, too. On the other hand, all the skills to solve a problem won't help if you don't have the willpower to do it."

Dr. Snyder found that people with high levels of hope share several attributes.

- Unlike people who are low in hope, they turn to friends for advice on how to achieve their goals.
- They tell themselves they can succeed at what they need to do.
- Even in a tight spot, they tell themselves things will get better as time goes on.
- They are flexible enough to find different ways to get to their goals.
- If hope for one goal fades, they aim for another. Those low on hope tend to become fixated on one goal and persist even when they find themselves blocked. They just stay at it and get frustrated.
- They show an ability to break a formidable task into specific, achievable chunks. People low in hope see only the large goal and not the small steps to it along the way.

People who get a high score on the hope scale have had as many hard times as those with low scores but have learned to think about it in a hopeful way, seeing a setback as a challenge, not a failure.

Daniel Goleman,
*The New York Times,*
December 24, 1991

**Whatever your level,**
**to get ahead you need:**

- **exposure to other possibilities and other dreams**
- **hard facts about those possibilities and dreams (through networking and research)**
- **the skills required in today's job market**
- **job-search training to help you get the work for which you are qualified**

*If you haven't the strength to impose your own terms upon life, then you must accept the terms it offers you.*

T. S. Eliot, *The Confidential Clerk*

*If you've always enjoyed writing and hate numbers, don't interview with investment bankers just because your parents think it's a good idea.*

Dr. Richard Bayer

# When You've Lost the Spirit to Job-Hunt

*"I can't explain* myself, *I'm afraid, Sir," said Alice, "because I'm not myself, you see."*
*"I don't see," said the Caterpillar.*

Lewis Carroll, *Alice in Wonderland*

They're all doing terrific! You're not. You're barely hanging on. You thought you were a winner, but now you're not so sure. How can you pull yourself out of this?

I've felt like that. Everyone in New York had a job except me. I would never work again. I was ruining interviews although I knew better—I had run The Five O'Clock Club for years in Philadelphia. Yet I was unable to job-hunt properly. I was relatively new to New York and divorced. Even going to my country house depressed me: A woman wanted me to sell it, join her cult, and have a 71-year-old roommate. It seemed to be my fate.

Then I got a call from my father—a hurricane was about to hit New York. When I told him my situation, he directed me to get rid of the cult lady and take the next train out. I got out just as the hurricane blew in, and he and I spent three beautiful days alone at my parents' ocean place. He encouraged me, including playing 10 motivational tapes on *being a winner*!

---

*The winners in life think constantly in terms of I can, I will and I am. Losers, on the other hand, concentrate their waking thoughts on what they should have or would have done, or what they can't do.*

Dr. Dennis Waitley, *The Psychology of Winning*

My father wined and dined and took care of me. We watched a six-hour tape of my family history—the births and birthdays, Christmases past, marriages, and parties. We talked about life and the big picture. I had no strength. He nurtured me and gave me strength.

What can *you* do if you can't get this kind of nurturing? Perhaps I've learned a few lessons that may help you.

## 1. Put Things in Perspective

*A depressing and difficult passage has prefaced every new page I have turned in life.*

Charlotte Brontë

You've probably worked a few years, and you'll probably work many more. In the grand scheme of things, this moment will be a blip: an aberration in the past.

Focusing on the present will make you depressed and will also make you a poor interviewee. You will find it difficult to brag about your past or see the future. You will provide too much information about what put you in this situation.

*Interviewers want to hear what you can do for them.* Focus on what you have done in the past and what you can do in the future. You *do* have a future, you know, though you may feel locked into your present situation. Even some young people say it is too late for them. But a lot can happen in the next 10 years—and *most* of what happens is up to you.

## 2. Get Support

*Woe to him that is alone when he falleth,*
*for he hath not another to help him up.*

The Wisdom of Solomon

The old support systems—extended families and even nuclear families—are disappearing. And we no longer look to our community for support.

Today, we are more alone; we are supposed to be tougher and take care of ourselves. But relying solely on yourself is not the answer. How can you fill yourself up when you are emotionally and spiritually empty?

Job hunters often need some kind of emotional and spiritual support because this is a trying time. Our egos are at stake. We feel vulnerable and uncared for. We need realistic support from people who know what we are going through.

---

*There is no such thing as a self-made man. I've had much help and have found that if you are willing to work, many people are willing to help you.*

O. Wayne Rollins

Rely on your Five O'Clock Club group. You'll be with others who know what you're going through. In addition, many places of worship have job-hunting groups open to anyone. During a later job hunt when I was employed, I reported my progress weekly to The Five O'Clock Club I formed in New York. It kept me going.

Statistics show that job hunters with a regular career-counseling support group get jobs faster and at higher rates of pay. A job-hunting group gives emotional support, concrete advice, and feedback. Often, however, that is not enough for those who are at their lowest.

---

*The more lasting a man's ultimate work,*
*the more sure he is to pass through a time, and*
*perhaps a very long one, in which there seems*
*to be very little hope for him.*

Samuel Butler

- If possible, rely on your friends and family. I scheduled lunches with friends and gave them an honest report or practiced my job-hunting lines with them.
- Don't abuse your relationships by relying on one or two people. Find lots of sources of support. Consider joining a church, synagogue, or mosque (they're *supposed* to be nice to you).

## 3. Remember That This Is Part of a Bigger Picture

*We, ignorant of ourselves, Beg often our own harms,*
*Which the Wise Power Denies us for our own good;*
*so we find profit by losing of our prayers.*

William Shakespeare, *Antony and Cleopatra*

*. . . so are My ways higher than your ways and*
*My thoughts than your thoughts.*

Isaiah 55:9

*You are a child of the universe no less than the trees and the stars; you have a right to be here. And whether or not it is clear to you, no doubt the universe is unfolding as it should.*

Max Ehrmann

Why me? Why now? Shakespeare thought there might be someone bigger than ourselves watching over everything—a Wise Power. My mother (and probably yours too) always said that "everything happens for the best."

---

*We know that in all things God works for the good of those who love Him.*

Romans 8:28

If you believe that things happen for a purpose, *think about the good in your own situation.* What was the "purpose" of my own unemployment? Because of it:

- I experienced a closeness with my father that still affects me.
- I became a better counselor.
- I stopped working 12-hour days.

Though shattered when they lost their jobs, many say in retrospect it was the best thing that could have happened to them. Some say the time of transition was the most rewarding experience of their lives.

---

*Every adversity has the seed of an equivalent or greater benefit.*

W. Clement Stone

Perhaps you, too, can learn from this experience and also make some sense of it. This is a time when people often

- decide what they *really* should be doing with their careers—I had resisted full-time career counseling because I liked the prestige of the jobs I had held.
- better their situations, taking off on another upward drive in their careers.
- develop their personalities; learn skills that will last their entire lives.
- reexamine their values and decide what is now important to them.

---

*For what shall it profit a man, if he shall gain the whole world, and lose his own soul?*

Mark 8:36

*The trouble with the rat race is that if you win, you're still a rat.*

Lily Tomlin

## 4. Continue to Do your Job

When you worked in a job, there were days you didn't feel like doing it, but you did it anyway because it was your responsibility. *Job hunting is your job right now.* Some days you don't feel like doing it, but you must. Make a phone call. Write a proposal. Research a company. Do your best every day. No matter how you feel. And somehow it will get done, as any job gets done. Some practical suggestions:

- Make your job hunting professional. Organize it. Get a special calendar to use exclusively to record what you are doing. Use The Five O'Clock Club's Interview Record in this book to track more professionally your efforts and results.
- Set goals. Don't think of whether you want to make calls and write letters. Of course you don't. Just do them anyway. Spend most of your time interviewing—that's how you get a job.

**Depression → Inactivity → Depression**

- If you're at the three-month mark or beyond, you may be at a low point. It's hard to push on. Get a fresh start. Pretend you're starting all over again.

---

*My life seems like one long obstacle course, with me as the chief obstacle.*

Jack Paar

- Finding a job is your responsibility. Don't depend on anyone else (search firms, friends) to find it for you.
- Watch your drinking, eating, smoking. They can get out of hand. Take care of yourself physically. Get dressed. Look good. Get some exercise. Eat healthful foods. You may need a few days off to recharge.
- Don't postpone having fun until you get a job. If you are unemployed, schedule at least three hours of fun a week. Do something you normally are unable to do when you are working. I went out to breakfast every morning, indulged

in reading the *Times,* and then went back to my apartment to job hunt. I also went to the auction houses, and bought a beautiful desk at Sotheby's when I sold my country house.

- Assess your financial situation. What is your backup plan if your unemployment goes on for a certain number of months? If need be, I had planned to get a roommate, sell furniture, and take out a loan. It turned out not to be necessary, but by planning ahead, I knew I would not wind up on the street.
- Remember: You are distracted. Job hunters get mugged, walk into walls, lose things. This is not an ordinary situation, and extraordinary things happen. Be on your guard.
- Observe the results of what you do in a job hunt. Results are indicators of the correctness of your actions and can help refine your techniques.
- Become a good job hunter so you can compete in this market. It takes practice, but the better you are, the less anxious you will be.

*All's well that ends well.*

William Shakespeare

*In the depths of winter*
*I discovered that there was in me an*
*invincible summer.*

Albert Camus

Finally, two sayings especially helped me when I was unemployed:

*You don't get what you want. You get what you need.*

and

*When God closes a door, He opens a window.*

Good luck.—Kate

# An Overview of the Job-Search Process

*The circumstances that surround*
*a man's life are not important.*
*How that man responds to those*
*circumstances*is *important.*
*His response is the ultimate determining*
*factor between success and failure.*

Booker T. Washington

The chart on page 17 outlines each part of the process. It's best to do every part, however quickly you may do it. Experienced job hunters pay attention to the details and do not skip a step. (Every step will be covered in detail in later chapters.)

The first part of the process is **assessment** (or evaluation). You evaluate yourself by doing the exercises, and you evaluate your prospects by doing some preliminary research in the library, on the Internet, or by talking to people.

**Assessment consists of the following exercises**:

- The Seven Stories Exercise
- Interests
- Values
- Satisfiers and Dissatisfiers
- Your Forty-Year Vision

If you are working privately with a career coach, he or she may ask you to do a few additional exercises, such as a personality test.

**Assessment results in:**

- a listing of all the targets you think are worth exploring
- a résumé that makes you look appropriate to your first target (and may work with other targets as well).

Even if you don't do the entire assessment, the Seven Stories Exercise is especially important because it will help you develop an interesting résumé. Therefore, we have included that exercise in this book.

Research will help you figure out which of your targets:

- are good fits for you
- offer some hope in terms of being a good market

You can't have too many targets—as long as you rank them. Then, for *each one,* conduct a campaign to get interviews in that target area.

---

*If you only care enough for a result you will almost certainly obtain it. If you wish to be rich, you will be rich; if you wish to be learned, you will be learned; if you wish to be good, you will be good.*

William James

## Phase I: Campaign Preparation

- Conduct research to develop a list of all the companies in your first target. Find out the names of people you should contact in the appropriate departments in each of those companies.
- Develop your cover letter. Paragraph 1 is the opening; Paragraph 2 is a summary about yourself appropriate for this target; Paragraph 3

contains your bulleted accomplishments ("You may be interested in some of the things I've done"); Paragraph 4 is the close. (Lots of sample letters are in this book.)

- Develop your plan for getting *lots of interviews in this target*. You have four basic choices: networking, direct contact, search firms, and ads (print, Internet, and your school).

You will read lots about each of these methods for getting interviews in this book.

---

*Sometimes it's best if a man just spends a moment or two thinking. It is one of the toughest things he will ever do, and that's probably why so few bother to do it.*

Alonzo Herndon
(born a slave; died a millionaire)
Founder, Atlanta Life Insurance Company

## Phase II: Interviewing

Most people think interviews result in job offers. But there are usually a few intervening steps before a final offer is made. Interviews should result in getting and giving information.

Did you learn the issues important to each person with whom you met? What did they think were your strongest positives? Where are they in the hiring process? How many other people are they considering? How do you compare with those people? Why might they be reluctant to bring you on board, compared with the other candidates? How can you overcome the decision makers' objections?

This is one of the most important and yet most overlooked parts of the job-search process. It is covered in extensive detail in this book.

---

*You ain't goin' nowhere . . . son.*
*You ought to go back to driving a truck.*

Jim Denny, Grand Ole Opry manager, firing Elvis Presley after one performance. An interview on October 2, 1954.

## Phase III: Follow-Up

Now that you have analyzed the interview, you can figure out how to follow up with each person with whom you interviewed. Aim to be following up with 6 to 10 companies. Five job possibilities will fall away through no fault of your own.

What's more, with 6 to 10 things going, you increase your chances of having 3 good offers to choose from. You would be surprised: Even in a tight market, job hunters are able to develop multiple offers.

When you are in the Interview Phase of Target 1, it's time to start Phase I of Target 2. This will give you more momentum and ensure that you do not let things dry up. Keep both targets going, and then start Target 3.

## Develop Your Unique Résumé

Read all of the case studies in this book. You will learn a powerful new way of thinking about how to position yourself for the kinds of jobs you want. Each of the résumés is for a unique person aiming at a specific target. Seeing how other people position themselves will help you think about what you want a prospective employer to know about you.

Now, it is best to go through the first part of the process, assessment. You will read actual case studies that will show you how real people benefited from doing the assessment, including the Forty-Year Vision.

Even if your targets are already defined, keep on reading.

---

*Everyone should learn to do one thing supremely well because he likes it, and one thing supremely well because he detests it.*

B. W. M. Young, Headmaster, Charterhouse School

*Life never leaves you stranded. If life hands you a problem, it also hands you the ability to overcome that problem. Are you ever tempted to blame the world for your failures and shortcomings? If so, I suggest you pause and reconsider. Does the problem lie with the world, or with you? Dare to dream.*

Dennis Kimbro, *Think and Grow Rich: A Black Choice*

# Phases of the Job Search and the results of each phase

## ASSESSMENT

**Consists of:**

- The Seven Stories Exercise
- Interests
- Values
- Satisfiers and Dissatisfiers
- Your Forty-Year Vision

**Results in:**

- As many targets as you can think of
- A ranking of your targets
- A résumé that makes you look appropriate to your first target
- A plan for conducting your search

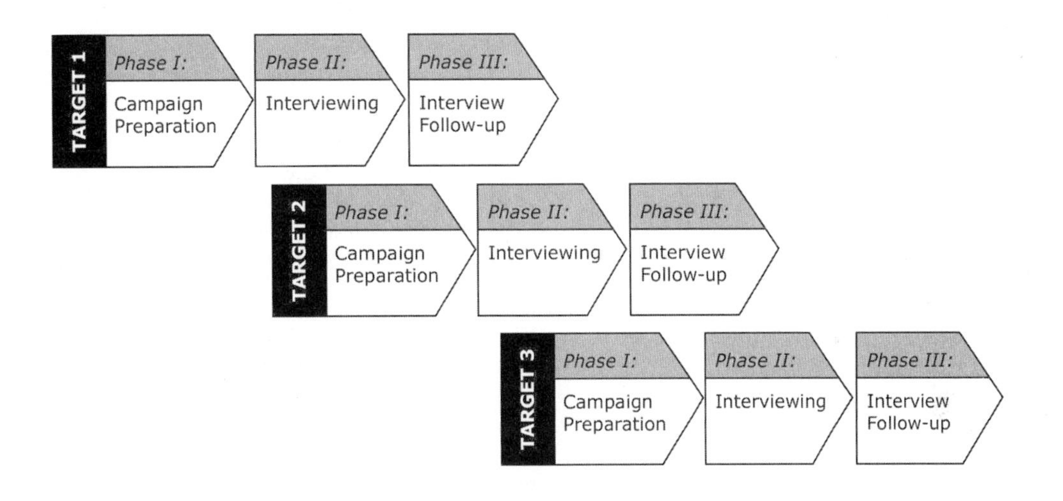


## RESULTS

***Phase I: Campaign Preparation.***

***Results in:***

- ❑ Research (list of companies)
- ❑ Résumé
- ❑ Cover letter
- ❑ Plan for getting interviews
  - networking
  - direct contact
  - search firms
  - ads

***Phase II: Interviewing.***

***Results in:***

- ❑ Giving them information to keep them interested in you
- ❑ Getting information so you can "move it along"
- ❑ Plan for follow-up (You may do several in-depth follow-ups with each person)

***Phase III: Follow-Up.***

***Results in:***

- ❑ Aiming to have 6 to 10 things in the works, and

Job Offers!

# Targeting the Jobs of the Future

*The time is not far off when you will be answering your television set and watching your telephone.*

Raymond Smith, chairman and chief executive of the Bell Atlantic Corporation, *The New York Times,* February 21, 1993

## The Times Are Changing

Ten years from now, half the working population will be in jobs that do not exist today. Positions and industries will disappear almost completely—edged out by technological advances or new industries. When was the last time you saw a typewriter repairman? Or even a typewriter? There are few TV or radio repair jobs either. They have been replaced by new jobs.

Some industries retrench—or downsize—slowly and trick us into thinking they are solid and dependable. At the turn of the last century, there were thousands of piano manufacturers. A few still remain, but that industry was affected by new industries: movies, TV, radio, and other forms of home entertainment, most recently, the Internet, CD-ROMs, and video game systems.

In 1900, most people probably thought: "But we'll *always* need pianos." People today think the same way about the industries they are in.

## Temporary Setbacks

Some industries and occupations ebb and flow with supply and demand. When there is a shortage in a well-paid field, such as nursing, engineering, or law, school enrollments increase, creating an excess. Then people stop entering these fields, creating a shortage. So, sometimes it's easy to get jobs, and sometimes it isn't.The overall economy may also temporarily affect a field or industry. Real estate, for example, may suffer in a down economy and pick up in a strong one.

---

*All our lives we are engaged in the process of accommodating ourselves to our surroundings; living is nothing else than this process of accommodation. When we fail a little, we are stupid. When we flagrantly fail, we are mad. A life will be successful or not, according as the power of accommodation is equal to or unequal to the strain of fusing and adjusting internal and external chances.*

Samuel Butler, *The Way of All Flesh*

## Ahead of the Market

When the Berlin Wall came down in 1989, there was a rush of companies wanting to capitalize on the potential market in Eastern Europe. Given all they were reading in the papers, job hunters thought it would be a good market for them to explore as well. They were ahead of the market. It took a few years before the market caught up with the concept. Now many people are employed in Eastern Europe or in servicing that market.

The same may be true for the area that you are in or are trying to get into: The market may not be there because it has not yet developed.

Another growth area is new media." This is such a rapidly changing area that it is still hard to define. As of this writing, it can include cable stations, a number of which are devoted to home shopping; "imaging" of medical records and credit card receipts; supermarket scanners and other devices that promote items or record what you buy; multimedia use of the computer (sound, motion and, color instead of just text, which you now take for granted); virtual reality; interactive TV; telephone companies (with cable already going into every home); cell phones; CD-ROMs (compact disks containing "read-only memory"), which put materials such as games and encyclopedias on CDs; the increasingly important Internet; and gadgets such as personal data assistants and DVD and MP3 players.

And let's not forget biotech, health care, and related areas (gyms, nutritionists, physical fitness instructors). Americans now take it as their right that they should have anything that makes them healthier. Such industries make up a significant part of the GDP and are projected to grow strongly. Often, large corporations have divisions or areas in a division that are in these new media areas. You can find out your company's involvement by looking at its website, talking to HR managers, looking through a company directory, and finding the appropriate people who are knowledgeable on the company's operations. This could be an excellent opportunity to use your skills in a growing area, as well as learn new skills and make an exciting career move.

---

*If you succeed in judging yourself rightly, then you are indeed a man of true wisdom.*

Antoine de Saint Exupéry, *The Little Prince*

## What about *Your* Industry or Profession?

Is your dream industry or field growing, permanently retrenching, or in a temporary decline because of supply and demand or other economic conditions? If you are lucky, your employer is ahead of the market, and the industry will pick up later. Often, you can find out just by reading your organization's annual report and other information it gives out to the public.

Most people in permanently retrenching industries, including the leaders, incorrectly think the decline is temporary. You have to decide for yourself. You could perhaps gain insight and objectivity by researching what those outside your industry have to say.

It has been predicted that if things continue as they are going, there will soon be a great divide in America, with technologically and internationally aware workers making fine salaries, while the unaware and unskilled earn dramatically lower wages. (Even high-level executives can be unaware and unskilled and thus face reductions in their salaries as they become less useful.) If this does come to pass, the best a career coach can do is to encourage people to try to be on the winning side of that divide.

---

*Today's workers need to forget jobs completely and look instead for work that needs doing—and then set themselves up as the best way to get that work done.*

William Bridges, *JobShift: How to Prosper in a Workplace without Jobs*

## Retrenching Markets Are All Alike

When an industry retrenches, the results are predictable. A retrenching market, by definition, has more job hunters than jobs. The more that market retrenches, the worse it gets.

Those who want to stay in the field have increasingly longer searches as more people chase fewer jobs. They will also tend to stay less time in their new jobs, as companies in the retrenching industry continue to downsize or go out of business.

Profit margins get squeezed as companies compete for a slice of a shrinking pie. Those companies become less enjoyable to work for because there is less investment in training and development, research, internal communications, and the like. Of course, salaries are cut.

Many young people are enticed into glamor fields, regardless of the practicality, or into fields their parents or friends are in, regardless of the fit for them personally despite the projections for those fields. Yes, you should pursue your dreams, but check them out a little first.

Most people target only their current industries, fields or professions at the start of their search. They consider other targets only after they have difficulty getting another job in their present field. They would probably have found something faster if they had looked in other fields from the beginning.

**Those in retrenching industries who also target new industries have a shorter search time.**

**The new fields are new to everyone. An outsider has a chance of becoming an insider.**

*One doesn't discover new lands without consenting to lose sight of the shore for a very long time.*

André Gide

## The Attributes of a High-Growth Industry

By definition, growth industries must hire from outside: They don't have enough people inside the industry. The new industry attracts new competitors—many of whom will fail—and there is a shakeout. But if the industry is still growing, those who got in early are the most knowledgeable and valuable and can command larger salaries. If the industry does *not* continue to grow, new entrants create a surplus of labor, and salaries decrease.

So long as the industry continues to grow, there is an open window: Those outside the industry can get in. As the industry stabilizes, there will be plenty of experienced people, companies will want only those with direct experience, and the window will close.

**HMOs, cellular technology, for-profit schools—and the Internet—were essentially nonexistent industries just 20 years ago.**

## Expanding Your Search Geographically; Targeting Small Companies

Studies show that more jobs are created in the suburbs than in major metropolitan areas, and there is greater job creation in the *new* suburbs than in the *old* suburbs. Oops! It's good to know the facts, because you can conduct your search accordingly. If you have been ignoring the suburbs, think about them.

Job growth has been in smaller companies. Large companies do most of the downsizing. **In New York City, for example, there are 193,000 companies. Only 270 of them employ 1,000 people or more**. James Brown, economist for the Department of Labor specializing in the New York City labor market, advised members of the mid-Manhattan Five O'Clock Club to look to the other 192,730 companies—those that employ fewer than 1,000 people.

*All our lives we are engaged in the process of accommodating ourselves to our surroundings; living is nothing else than this process of accommodation.*
*When we fail a little, we are stupid. When we flagrantly fail, we are mad. A life will be successful or not, according as the power of accommodation is equal to or unequal to the strain of fusing and adjusting internal and external chances.*

Samuel Butler,
*The Way of All Flesh*

Think about your geographic area, and think about the companies you are targeting. Most jobs hunters naturally think about the big companies that are in the news, but perhaps you should think about the new "hidden job market": the suburbs and companies with fewer than 1,000 employees.

---

*For workers, there are dark spots, but the overall picture is still far brighter than commonly believed. Real wages are starting to turn up, after years of decline. The old factory jobs are disappearing, but new jobs in other industries are being generated at an unprecedented rate. Rather than becoming a nation of hamburger flippers, we are becoming a nation of schoolteachers, computer programmers, and health-care managers. About 11 million new jobs have been created since 1989, and of those, approximately two-thirds are managerial and professional positions. There is a tremendous surge in creativity and new opportunities, ranging from new forms of entertainment to cheap global communications.*

Michael Mandel, *The High-Risk Society*

## Bull Market for Labor Likely to Continue into the Foreseeable Future

Richard Bayer, an economist and the chief operating officer for The Five O'Clock Club, is optimistic. He notes that both the Bureau of Labor Statistics and the Conference Board project labor shortages over the next 10 years.

Predictions are, of course, uncertain, and there could easily be a recession or two in this time frame, but the overall employment trend line remains strongly positive.

- The demand for labor will continue to grow. The supply of labor will barely be adequate to meet the demand.
- There will almost surely be pockets of "skills mismatch," in which some positions are very difficult to fill.
- Overall, the educational level required to function in this new economy will rise.
- Although workers will continue to be needed at all levels, the larger increases in employment are coming in the various managerial, professional, and skilled technical ranks. This goes against the myth that the new economy is producing mainly low-skill and low-wage jobs.
- The occupations with the greatest declines tend to be lower skilled and lower paid: garment workers, customer-service (those who answer 800 telephone calls), farmworkers, textile machine operators.

So, what might the implications of all this be for Five O'Clock Clubbers and others?

This is a great time to be alive and have a career! The efforts you put into your education, into career development, into networking, and into targeting a meaningful job have never had such a strong chance of bearing good fruit!

---

*There is guidance for each of us, and by lowly listening, we shall hear the right word.*

Ralph Waldo Emerson

## Getting More Sophisticated

Whether you are relatively new to the labor force or have been working a while, think past the obvious and think more deeply about the changes that are occurring.

Listed here are a few of the industries business experts project will grow in the near future. Try to discover other areas that may be affected by these or how your own job may be affected by growth in these areas. Each is huge and changing and can be better defined by your investigation through networking, as well as by Internet and library research.

- Health care, biotech, or anything having to do with either. Health care is considered a sure bet because of the aging population and the advances being made in medical technology.

- Anything high-tech, or the high-tech aspect of whatever field or industry you are in.
- The international aspect of the field or industry you are considering.
- The environmental area; waste management.
- Safety and security (especially since the September 11th attack on America).
- Telecommunications, the new media, and global communications (movie studios, TV networks, cable companies, computer companies, consumer electronics companies, and publishers).
- Education in the broadest sense (as opposed to the traditional classroom), including computer-assisted instruction. (Researchers have found that illiterates learn to read better with computer-assisted instruction than they do in a classroom.)

  Because all of us will have to keep up-to-date in more areas in order to do our jobs well, technology will play an important part in our continuing education. Further, with America lagging so far behind other countries educationally, both the for-profit and not-for-profit sectors are working hard to revamp our educational system.
- Alternative means of distributing goods. Instead of retail stores, think not only about direct mail but also about purchasing by TV or the Internet.
- Anything serving the aging population, both products and services.

In studying the preceding list, think of how you can combine different industries to come up with areas to pursue. For example, combine the aging population with education, the aging population with telecommunications, or health care with education. The more you research, the more sophisticated your thoughts will get.

If you combine education with the new media, you will be thinking like many experts. Students in schools are learning from interactive multimedia presentations on computers—presentations as exciting as computer games and MTV combined, and almost as up-to-date as the morning news (most textbooks are years out of date). Teachers will do what computers cannot do: facilitate the groups, encourage, reinforce learning.

A computer-based approach can be used to train and update the knowledge of America's workers: Employees can learn when they have the time and at their own pace, rather than leaving their jobs in large numbers to learn in a classroom situation.

When you read predictions that there will be huge growth in a certain industry—say, home health care workers, personal and home care aides, and medical assistants, medical secretaries, radiology technologists and technicians, and psychologists—you may think: "I don't want to be any of those." Think more creatively. Companies will have to spring up to supply and train those workers. (Some of the training could be done on multimedia.) People will be needed to manage the companies, regulate the care given, coach patients on how to select and manage such workers, and so on. If you read about the tremendous growth in the temporary help business, you *may* become a temporary worker yourself, or you could go to work running one of the temporary help companies.

Think about the field you are interested in and how it is being affected by technology. Virtually every job and industry—whether it is publishing, entertainment, manufacturing, or financial services—is being impacted by technology and by the global marketplace. If you are not aware, you will be blindsided.

---

*The trouble with the future is that it usually arrives before we're ready for it.*

Arnold H. Glasow

## Some Areas Are Safer Bets

The rate of change is so fast that technologies you read about may never reach the mainstream or may be replaced with new developments. However, some areas are safer bets than others. "Hard skills" are more marketable than "soft skills." For example, a person who wants to get a job as a general writer will have more difficulty than someone who can bring more to the party—such as some specialization or computer skills.

---

*When there is no vision, the people perish.*

Old Testament, .Proverbs 29:18

## Figure It Out

It's your job to figure out how your dream industry or field is being affected by technology, global competition, and the market in general. Think where you fit into the future. Do research.

We are now on the ground floor of many industries, and it is an exciting time for those who choose to take advantage of the revolutionary changes that are taking place.

So, once again, remember the definition of job-hunting that The Five O'Clock Club developed:

**Job-hunting in a changing economy means continuously becoming aware of market conditions inside as well as outside your present organization and learning more about what you have to offer.**

## A New Way of Thinking

Any assignment (or job) you get is a temporary one. You're doing work, but you don't have a permanent job. It's like an actor who lands a part. He or she does not really know how long it may last. Furthermore, actors tend to worry about whether a role will typecast them and potentially cause them to lose future roles. Or they may intentionally decide to be typecast, hoping it will increase their chances going forward. Actors understand that they will most likely have to land another role after this one, and they constantly think about how a certain role will position them for the future. And so must you. Your next job is only a temporary assignment.

---

*Work today is not just doing;*
*it is, more than ever, thinking.*
*Today's corporation needs thinking, flexible, proactive workers. It wants creative problem solvers, workers smart and skilled enough to move with new technologies and with the ever-changing competitive environment.*
*It needs workers accustomed to collaborating with co-workers, to participating in quality circles, to dealing with people high and low. Communication skills and people skills have become parts of the necessary repertoire of the modern worker.*

Hedrick Smith, *Rethinking America*

# Learning to Track Trends

*The factory of the future will have only two employees, a man and a dog. The man will be there to feed the dog. The dog will be there to keep the man from touching the equipment.*

Warren Bennis

In this volatile market, where jobs are disappearing every day, new jobs are appearing. Select a field that will position you for the long run. The people in our stories are picking up skills and experience that will be transferable to other jobs, and they will be extremely marketable.

Virtually every industry is in turmoil. Read what experts write about the industries that interest you. What are the trends? What outside forces are affecting the industry? How might you be affected? How can you prepare for the future?

---

*Within the next decades education will change more than it has changed since the modern school was created by the printed book over three hundred years ago. An economy in which knowledge is becoming the true capital and the premier wealth-producing resource makes new and stringent demands on the schools for education performance and educational responsibility. . . . How we learn and how we teach are changing drastically and fast—the result, in part, of new theoretical understanding of the learning process, in part of new technology.*

Peter Drucker,
*The New Realities*

## The Growth of the Web

A few years ago, the pace of technological change started to pick up: There was a confluence of technological work in various arenas that began to bear fruit.

You may know that the Internet itself was envisioned in 1945 by Vannevar Bush, an electrical engineer. Hypertext, the basis for interactivity on the Internet, was developed in 1965! The World Wide Web was created in 1989 using hypertext. HTML, the "hypertext markup language," was developed in 1990. Yet, interactive business applications on desktop computers were in relatively wide commercial use by 1980.

**Here's one way to look at it:**
**Radio → TV → Computers → Internet**

The long-accepted concept of computer-based interactivity, combined relatively recently with HTML and URLs, laid the groundwork for the surge we are experiencing today.

In the mid-1990s, we told concerned Five O'Clock Clubbers who were targeting Internet-related companies that even if the Internet didn't make it, their new skills would be transferable to whatever interactive technologies took its place.

Clearly, "interactive" was here to stay: Computer interactivity had been popular in business applications for more than 20 years! But the Internet was not just another interactive medium, such as ATMs, interactive kiosks, and telephones, or even CD-ROMs. The Internet was an international infrastructure for commerce and ideas, an intelligent medium that made people smarter and proactive. It was a core medium that would change everything.

## The Same Development Pattern in Other Industries

The development of the Internet—a long gestation period followed by a "sudden" appearance on the market—was paralleled by developments in a number of unrelated industries, and the results added to the cataclysm. Probably half of the jobs that exist today did not exist 10 years ago.

- HMOs and alternative medicine have changed the face of **health care**. Just a few years ago, hospitals were merging or shutting down. But the aging population and the increase in elective surgery changed that trend and encouraged hospitals to offer services that would attract patients who can afford to pay. More hospitals are specializing—in eye and ear, heart, cancer, and so on—to increase profitability, which puts a squeeze on general hospitals that have to handle the less profitable business. Congress may soon limit this trend.

  Still, employers—and the country—have had to find ways to cut health care costs, and innovations abound. Hospitals are spending money on technology to streamline operations, including launching electronic patient-record systems. Insurance companies have added help lines, hoping to reduce the number of actual doctor visits.

  But good help is hard to find. Because of rising malpractice insurance ($35,000+ per year) and the restrictive fees paid by HMOs, some private-practice doctors left the profession and went into pharmaceutical sales or medical research. The nursing shortage continues, with bonuses and other lures becoming common.
- **Telecom**, with cellular phones that can take photographs and access the Internet with an international reach, looks nothing like it did only a few years ago.
- **Education** will be permanently changed by for-profit schools, the erosion of tenure, and the technological advances that are impacting the industry—with or without the approval of powerful unions.
- ***Retail*** no longer necessarily means going into a store or even talking to a person. Alternative distribution methods have been in the works for decades—through direct mail and other means—and now through the Internet. People don't need stores to buy computers, travel agents to arrange travel, or stockbrokers to purchase stocks. Automobiles are "sold" over the Internet, a new direct-marketing approach; showrooms are there so you can kick the tires. But the marketing approaches keep evolving. The direct-mail industry was badly hurt by the Internet. But by 2004, popular Internet sites, such as Ebay and Amazon, mailed millions of glossy catalogues to homes to promote their websites. Internet companies were using direct mail!
- The **entertainment** industry has morphed in unpredictable ways, and media growth is being driven by technology, not programming. For example, 20 years ago, there were 3 broadcast networks and 20 cable channels. DVDs did not exist. Today, there are 6 broadcast networks, 300 cable channels (perhaps going to a 600+ channel universe), PCs in virtually every home, DVD players, and VCRs. A large number of families have installed video game consoles. Cell phones, PDAs, and iPods are all part of the entertainment arena. Traditional marketing approaches are becoming less efficient. And as of this writing, content is the entertainment king, allowing companies to exploit content over multiple media.

  Pirated software, music, and movies have plagued those industries, and new technology may be the primary answer because legislation does not seem to be working. As of this writing, the music industry is testing the sale of new releases as digital only—no CD, just the digital music. This is after hundreds of record stores closed, while those that remained have devoted more shelf space to DVDs and video games, leaving less space for CDs.

Movie theaters look nothing like their old-time counterparts. Instead of the good old days, when people listened to an organist and saw two cartoons and a double feature, we now sit through paid advertisements and have more comfortable chairs, stadium seating, and a broader variety of refreshments—almost a meal.

- The **publishing** industry (books, magazines) is under new pressure , competing with the Internet, video games, and DVDs. And Amazon.com is now selling used books—some just a few days old—which further undercuts traditional publishing. E-books were supposed to be the thing of the future, but so far they have not caught on.
- The **advertising** industry continues to evolve. It's been decades since the industry relied on the three major networks for their revenue. The latest trend is implanting marketing messages in video games, movies, and TV shows. In addition, some print advertising is starting to look like editorials.

Who could have dreamed of today's situation just five years ago? But these changes created open windows in the new areas while traditional fields retrenched and revamped.

---

*Cato learned Greek at eighty; Sophocles*
*Wrote his grand Oedipus, and Simonides*
*Bore off the prize of verse from his compeers,*
*When each had numbered more than*
*four score years. . . .*
*Chaucer, at Woodstock with the nightingales,*
*At sixty wrote the Chaucer Tales;*
*Goethe at Weimar, toiling to the last,*
*Completed Faust when eighty years were past.*

Henry Wadsworth Longfellow,
*Morituri Salutamus*

## Professions Also Get Outmoded Overnight

*Strangely enough, this is the past that somebody in the future is longing to go back to.*

Ashleigh Brilliant

It used to be that once a person had found a profession, that was the source of stability. That is absolutely no longer the case; professions change overnight. Ask physicians or attorneys about their early visions of those professions, and you will quickly hear how their fields have dramatically changed. Physicians in their 50s and 60s say they are lucky to have been part of the "golden age" of medicine—when doctors could see whomever they wanted, recommend whatever they felt was in their patients' best interests, get referrals from other physicians, and earn good money. Now, nothing is the same.

Fifteen years ago, we rarely saw an attorney at The Five O'Clock Club, and until five years ago, we had no physicians. Now, we have plenty of both—and computer programmers as well. Their professions have changed—quickly.

---

*In this high-risk society, each person's main asset will be his or her willingness and ability to take intelligent risks. Those people best able to cope with uncertainty . . . will fare better in the long run than those who cling to security.*

Michael Mandel, *The High-Risk Society*

## The High-Risk Society

In 1996, Michael Mandel wrote in *The High-Risk Society* that the times are good, but prosperity has come at a high price: more intense, more pervasive economic uncertainty than Americans have suffered at any time in the past 50 years.

He pointed out that prosperity and security no longer go hand in hand: "Today, the very forces behind economic turbulence are also the world's greatest engines of growth. As a result, success hinges on your willingness to embrace risk—rather than flee from it."

Those who keep up and see where the future is heading—in both their professions and their industries—can benefit from the changes that are going to take place anyway.

Now, we all expect new developments, and we expect uncertainty. We expect our fields and industries to change. This time, we're ready.

Our eyes are open now. We keep up-to-date. We stay in touch. We're thinking about our next move even before we start a new position. We know that we have to take charge of our careers, and that doesn't seem so bad anymore. We've got perspective.

God bless you as you face the uncertain future. It's better than trying to stay in the non-existent past.

---

*The essence of the high-risk society is choice: the choice between embracing uncertainty and running from it.*

Michael Mandel, *The High-Risk Society*

## When to See a Counselor Privately

Just as you have a doctor to help you with medical problems (or to prevent problems), consider developing a relationship with a counselor who gets to know you over the long term. Speak to your counselor when you have specific problems, such as those that follow, or for a checkup to make sure everything is okay. Schedule a private session to:

- solve present job problems (do a better job of managing up, down, and across)
- determine your career path (plan now; avoid the rush)

And when you are job hunting, to:

- prepare your résumé
- plan your marketing campaign
- practice for an important interview
- plan your salary negotiation

If you need help, visit the coaching section of our website: www.FiveOClockClub.com.

When you become a member, we will refer you to two Five O'Clock Club–certified counselors. You can choose one to help you with job search and career planning.

---

*The line between the self-employed condition and working for an "employer" has become unclear: Communications technology and flextime arrangements allow official, full-time employees to telecommute and to do their forty hours a week without leaving home. At the same time, self-employed people may get contracts that not only require them to perform the tasks that used to be done by a jobholder, but also give them an in-house office, membership on a task force within the organization, and even a discount at the employee store.*

William Bridges, *JobShift: How to Prosper in a Workplace without Jobs*

PART TWO

# Deciding What You Want

## START BY UNDERSTANDING YOURSELF

# Case Studies

## *Targeting the Future*

*While your basic emotional temperament may not change much during your lifetime, you can make significant day-to-day adjustments in the way you perceive events and respond to them. When you face an emotionally trying situation, guard against exaggerating or over-generalizing, and focus instead on your specific options for taking direct action. Avoid putting yourself down by doing something that will exercise your good traits. And seek the company of others, whether it's to gather more rational views on the situation or simply to change your mood.*

Jack Maguire, *Care and Feeding of the Brain*

What changes are taking place in your industry or function? If you think your industry or function will continue to retrench, find a "new horse to ride": an industry or function that is on a growth curve or one that will give you transferable skills.

*The person who fears to try is thus enslaved.*

Leonard E. Read

*Progress might have been all right once,*
*But it has gone on too long.*

Ogden Nash

## What about Your Dream Field, Industry, or Geographic Area?

A job target is "a clearly selected geographic area, an industry or organization size, and a function or position within that industry." An accountant, for example, may target a certain industry (such as telecommunications or hospitals) or may see himself in the accounting function and may not care which industry he is in but prefer instead to focus on "organization size." This means he wants to target a small, medium, or large organization, regardless of industry.

Examine your targets to see how each is doing. Perhaps, for example, your industry is okay, but large organizations are not doing well while smaller organizations are hiring. In this case, target the smaller organizations.

## It's Time to Take Control of Your Own Career

*If you succeed in judging yourself rightly, then you are indeed a man of true wisdom.*

Antoine de Saint Exupéry, *The Little Prince*

Get in the habit of reading the papers and noticing what news may affect the industry or field you are in. Learn about some of the industries of the future.

Even if all you want is a job right now, instead of a career, do the exercises in the next section. Be sure to include at least the Seven Stories Exercise, Interests, Values, and Forty-Year Vision. They won't take a long time to do, and they will shorten the length of your search.

*Illness strikes men when they are exposed to change.*

Herodotus, Greek historian

*When I examined myself and my methods of thought, I came to the conclusion that the gift of fantasy has meant more to me than my talent for absorbing positive knowledge.*

Albert Einstein

## Retraining Is for Everybody—Even Executives

When people talk about retraining in America, they are usually talking about lower level workers who don't have computer skills. Retraining is necessary at all levels. Do research to learn the terminology of the industry you want to enter so you can be an insider, not an outsider.

By definition, new industries must hire people from outside the industry. A job hunter who studies the field and develops a sincere interest in it has a good chance of being hired.

Careful research is a critical component that becomes a central part of every sophisticated person's job search.

If you just think off the top of your head about the areas you should be targeting, your ideas will probably be superficial—and outdated.

Change is happening at an increasingly faster rate. Industries disappear, and new ones spring up quickly. Instead of simply hunting for the next job, think about your long-range career.

You can pick the *right horse to ride* into your future rather than hanging on for dear life in a declining market. If you pick the right horse, you'll have a much easier ride.

## Achieving Stability in a Changing World

How can you keep yourself stable in a constantly changing economy? If the world is being battered, organizations are being battered, and many CEOs cannot keep their jobs, what are you going to do?

The benefit of doing the following exercises is that they give you confidence and a sense of stability in a changing world. You will learn to know yourself and become sure of exactly what you can take with you wherever you go.

---

*One doesn't discover new lands without consenting to lose sight of the shore for a very long time.*

André Gide

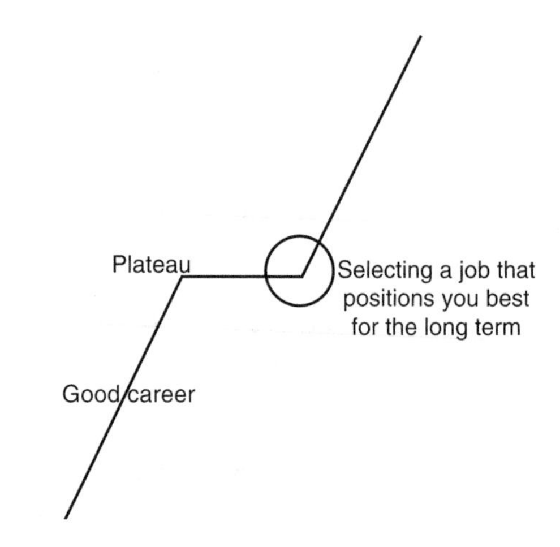


## The Result of Assessment Is Job Targets

If you go through an assessment with a career coach or vocational testing center and do not wind up with tentative job targets, the assessment has not helped you very much. You must go one more step and decide what to *do* with this information.

## The Result of Assessment Is Power

The more you know about yourself, the more power you have to envision a job that will suit you. The exercises give you power.

People find it hard to believe that I went through a period of about 30 years when I was painfully shy. In graduate school, I was afraid when they took roll because I obsessed with whether I should answer "here" or "present." When I had to give a presentation, the best I could do was read the key words from my index cards. (Today, my throat is actually hoarse from all the public speaking I do.) I will be forever grateful for the kindness of strangers who told me I did well when I knew I was awful.

The only thing that ultimately saved me was the Seven Stories Exercise. When I was little, I had led groups of kids in the neighborhood, and I did it well. It gave me strength to know that I was inherently a group leader regardless of how I was behaving now. (I was in my 30s at the time.)

**The Seven Stories Exercise grounds you, and the Forty-Year Vision guides you.** When people said, "Would you like to lead groups?" I said to myself, "Well, I led groups when I was 10. Maybe I can do it again." The transition was painful and took many years, but my Seven Stories Exercise kept me going. And my Forty-Year Vision let me know there was plenty of time to do it.

---

*Enjoy yourself. If you can't enjoy yourself, enjoy somebody else.*

Jack Schaefer

*I was going to buy a copy of* The Power of Positive Thinking, *and then I thought: What the hell good would that do?*

Ronnie Shakes

# Deciding What You Want: Selecting Your Job Targets

*It may sound surprising when I say, on the basis of my own clinical experience as well as that of my psychological and psychiatric colleagues, "that the chief problem of people in the middle decade of the twentieth century is emptiness." By that I mean not only that many people do not know what they want; they often do not have any clear idea of what they feel.*

Rollo May, *Man's Search for Himself*

Studies have shown that up to 85 percent of all American workers are unhappy in their jobs. After going through an evaluation process (assessment), some find that a small change is all that is needed. On the other hand, some want to make a major career change.

The exercises in this book will help you assess yourself in an organized way so that you can better understand the situations in which you perform your best and are happiest.

*Your health is bound to be affected if, day after day, you say the opposite of what you feel, if you grovel before what you dislike and rejoice at what brings you nothing but misfortune.*

Boris Pasternak, *Dr. Zhivago*

## Getting Started

You may do certain exercises in this book and skip others. But don't skip the Seven Stories Exercise, and try to do the Forty-Year Vision. If you have had problems with bosses or teachers, analyze those situations. Examining your values may also be an issue at this time. Your insights about yourself from the Seven Stories Exercise will serve as a template for selecting the right job.

After you do the exercises, brainstorm a number of possible job targets. Then research each target to find out what the job possibilities are for someone like you. This book will guide you through the entire process.

*To have a great purpose to work for, a purpose larger than ourselves, is one of the secrets of making life significant; for then the meaning and worth of the individual overflow his personal borders, and survive his death.*

Will Durant

## Consider Your History

If you have enjoyed certain jobs, attempt to understand exactly what about them you enjoyed. This will increase your chances of replicating the enjoyable aspects.

For example, an accounting assistant will probably not be happy in just any accounting job. If what he really enjoyed was *helping* the business manager make the business profitable, and if this thread of helping reappears in his enjoyable experiences (Seven Stories Exercise), then he would be unhappy in a job where he was *not* helping.

If, however, his enjoyment primarily came from reconciling numbers and resolving messes while working alone, then he needs a job that has accounting messes to be resolved and the promise of more messes to come.

Furthermore, if he wants to do again those things he enjoyed, he can state them in the summary on his résumé. For instance:

Accounting Assistant
Serve as right-hand to Business Manager, improving organization's profitability.
*or*
Accounting Assistant
Reconcile accounts and resolve problem situations

---

*Wherever I went, I couldn't help noticing, the place fell apart. Not that I was ever a big enough wheel in the machine to precipitate its destruction on my own. But that they let me—and other drifters like me—in the door at all was an early warning signal. Alarm bells should have rung.*

Michael Lewis, *Liar's Poker*

## The Results of Assessment: Job Targets—*Then* a Résumé

A job target contains three elements:

- industry or organization size (small, medium, or large organization)
- position or function
- geographic location

## Industry or Organization Size

A person could be a lawyer, but it makes a great deal of difference whether that person is a lawyer in a corporation, in a stuffy law firm, or in a not-for-profit organization. Your environment affects your satisfaction level.

By the same token, some people are better suited to working in a large organization, and others are better suited to a small one. Those who are unhappy may simply need to work in an organization of a different size.

## Position or Function

Some people are urged to go into finance or work the family farm, when those fields may not be at all appropriate for the individual. When you do the Seven Stories Exercise, you will notice whether there is any support for the fields others have chosen for you.

If you already have experience in one field, you may be reluctant to find something else. Even very young people feel it is "too late to start over." But you owe it to yourself to find your rightful place in the world. It may be that you have to take a job in one field while you get experience in your dream field on the side. In general, it is relatively easy to get experience in the new field if you really want it.

## Geographic Location

Is one geographic area the same as another to you? Probably not. Assess your feelings about this because nothing will affect your lifestyle more than the geographic area you choose. On the other hand, you may accept living in an otherwise unacceptable location so you can get the experience you need.

---

*A man is what he thinks about all day long.*

Ralph Waldo Emerson

## Looking Ahead: A Career Instead of a Job

Assessment will help you decide what you want to do in your next job as well as in the long run. Through your Forty-Year Vision, you may uncover some hidden dream that may dramatically influence what you will want to do in both the short and long run. I did my own Forty-Year Vision about 15 years ago, and the idea I had about my future still drives me today, even though that vision was actually rather vague at the time. Knowing where you would like to wind up in 10, 20, 30, or 40 years can broaden your ideas about the kinds of jobs you would be interested in today. The Forty-Year Vision is powerful.

The Seven Stories Exercise is equally powerful. Without it, many job hunters develop stilted descriptions of what they have accomplished. But the exercise frees you up to brag a little and express things very differently. The results will add life to your résumé and your interviews, and also dramatically increase your self-confidence.

## No Easy Way

It would be nice if you could simply take a test that would tell you what you should be. Unfortunately, there is no such sure-fire test. But fortunately, in today's rapidly changing world, we are allowed to be many things: We can be a doctor *and* a concert violinist. We have an abundance of choices.

## A Clear Direction

People are happy when they are working toward their goals. When they get diverted from their goals, they are unhappy. Life has a way of sneaking up and distracting you. Many people are unhappy in their jobs because they don't know where they are going.

A happy person going toward his or her goal.

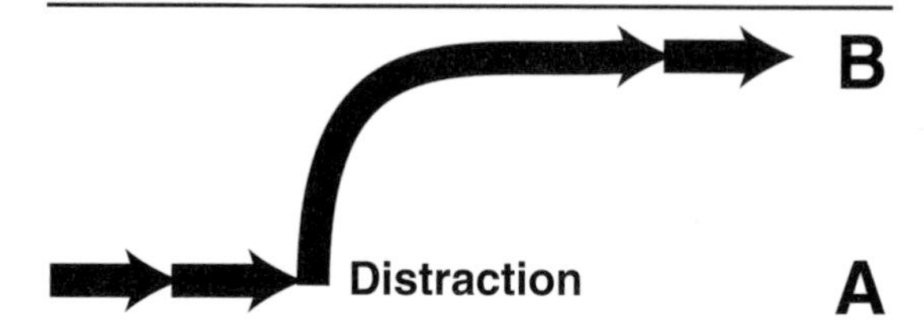


An unhappy person being deflected from his or her goal.

People without goals are more irked by petty problems on their jobs. Those with goals are less bothered because they have bigger plans. To control your life, you have to know where you are going and be ready for your next move—in case the ax falls on you.

Even after you take that next job, continue to manage your career. Organizations rarely build career paths for their employees any more. Make your own way.

# Exercises to Analyze Your Past and Present

## *The Seven Stories Exercise*

*What seems different in yourself; that's the rare thing you possess. The one thing that gives each of us his worth.*

André Gide

Things are very different today than they were when your parents and teachers were growing up. In fact, half the jobs of today did not even exist 10 years ago. Here are a few examples:

- The Internet started to grow in 1995 and that industry still employs more people than the publishing or advertising industries.
- The telecommunications and health care industries are nothing like what they were even a few years ago.
- Service businesses are growing too, and the jobs include more than hamburger flippers and home health care workers. For example, an African American millionaire who died recently had started a very exclusive limousine and concierge business serving the rich and famous and had dozens of employees.
- Entire *professions* have changed. Being a doctor or lawyer is no longer what it used to be.

**Young people tend to select careers they think they already know: what they see in their neighborhoods, on TV, or what relatives do.**

We can't know what the careers of the future will be—because they're in the future—but we do know how to think about them.

## A Way to *Think* about Career Choices

I recently met with a 30-year-old attorney. He had excelled in law school and was now working for a prestigious law firm. But he was miserable and derived no enjoyment from his work. He had gone into law because it was expected of him, but his heart was not in it. It was the wrong field for him.

Young people tend to select careers they think they already know: They select what they see around their neighborhoods or what they see on television. Sometimes they are urged to go into the same fields as their parents or other relatives. However, you will be happier *and* more successful if you choose a field based on what *you* personally enjoy doing and also do well, and based on *your* interests, abilities, and values.

You *can* develop a broader vision of the possibilities that lie ahead. You can develop *a way to think* about career choices and avoid serious errors.

To be successful and satisfied, you need to develop both self-awareness and an awareness of the world. You need to understand what you enjoy doing and also do well (self-awareness) and you need to find out more about what is going on in the world, beyond video games and celebrity sneakers.

**We can't know what the careers of the future will be—because they're in the *future*—but we *do* know how to think about them.**

## An Exercise for Developing Awareness of the World

The world today is complex and interesting, and there's plenty of opportunity to go around. You can become more aware of the different ways people earn a living today. This will help you imagine greater possibilities for yourself.

Virtually everything a person looks at can be seen in terms of careers. Here are a few examples.

- Someone developed, produced, marketed, and distributed the programs kids use on the Internet or the games they're playing on their CD-ROMs.
- In fact, someone made, marketed, and distributed just about everything you see, from the telephones in your home to the home itself. This includes manufactured goods such as furniture and fixtures, paint and wallpaper, steps and doors. It also includes "brainware," such as the writing in magazines and newspapers and the computer programs in calculators and remote controls.
- A lot of jobs have to do with health care (all the jobs in hospitals and HMOs, for example), telecommunications (who's behind all those reduced telephone rates?), and education (not just teachers, but the administrators, too).
- What about museums and bookstores, post offices, and Wall Street, small as well as giant retail stores?

And this just touches the surface. People work as economists and clergy. They take care of babies, the elderly and sick, animals and plants.

Here are a couple of exercises to stimulate your thinking.

- Try naming all the jobs you can think of in a particular organization. In a hospital, for example, there are various kinds of medical personnel, but the back office staff as well (accounting perations, computers, security, and so on).
- Take a look at the display ads in the employment section of the newspaper. The huge variety of career positions is food for thought.

**You can become more aware of the different ways people earn a living today.**

---

*One's prime is elusive. . . . You must be on the alert to recognize your prime at whatever time of life it may occur.*

Muriel Spark, *The Prime of Miss Jean Brodie*

## The Seven Stories: An Exercise for Developing Self-Awareness

In addition to becoming aware of the outside world, you need to become more *self*-aware. You need to figure out the things you enjoy doing and also do well, and the best exercise for doing this is the Seven Stories Exercise in this section.

You will start by analyzing your accomplishments. Think about the answer to this: "Tell me something you've done in your life that is an accomplishment, but it must be something you enjoyed doing and also did well." Be as specific as possible. For example, "writing" is not good enough, but "Writing an essay on my summer vacation" is an accomplishment you can analyze. After you name a few accomplishments, rank them in the order of the ones you enjoyed the most and did the best. Then answer the following questions about *each:*

- What was the main *accomplishment* for you?
- What did you *enjoy the most?*
- What did you *do the best?*

- What *led up to your doing this thing?* (e.g., I was assigned to do it, thought it up myself, etc.)
- What was your *relationship with others?* (e.g., I was the leader, worked alone, inspired team members, etc.)
- Describe the *environment* in which you performed.
- What was the *subject matter?* (e.g., music, mechanics, trees, numbers, etc.)

**You will see threads that run throughout the stories**. Pay attention to those threads. "Oh, I see that I enjoyed working alone on that project. And it appears that I like to add things up."

**To be successful and satisfied, young people need to develop both self-awareness and an awareness of the world.**

Your *motivated abilities* (that is, the things you enjoy doing and also do well) may or may not change over time. However, self-knowledge is a worthwhile skill to develop. The more aware you are about yourself, the better you will be at selecting careers that are appropriate. You are simply trying to understand yourself and see yourself better. If you work with a parent or teacher on this, they should reflect back to you what you say about yourself and what they observe.

Let's look at the example of Suzanne who described a dramatic accomplishment: "When I was nine years old, I was living with my three sisters. There was a fire in our house and our cat had hidden under the bed. We were all outside, but I decided to run back in and save the cat. And I did it."

No matter what the story is, delve in a little by asking yourself these two questions: What gave you the sense of accomplishment? and What about that made you proud? These questions give you a quick fix on yourself. You can also ask the questions listed earlier.

I asked Suzanne these questions. She said at first: "I was proud because I did what I thought was right." When I probed a little, she added: "I had a sense of accomplishment because I was able to make an instant decision under pressure. I was proud because I overcame my fear."

I asked Suzanne for another story to see what patterns might emerge when we put the two together. In both stories, Suzanne showed that she was good at making decisions in tense situations. She showed a good intuitive sense. She's decisive and likes fast-paced, energetic situations. She likes it when she overcomes her own fears as well as the objections of others.

We needed more than two stories to see if these patterns ran throughout Suzanne's life and to see what other patterns might emerge. After the full exercise, Suzanne felt for sure that she wanted excitement in her jobs, a sense of urgency—that she wanted to be in a position where she had a chance to be decisive and operate intuitively. Those are the conditions she enjoys and under which she operates at her best. Suzanne can confidently say that she thrives on excitement, high pressure, and quick decision making. She'll probably do better in jobs that have those elements and match her skills, interests, and values.

**Try naming all the jobs you can think of in a particular organization, such as a hospital.**

---

*It has long been an axiom of mine that the little things are infinitely the most important.*

A. Conan Doyle, *A Case of Identity*

## Another Exercise for Developing Self-Awareness

When you were a child, you were probably asked the question that has become a cliché: "What would you like to be when you grow up?" Whatever job you named (policeman, dancer, football star), think of what appealed to you about that job. If you wanted to be a firefighter, was it because you wanted to help people, liked excitement, wanted a uniform—or what? If you wanted to become a model, was it because you liked beauty, attention, poise—or what?

Then you can think about the fields that interest you today.

- Examine those jobs to determine whether they actually have the elements you *think* they have (you may think a surgeon performs experiments and a firefighter rescues cats from trees).
- Think of other occupations that would contain the same elements that have appeal for you (such as, experimentation, helping animals).

If you want to be a football star because you like the physical activity, think of other jobs that have physical activity or simply realize that some interests should become hobbies rather than the means of earning a living.

Remember that you may have lots of jobs and lots of careers. As I said earlier, you can be a doctor *and* a concert violinist. Whatever you decided when you were five years old has probably changed, and what you think you want now may change later. That's okay. You can't guess what lies ahead! But it's not too soon to start thinking about yourself, the world outside, and your career. Having a job is not enough. You need a *direction.*

This new mind-set—examining yourself early and often—increases the chances that you will select satisfying occupations and be able to adapt as the workplace evolves.

*We are challenged on every hand to work untiringly to achieve excellence in our lifework. . . . If a man is called to be a street sweeper, he should sweep streets even as Michelangelo painted, or Beethoven composed music, or Shakespeare wrote poetry. He should sweep streets so well that all the host of heaven and earth will pause to say, "Here lives a great street sweeperwho did his job well."*

Rev. Martin Luther King Jr.

*Our deepest fear is not that we are inadequate. Our deepest fear is that we are powerful beyond measure. It is our light, not our darkness, that most frightens us. We ask ourselves, "Who am I to be brilliant, gorgeous, talented and fabulous?"*
*Actually, who are you not to be? You are a child of God. Your playing small doesn't serve the world. There's nothing enlightened about shrinking so that other people won't feel insecure around you.*
*We were born to make manifest the glory of God that is within us. It's not just in some of us; it's in everyone. And as we let our own light shine, we unconsciously give other people permission to do the same. As we are liberated from our own fear, our presence automatically liberates others.*

Nelson Mandela
1994 Inaugural Speech

*The Ugly Duckling was so happy and in some way he was glad that he had experienced so much hardship and misery; for now he could fully appreciate his tremendous luck and the great beauty that greeted him.*
*. . . And he rustled his feathers, held his long neck high, and with deep emotion he said: " I never dreamt of so much happiness, when I was the Ugly Duckling!"*

Hans Christian Anderson, *The Ugly Duckling*

# The Seven Stories Exercise Worksheet

Here is an opportunity to examine the most satisfying activities of your life and discover those skills you will want to use as you grow older. You will be looking at the times when you feel you did something very well that you also enjoyed doing. It doesn't matter what other people thought, or when in your life the experiences took place. **All that matters is that you felt happy about doing whatever it was and thought you did it well**. Think about when you were younger. When I did my own Seven Stories Exercise, I remembered the time when I was 10 years old, led a group of kids in the neighborhood, enjoyed it, and did it well. It might take you a few days to think of things to put on your list. Carry around a piece of paper to jot down ideas as you think of them.

## Section I

List below all the activities that meet the definition. Come up with at least 10. We ask for 10 stories so you won't be too selective. Just write down anything that occurs to you, no matter how trivial it may seem. Try to **think of concrete examples**, situations, and tasks, not generalized skills or abilities. It may be helpful if you say to yourself, "**There was the time when I**. . . ." Here are a few examples:

*RIGHT*
- *Wrote an essay on my favorite things.*
- *Improved my grade in math.*
- *Rode my bike in a fund-raising marathon.*
- *Made a basket in second grade.*

*WRONG*
- *Writing.*
- *Math.*
- *Bicycling.*
- *Working on projects alone.*

1. ______________________________
2. ______________________________
3. ______________________________
4. ______________________________
5. ______________________________
6. ______________________________
7. ______________________________
8. ______________________________
9. ______________________________
10. ______________________________

## Section II

For each accomplishment, describe what you did. Write the specifics, noting each step in detail. Notice the role you played and your relationship with others (member of team, working alone, leader, etc.), the subject matter, the skills used, and so on. Notice the threads that run through the stories so you can discover the things you do well that also give you satisfaction. What did you enjoy the most in each story? Do the best?

# Analyzing Your Seven Stories

Now it is time to analyze your stories. You are trying to look for the threads that run through them so that you will know the things you do well that also give you satisfaction. Some of the questions here sound similar. That's okay. They are a catalyst to make you think more deeply about the experience. The questions don't have any hidden psychological significance.

If your accomplishments happen to be mostly work related, this exercise will form the basis for your *positioning* or summary statement in your résumé, and also for your Two-Minute Pitch.

If these accomplishments are mostly not work related, they will still give you some idea of how you may want to slant your résumé, and they may give you an idea of how you will want your career to go in the long run.

For now, simply go through each story without trying to force it to come out any particular way. Just think hard about yourself. And be as honest as you can. When you have completed this analysis, the words in the next exercise may help you think of additional things. **Do this page first.**

**Story #1.** ______________________________

What was the ***main accomplishment*** for you?______________________________

______________________________

What about it did you ***enjoy most?***______________________________

______________________________

What did you ***do best?***______________________________

______________________________

What was your ***key motivator?***______________________________

______________________________

What ***led up to your getting involved?*** (e.g., assigned to do it, thought it up myself, etc.)__________

______________________________

What was your ***relationship with others?*** (e.g., leader, worked alone, inspired others, team member, etc.)

______________________________

Describe the ***environment*** in which you performed. ______________________________

______________________________

What was the ***subject matter?*** (e.g., music, mechanics, trees, budgets, etc.)______________________________

______________________________

**Story #2.** ______________________________

Main accomplishment? ______________________________

Enjoyed most? ______________________________

Did best? ______________________________

Key motivator? ______________________________

What led up to it? ______________________________

Your role? ______________________________

The environment?______________________________

The subject matter?______________________________

**Story #3.** ______________________________
Main accomplishment? ______________________________
Enjoyed most? ______________________________
Did best? ______________________________
Key motivator? ______________________________
What led up to it? ______________________________
Your role? ______________________________
The environment? ______________________________
The subject matter? ______________________________

**Story #4.** ______________________________
Main accomplishment? ______________________________
Enjoyed most? ______________________________
Did best? ______________________________
Key motivator? ______________________________
What led up to it? ______________________________
Your role? ______________________________
The environment? ______________________________
The subject matter? ______________________________

**Story #5.** ______________________________
Main accomplishment? ______________________________
Enjoyed most? ______________________________
Did best? ______________________________
Key motivator? ______________________________
What led up to it? ______________________________
Your role? ______________________________
The environment? ______________________________
The subject matter? ______________________________

**Story #6.** ______________________________
Main accomplishment? ______________________________
Enjoyed most? ______________________________
Did best? ______________________________
Key motivator? ______________________________
What led up to it? ______________________________
Your role? ______________________________
The environment? ______________________________
The subject matter? ______________________________

**Story #7.** ______________________________
Main accomplishment? ______________________________
Enjoyed most? ______________________________
Did best? ______________________________
Key motivator? ______________________________
What led up to it? ______________________________
Your role? ______________________________
The environment? ______________________________
The subject matter? ______________________________

---

*We are here to be excited from youth to old age, to have an insatiable curiosity about the world. . . . We are also here to help others by practicing a friendly attitude. And every person is born for a purpose. Everyone has a God-given potential, in essence, built into them. And if we are to live life to its fullest, we must realize that potential.*

Norman Vincent Peale

# Skills from Your Seven Stories

The numbers across the top represent each of your seven stories. Start with Story #1 and check off all of your specialized skills that appear in that story. When you've checked off the skills for all seven stories, total them.

| Story # | 1 | 2 | 3 | 4 | 5 | 6 | 7 | Total |
|---|---|---|---|---|---|---|---|---|
| Administration | | | | | | | | |
| Advising/Consulting | | | | | | | | |
| Analytical | | | | | | | | |
| Artistic Ability | | | | | | | | |
| Budgetary | | | | | | | | |
| Client Relations | | | | | | | | |
| Communication | | | | | | | | |
| Community Relations | | | | | | | | |
| Contract Negotiation | | | | | | | | |
| Control | | | | | | | | |
| Coordination | | | | | | | | |
| Creativity | | | | | | | | |
| Decisiveness | | | | | | | | |
| Design | | | | | | | | |
| Development | | | | | | | | |
| Financial | | | | | | | | |
| Foresight | | | | | | | | |
| Frugality | | | | | | | | |
| Fund-Raising | | | | | | | | |
| Human Relations | | | | | | | | |
| Information Mgmt. | | | | | | | | |
| Imagination | | | | | | | | |
| Individualism | | | | | | | | |
| Initiative | | | | | | | | |
| Inventiveness | | | | | | | | |
| Leadership | | | | | | | | |
| Liaison | | | | | | | | |
| Logic | | | | | | | | |
| Management | | | | | | | | |
| Marketing | | | | | | | | |
| Mathematical | | | | | | | | |
| Mechanical | | | | | | | | |
| Motivational | | | | | | | | |
| Negotiation | | | | | | | | |
| Observation | | | | | | | | |
| Organization | | | | | | | | |
| Other Talents | | | | | | | | |

*Note:* Job hunters enjoy exercises like this because they are simple. But **your experiences are more complex than the words on this page**. These words alone do not reflect the richness of what you have to offer. So Pay more attention to **the more in-depth answers you came up with on the preceding page,** and continue to analyze your stories throughout your life. You will find deeper and deeper answers about yourself.

| Story # | 1 | 2 | 3 | 4 | 5 | 6 | 7 | Total |
|---|---|---|---|---|---|---|---|---|
| Operations Mgmt. | | | | | | | | |
| Org. Design/Devel. | | | | | | | | |
| Ownership | | | | | | | | |
| Perceptiveness | | | | | | | | |
| Perseverance | | | | | | | | |
| Persuasiveness | | | | | | | | |
| Planning | | | | | | | | |
| Policy Making | | | | | | | | |
| Practicality | | | | | | | | |
| Presentation | | | | | | | | |
| Problem Solving | | | | | | | | |
| Procedures Design | | | | | | | | |
| Production | | | | | | | | |
| Program Concept | | | | | | | | |
| Program Design | | | | | | | | |
| Project Management | | | | | | | | |
| Promotion | | | | | | | | |
| Public Relations | | | | | | | | |
| Public Speaking | | | | | | | | |
| Quality Assessment | | | | | | | | |
| Research | | | | | | | | |
| Resourcefulness | | | | | | | | |
| Sales Ability | | | | | | | | |
| Service | | | | | | | | |
| Showmanship | | | | | | | | |
| Speaking | | | | | | | | |
| Staff Dev./Mgmt. | | | | | | | | |
| Strategic Planning | | | | | | | | |
| Stress Tolerance | | | | | | | | |
| Systems | | | | | | | | |
| Teamwork | | | | | | | | |
| Tenacity | | | | | | | | |
| Training | | | | | | | | |
| Travel | | | | | | | | |
| Troubleshooting | | | | | | | | |
| Writing | | | | | | | | |
| Other Talents | | | | | | | | |

Top six or seven Specialized Skills, according to which had the most checkmarks:

1. ____________________
2. ____________________
3. ____________________
4. ____________________
5. ____________________
6. ____________________
7. ____________________

# Your Current Work-Related Values

What is important to you? Your values change as you grow and change, so they need to be reassessed continually. At various stages in your career, you may value money, or leisure time, or independence on the job, or working for something you believe in. See what is important to you *now.* This will help you not be upset if, for instance, a job provides you with the freedom you wanted, but not the kind of money your friends are making.

Sometimes we are not aware of our own values. It may be that, at this stage of our life, time with our family is most important to you. For some people, money or power is most important, but they may be reluctant to admit it—even to themselves.

Values are the driving force behind what we do. It is important to truthfully understand what we value in order to increase our chances of getting what we want.

Look at the following list of values. Think of each in terms of your overall career objectives. Rate the degree of importance you would assign to each for yourself, using this scale:

1—Not at all important in my choice of job
2—Not very but somewhat important
3—Reasonably important
4—Very important

Add other values that don't appear on the list or substitute wording you are more comfortable with.

___ the chance to advance
___ work on frontiers of knowledge
___ having authority (responsibility)
___ helping society
___ helping others
___ meeting challenges
___ working for something I believe in
___ public contact
___ enjoyable colleagues
___ competition
___ ease (freedom from worry)
___ influencing people
___ enjoyable work tasks
___ working alone
___ being an expert
___ personal growth and development
___ independence
___ artistic or other creativity
___ learning
___ location of workplace
___ tranquility
___ money earned
___ change and variety
___ have time for personal life
___ fast pace
___ power
___ adventure/risk taking
___ prestige
___ moral fulfillment
___ recognition from superiors, society, peers
___ security (stability)
___ physical work environment
___ chance to make impact
___ clear expectations and procedures

Of those you marked "4," circle the five **most** important to you today:

- If forced to compromise on any of these, which one would you give up? ____________________
- Which one would you be most reluctant to give up? ____________________

Describe in 10 or 20 words what you want most in your life and/or career.

# Other Exercises
# Interests, Satisfiers, and Bosses

## Interests Exercise

For many people, interests should stay as interests—things they do on the side. For others, their interests may be a clue to the kinds of jobs they should do next or in the long run. Only you can decide whether your interests should become part of your work life.

List all the things you really like to do—anything that makes you feel good and gives you satisfaction. List those areas in which you have developed a relatively in-depth knowledge or expertise. For ideas, think of your day, your week, the seasons of the year, places, people, work, courses, roles, leisure time, friends, and family. Think of how you spend your discretionary time.

- Think about the books you read, the magazines you subscribe to, the section of the newspaper you turn to.
- Think about knowledge you've built up simply because you're interested in it.
- Think about the volunteer work you do—what are the recurring assignments you tend to get and enjoy?
- Think about your hobbies—are there one or two you have become so involved in that you have built up a lot of expertise/information in those areas?
- What are the things you find yourself doing all the time and enjoying, even though you don't have to do them?

Your interests may be a clue to what you would like in a job. Rob worked at a law firm but loved everything about wine. He left the law firm to become a lawyer in a wine company. Most people's interests should stay as interests, but you never know until you think about it.

______________________________

______________________________

______________________________

______________________________

______________________________

## Satisfiers and Dissatisfiers Exercise

Simply list every job you have ever had. List what was satisfying and dissatisfying about each job. Some people are surprised to find that they were sometimes most satisfied by the vacation, pay, title, and other perks but were not satisfied with the job itself.

| **Job** | **Satisfiers** | **Dissatisfiers** |
|---|---|---|
| | | |
| | | |
| | | |
| | | |

## Bosses Exercise

Make a list of all the *bosses* you have ever had in work situations. Use a very broad definition. They don't have to have been *bosses* in the strictest sense of the word. Include bosses from part-time jobs, summer jobs, and even professors with whom you worked closely as a student.

Examine those bosses you have had a good relationship with and those you have not, and determine what you need in your future relationship with bosses. If you have had a lot of problems with bosses, discuss this with your counselor.

| **Boss** | **Good Relationship** | **Poor Relationship** |
|---|---|---|
| | | |
| | | |
| | | |
| | | |

# Looking into Your Future

*There are more things in heaven and earth, Horatio, than are dreamt of in your philosophy.*

William Shakespeare, *Hamlet*

Your motivated abilities tell you the *elements* you need to make you happy, your values exercise tells you the values that are important to you right now, and the interests exercise may give you a clue to other fields or industries to explore. But none of them gives you a feel for the *scope* of what may lie ahead.

Dreams and goals can be great driving forces in our lives. We feel satisfied when we are working toward them—even if we never reach them. People who have dreams or goals do better than people who don't.

Setting goals will make a difference in your life, and this makes sense. Every day we make dozens of choices. People with dreams make choices that advance them in the right direction. People without dreams also make choices—but their choices are strictly present-oriented with little thought of the future. When you are aware of your current situation, and you also know where you want to go, a natural tension leads you forward faster.

When you find a believable dream that excites you, don't forget it. In the heat of our day-to-day living, our dreams slip out of our minds. Happy people keep an eye on the future as well as the present.

## *Freeing-Up* Exercises

Here are a few exercises to inspire you and move you forward, add meaning to your everyday life, and give it some long-term purpose.

It's okay if you never reach your dreams. In fact, it can be better to have some dreams that you will probably never reach, so long as you enjoy the *process* of trying to reach them. For example, a real estate developer may dream of owning all the real estate in Phoenix. He may wind up owning much more than if he did not have that dream. If he enjoys the *process* of acquiring real estate, that's all that matters.

### Exercise #1—Write Your Obituary

*Every now and then I think about my own death, and I think about my own funeral. . . . I ask myself, "What is it that I would want said?"*

*Say I was a drum major for justice; say that I was a drum major for peace; say that I was a drum major for righteousness. All of the other shallow things will not matter. . . . I just want to leave a committed life behind.*

Rev. Martin Luther King Jr.

Rev. Martin Luther King Jr. knew how he wanted to be remembered. He had a dream, and it drove his life. Write out what you would want the newspapers to say about *you* when you die. Alfred Nobel had a chance to *rewrite* his obituary. The story goes that his cousin, who was also named

Alfred, died. The newspapers, hearing of the death of Alfred Nobel, printed the prepared obituary—for the wrong man. Alfred read it the day after his cousin's death. He was upset by what the obituary said because it starkly showed him how he would be remembered: as the well-known inventor of a cheap explosive called dynamite.

Alfred resolved to change his life. Today, he's remembered as the Swedish chemist and inventor who provided for the Nobel Prizes.

Write your obituary as you want to be remembered after your death. Include parts that are *not* related to your job. If you don't like the way your life seems to be headed, change it—just as Alfred Nobel did. Write your own obituary, and *then make a list of the things you need to do to get there.*

### Exercise #2—Invent a Job

If you could have any job in the world, what would it be? Don't worry about the possibility of ever finding that job—make it up! Invent it. Write it out. It may spark you to think of how to create that job in real life.

### Exercise #3—If You Had a Million

If you had a million dollars (or maybe 10 million) but still had to work, what would you do?

When I asked myself this question some time ago, I decided I'd like to continue doing what I was doing at work but would like to write a book on job hunting because I felt I had something to say. I did write that book—and I've gone on to write others!

People often erroneously see a lack of money as a stumbling block to their goals. Think about it: Is there some way you could do what you want without a million dollars? Then do it!

### Exercise #4—Your Fifteen-Year and Forty Year Visions

Take a look at this very important exercise, which starts on the next page.

# Your Fifteen-Year Vision® and Your Forty-Year Vision®

*In my practice as a psychiatrist, I have found that helping people to develop personal goals has proved to be the most effective way to help them cope with problems.*

Ari Kiev, M.D., *A Strategy for Daily Living*

If you could imagine your ideal life five years from now, what would it be like? How would it be different from the way it is now? If you made new friends during the next five years, what would they be like? Where would you be living? What would your hobbies and interests be? How about 10 years from now? Twenty? Thirty? Forty? Think about it!

Some people feel locked in by their present circumstances. Many say it is too late for them. But a lot can happen in 5, 10, 20, 30 or 40 years. Reverend King had a dream. His dream helped all of us, but his dream helped him, too. He was living according to a vision (which he thought was God's plan for him). *It gave him a purpose in life.* Most successful people have a vision.

A lot can happen to you over the next few decades—and most of what happens is up to you. If you see the rest of your life as boring, I'm sure you will be right. Some people pick the *sensible* route or the one that fits in with how others see them, rather than the one that is best for them.

On the other hand, you can come up with a few scenarios of how your life could unfold. In that case, you will have to do a lot of thinking and a lot of research to figure out which path makes most sense for you and will make you happiest.

When a person finds a vision that is right, the most common reaction is fear. It is often safer to *wish* a better life than to actually go after it.

I know what that's like. It took me two years of thinking and research to figure out the right path for myself—one that included my motivated abilities (Seven Stories Exercise) as well as the sketchy vision I had for myself. Then it took *10 more years* to finally take the plunge and commit to that path—running The Five O'Clock Club. I was 40 years old when I finally took a baby step in the right direction, and I was terrified.

You may be lucky and find it easy to write out your vision of your future. Or you may be more like me: It may take a while and a lot of hard work. You can speed up the process by reviewing your assessment results with a Five O'Clock Club career counselor. He or she will guide you along. Remember, when I was struggling, the country didn't *have* Five O'Clock Club counselors or even these exercises to guide us.

Test your vision and see if that path seems right for you. Plunge in by researching it and meeting with people in the field. If it is what you want, chances are you will find some way to make it happen. If it is not exactly right, you can modify it later—after you have gathered more information and perhaps gotten more experience.

## Start with the Present

Write down, in the present tense, the way your life is right now and the way you see yourself at each of the time frames listed. **This exercise should take no more than one hour**. Allow your unconscious to tell you what you will be doing in the future. Just quickly comment on each of the questions listed on the following page, and then move on to the next. If you kill yourself off too early (say, at age 60), push it 10 more years to see what would have happened if you had lived. Then push it another 10, just for fun.

When you have finished the exercise, ask yourself how you feel about your entire life as you laid it out in your vision. Some people feel depressed when they see on paper how their lives are going, and they cannot think of a way out. But they feel better when a good friend or a Five O'Clock Club counselor helps them think of a better future to work toward. If you don't like your vision, you are allowed to change it—it's your life. Do what you want with it. Pick the kind of life you want.

Start the exercise with the way things are now so you will be realistic about your future. Now, relax and have a good time going through the years. Don't think too hard. Let's see where you wind up. You have plenty of time to get things done.

**The 15-year mark proves to be the most important for most people. It's far enough away from the present to allow you to dream.**

# Your Fifteen- and Forty-Year Vision Worksheet

1. The year is <u>xxxx</u> (current year).
   You are ___________ years old right now.

- Tell me what your life is like right now. (Say anything you want about your life as it is now.)
- Who are your friends? What do they do for a living?
- What is your relationship with your family, however you define "family"?
- Are you married? Single? Children? (List ages.)
- Where are you living? What does it look like?
- What are your hobbies and interests?
- What do you do for exercise?
- How is your health?
- How do you take care of your spiritual needs?
- What kind of work are you doing?
- What else would you like to note about your life right now?

Year: ________ Your Age ________________

______________________________________________

______________________________________________

______________________________________________

______________________________________________

______________________________________________

______________________________________________

______________________________________________

______________________________________________

______________________________________________

______________________________________________

______________________________________________

______________________________________________

______________________________________________

______________________________________________

______________________________________________

Don't worry if you don't like everything about your life right now. Most people do this exercise because they want to improve themselves. They want to *change* something. What do *you* want to change? **Please continue.**

2. The year is <u>xxxx</u> (current year + **5**).
   You are _______ years old.
   (Add 5 to present age.)
   **Things are going well for you.**

- What is your life like now at this age? (Say anything you want about your life as it is now.)
- Who are your friends? What do they do for a living?
- What is your relationship with your "family"?
- Married? Single? Children? (List their ages now.)
- Where are you living? What does it look like?
- What are your hobbies and interests?
- What do you do for exercise?
- How is your health?
- How do you take care of your spiritual needs?
- What kind of work are you doing?
- What else would you like to note about your life right now?

Year: ________ Your Age ________________

______________________________________________

______________________________________________

______________________________________________

______________________________________________

______________________________________________

______________________________________________

______________________________________________

______________________________________________

______________________________________________

______________________________________________

______________________________________________

______________________________________________

______________________________________________

______________________________________________

______________________________________________

(continues)

| | |
|---|---|
| 3. The year is **<u>xxxx</u>** (current year + **15**).<br>You are ________ years old.<br>(Current age plus 15.)<br>• What is your life like now at this age? (Say anything you want about your life as it is now.)<br>• Who are your friends? What do they do for a living?<br>• What is your relationship with your "family"?<br>• Married? Single? Children? (List their ages now.)<br>• Where are you living? What does it look like?<br>• What are your hobbies and interests?<br>• What do you do for exercise?<br>• How is your health?<br>• How do you take care of your spiritual needs?<br>• What kind of work are you doing?<br>• What else would you like to note about your life right now? | Year: ________ Your Age ________ |

The 15-year mark is an especially important one. This age is far enough away from the present that people often loosen up a bit. It's so far away that it's not threatening. Imagine *your* ideal life. What is it like? Why were you put here on this earth? What were you meant to do here? What kind of life were you meant to live? Give it a try and see what you come up with. If you can't think of anything now, try it again in a week or so. On the other hand, if you got to the 15-year mark, why not keep going?

| | |
|---|---|
| 4. The year is **<u>xxxx</u>** (current year + **25**).<br>You are ________ years old!<br>(Current age plus 25.) | Year: ________ Your Age ________<br>Using a blank piece of paper, answer all of the questions for this stage of your life. |
| 5. The year is **<u>xxxx</u>** (current year + **35**).<br>You are ________ years old!<br>(Current age plus 35.) | Repeat. |
| 6. The year is **<u>xxxx</u>** (current year + **45**).<br>You are ________ years old!<br>(Current age plus 45.) | Repeat. |
| 7. The year is **<u>xxxx</u>** (current year + **55**).<br>You are ________ years old!<br>(Current age plus 55.) | Keep going. How do you feel about your life? You are allowed to change the parts you don't like. |
| (Keep going—don't die until you are past 80!) | |

You have plenty of time to get done everything you want to do. Imagine wonderful things for yourself. You have plenty of time. Get rid of any *negative programming*. For example, if you imagine yourself having poor health because your parents suffered from poor health, see what you can do about that. If you imagine yourself dying early because that runs in your family, see what would have happened had you lived longer. It's your life—your only one. As they say, "This is the real thing. It's not a dress rehearsal."

# Case Study: Howard Developing a Vision

*In the thick of active life, there is more need to stimulate fancy than to control it.*

George Santayana, *The Life of Reason*

Howard attended a Five O'Clock Club group that specializes in helping people who are not yet in professional-level jobs. He had done the Seven Stories and other exercises and had tried to do the Forty-Year Vision. Like most people, he had left out important parts, such as what he would be doing for a living. That's okay. I asked him if he would mind doing it in the small discussion group.

At the time, Howard was 35 years old and worked in a lower level job in the advertising industry. He wanted to advance in his career by getting another job in advertising. Based on our research into the jobs of the future, which showed that his current industry was a shaky choice, we asked him to postpone selecting an industry while we helped him complete his Forty-Year Vision.

---

*HAPPY: All I can do now is wait for the merchandise manager to die. And suppose I get to be merchandise manager? He's a good friend of mine, and he just built a terrific estate on Long Island. And he lived there about two months and sold it, and now he's building another one. He can't enjoy it once it's finished. And I know that's just what I would do. I don't know what the hell I'm workin' for.*

Arthur Miller, *Death of a Salesman*

Howard was just getting started on his career even though he was 35. You're just getting started, too. Regardless of your age, take pen to paper and force yourself to write something. You can always change it later.

## Filling in His Forty-Year Vision

Kate: "Howard, you're 35 years old right now. Tell me: Who are your friends, and what do they do for a living?"

Howard: "John is a messenger, Keith minds the kids while his wife works, and Greg delivers food."

Kate: "What do you do for a living?"

Howard: "I work in the media department of an advertising agency."

Kate: "Okay. Now, let's go out a few years. You're 40 years old, and you've made a number of new friends in the past 5 years. Who are these people? What are they doing for a living?"

Howard: "One friend is a medical doctor; another works in finance or for the stock exchange; and a third is in a management position in the advertising industry."

Kate: "That's fine. Now, let's go out further. You're 50 years old, and you have made a lot of new friends. What are they doing for a living?"

Howard: "One is an executive managing 100 to 200 people in a corporation and is very well respected; a second one is in education—he's the principal or the administrator of an experimental high school and gets written up in the newspapers all the time; a third is a vice president in finance or banking."

Kate: "Those are important-sounding friends you have, Howard. But who are you and what are you doing that these people are associating with you?"

Howard: "I'm not sure."

Kate: "Well, how much money are you making at age 50 in today's dollars?"

Howard: "I'm making $150,000 a year."

Kate: "I'm impressed. What are you doing to earn that kind of money, Howard? What kind of place are you working in? Remember, you don't *have* to be specific about the industry or field you're in. For example, how do you dress for work?"

Howard: "I wear a suit and tie every day. I have a staff of 60 people working for me: 6 departments, with 10 people in each department."

Kate: "And what are those people doing all day?"

Howard: "They're doing paperwork, or computer work."

Kate: "That's great, Howard. We now have a pretty good idea of what you'll be doing in the future. We just need to fill in some details."

I said to the group: "Perhaps Howard won't be making $150,000, but he'll certainly be making a lot by his own standards. And maybe it won't be 60 people, but it will certainly be a good-sized staff. What Howard is talking about here is a concept. The details may be wrong, but the concept is correct."

---

*If I see what I want real good in my mind, I don't notice any pain in getting it.*

George Foreman, former heavyweight boxing champion of the world

Howard said: "But I'm not sure if that's what I really want to do."

Kate: "It may not be exactly what you want to do, Howard, but it's in the right direction and contains the elements you really want. What you just said fits in with your Seven Stories Exercise (one story was about your work with computers; another was about an administrative accomplishment). Think about it for next week, but I'll tell you this: You won't decide you want to be a dress designer, like Roxanne here. Nor will you say you want to sell insurance, like Barry. What you will do will be very close to what you just described.

"If you come back next week and say that you've decided to sell ice cream, for example, I'll tell you that you simply became afraid. Fear often keeps people from pursuing their dreams. Over the week, read about the jobs of the future, and let me know the industries you may want to investigate for your future career. It's usually better to pick growth industries rather than declining ones. You stand a better chance of rising with the tide."

## The Next Week

When it was Howard's turn in the group the next week, he announced that he had selected health care as the industry he wanted to investigate. That sounded good because it is a growth field and because there will be plenty of need for someone to manage a group of people working on computers.

We brainstormed the areas within health care that Howard could research. He could work in a hospital, an HMO, a health care association, and so on. He could learn about the field by reading the trade magazines having to do with health care administration, and he could start networking by meeting with someone else in the group who had already worked in a hospital.

## Week #3

Howard met with the other person in the group and got a feel for what it was like to work in a hospital. He also got a few names of people he could talk to—people at his level who could give him basic information. He had spent some time in a library reading trade magazines having to do with health care administration.

Howard needed to do a lot more research before he would be ready to meet with higher level people—those in a position to hire him.

## Week #4

Howard announced to the group that he had done more research, which helped him figure out that he should start in the purchasing area of a hospital, as opposed to the financial area, for example. In previous jobs, he had worked both as a buyer and as a salesman, so he knew both sides of the picture. He would spend some time researching the purchasing aspect of health care. That could be his entry point, and he could make other moves after he got into the field.

*A human being certainly would not grow to be seventy or eighty years old if his longevity had no meaning for the species.*

C. G. Jung

## Week #5

Today Howard is ready to meet with higher level people in the health care field. As he networks around, he will learn even more about the field and select the job and the organization that will position him best for the long run—the situation that fits in best with his Forty-Year Vision.

After Howard gets his next job, he will occasionally come to the group to ask the others to help him think about his career and make moves within the organization. He will be successful in living his vision if he continues to do what needs to be done, never taking his eye off the ball.

If Howard sticks with his vision, he will make good money and live in the kind of place where he wants to live. Like many people who develop written plans, Howard has the opportunity to have his dream come true.

## You Can Do It Too

As I mentioned earlier, the group that Howard attended was a special Five O'Clock Club program that works mostly with adults who are not yet in the professional or managerial ranks and helps them get into professional-track jobs.

For example, Emlyn, a 35-year-old former babysitter, embarked on and completed a program to become a nurse's aide. This is her first step toward becoming an R.N., her ultimate career goal.

Calvin, who suffers from severe rheumatoid arthritis, hadn't worked in 10 years. Within 5 weeks of starting with us, he got a job as a consumer advocate with a center for the disabled and has a full caseload. We are continuing to work with him.

These ambitious, hardworking people did it, and so can you. It's not easy, but what else are you doing with your 24 hours a day? The people who did it followed this motto: "Have a dream. Make a plan. Take a step. Keep on climbing."

You can complain that you haven't gotten lucky breaks, but Howard, Emlyn, and Calvin didn't either.

They made their own breaks, attended a branch of The Five O'Clock Club, and kept plugging ahead despite difficulties. If they can do it, you can do it, too.

*You can either say the universe is totally random and it's just molecules colliding all the time and it's totally chaos and our job is to make sense of that chaos, or you can say sometimes things happen for a reason and your job is to discover the reason. But either way, I do see it meaning an opportunity and that has made all the difference.*

Christopher Reeve, former star of *Superman,* in an interview with Barbara Walters. Reeve became a quadriplegic after a horseback-riding accident.

*This is a real test of the wedding vows. He's my partner. He's my other half, literally. It's not within the realm of my imagination to do anything less than what I'm doing.*

Mrs. Christopher Reeve (Dana), in that same interview

*We live in an age when art and the things of the spirit come last. The truth still holds, however, that through dedication and devotion one achieves another kind of victory. I mean the ability to overcome one's problems and meet them head on."Serve life and you will be sustained."That is a truth which reveals itself at every turn in the road. I speak with inner conviction because I have been through the struggle. What I am trying to emphasize is that, whatever the nature of the problem, it can only be tackled creatively. There is no book of "openings," as in chess lore, to be studied. To find an opening one has to make a breach in the wall—and the wall is almost always in one's own mind. If you have the vision and the urge to undertake great tasks, then you will discover in yourself the virtues and the capabilities required for their accomplishment. When everything fails, pray! Perhaps only when you have come to the end of your resources will the light dawn. It is only when we admit our limitations that we find there are no limitations.*

Henry Miller, *Big Sur and the Oranges of Hieronymous Bosch*

# Self-Assessment Summary

Summarize the results of all of the exercises. This information will help define the kind of environment that suits you best, and will also help you brainstorm some possible job targets. Finally, it can be used as a checklist against job possibilities. When you are about to receive a job offer, use this list to help you analyze it objectively.

1. **What I need in my relationship with bosses:** ______________________

2. **Job satisfiers/dissatisfiers:**

   Satisfiers: ______________________

   Dissatisfiers: ______________________

3. **Most important work-related values:** ______________________

4. **Special interests:** ______________________

5. **Threads running through the Seven Stories analysis:**
   Main accomplishments: ______________________
   Key motivators: ______________________
   Enjoyed most; did best: ______________________
   My role: ______________________
   The environment: ______________________
   The subject matter: ______________________

6. **Top six or seven Specialized Skills:**

   ______________________
   ______________________
   ______________________
   ______________________
   ______________________
   ______________________
   ______________________

7. **From Fifteen- or Forty-Year Vision:**

   Where I see myself in the long run: ______________________
   ______________________
   ______________________

   What I need to get there: ______________________
   ______________________
   ______________________

8. **My basic personality and the kinds of work cultures into which it will fit:** ______________________
   ______________________
   ______________________

# How to Change Careers

*If an idea, I realized, were really a valuable one, there must be some way of realizing it.*

Elizabeth Blackwell
(the first woman to earn a medical degree)

So you thought you would spend a few years trying out various fields and pick the one that you liked the most. The problem is that once you landed that first accounting job, your resume said "accountant." Now you're having a hard time being considered for a technology or sales job instead.

All things being equal, finding a job similar to your old one is quicker. A career change will probably take more time. What's more, the job-hunting techniques are different for both.

---

*When a large American steel company began closing plants in the early 1980's, it offered to train the displaced steelworkers for new jobs. But the training never "took"; the workers drifted into unemployment and odd jobs instead. Psychologists came in to find out why, and found the steelworkers suffering from acute identity crises. "How could I do anything else?" asked the workers. "I am* a lathe operator."

Peter Senge, *The Fifth Discipline*

## It's Not Easy to Categorize Job Hunters

The easier it is to categorize you, the easier it is for others to see where you fit in their organizations and for you to find a job. Search firms, for example, generally will not handle career changers. They can more easily market those who want to stay in the same function in the same industry.

## You Must Offer Proof of Your Interest and Competence

*Civility is not a sign of weakness, and sincerity is always subject to proof.*

John F. Kennedy
Inaugural Address, January 20, 1961

Many job changers essentially say to a prospective employer, "Give me a chance. You won't be sorry." They expect the employer to hire them on faith, and that's unrealistic. The employer has a lot to lose. First, you may lose interest in the new area after you are hired. Second, you may know so little about the new area that it turns out not to be what you had imagined. Third, you may not bring enough knowledge and skill to the job and fail—even though your desire may be sincere.

The hiring manager should not have to take those risks. It is the job hunter's obligation to prove that he or she is truly interested and capable.

## How You as a Career Changer Can Prove Your Interest and Capability

- Read the industry's trade journals.
- Get to know the people in that industry or field.
- Join its organizations; attend the meetings.

- Be persistent.
- Show how your skills can be transferred.
- Write proposals.
- Be persistent.
- Take relevant courses, part-time jobs, or do volunteer work related to the new industry or skill area.
- Be persistent!

Ted wanted to move from the cosmetics industry to the casino industry. As a career changer, he had to offer proof to make up for his lack of experience. One proof was that he had read the industry's trade newspapers for years. When he met people in his search, he could truthfully tell them that he had followed their careers. He could also say he had hope for himself because he knew that so many of them had come from outside the industry.

Another proof of his interest was that he had sought out so many casino management people at trade association meetings and by contacting them directly. After a while, he ran into people he had met on previous occasions. Employers want people who are sincerely interested in their industry, their company, and the function the new hire will fill. Sincerity and persistence count, but they are usually not enough.

Another proof Ted offered was that he figured out how to apply his experience to the casino industry and its problems. Writing proposals to show how you would handle the job is one way to prove you are knowledgeable and interested in an area new to you. Some people prove their interest by taking courses, finding part-time jobs, or doing volunteer work to learn the new area and build marketable skills.

Ted initially decided to *wing it* and took trips to Atlantic City and Las Vegas hoping someone would hire him on the spot. That didn't work and took two months and some money. Then he began a serious job hunt—following the system that will be explained in the pages that follow. He felt he was doing fine, but the hunt was taking many months, and he was not sure it would result in an offer.

After searching in the casino industry for six months, Ted began a campaign in his old field—the cosmetics industry. Predictably, he landed a job there quickly. Ted took this as a sign that he didn't have a chance in the new field. He lost sight of the fact that a career change is more difficult and takes longer.

Ted accepted the cosmetics position, but his friends encouraged him to continue his pursuit of a career in the casino industry—a small industry with relatively few openings compared with the larger cosmetics industry.

Shortly after he accepted the new position, someone from Las Vegas called him for an interview, and he got the job of his dreams. His efforts paid off because he had done a thorough campaign in the casino industry. It just took time.

Ted was not unusual in giving up on a career change. It can take a long time, and sometimes the pressure to get a paycheck will force people to take inappropriate jobs. That's life. Sometimes we have to do things we don't want to. There's nothing wrong with that.

What *is* wrong is forgetting that you had a dream. What *is* wrong is expecting people to hire you on faith and hope, when what they deserve is proof that you're sincere and that hiring you has a good chance of working. *What is wrong is underestimating the effort it takes to make a career change.*

In the future, most people will have to change careers. Your future may hold an involuntary career change, as new technologies make old skills obsolete. Those same new technologies open up new career fields for those who are prepared—and ready to change. Know what you're up against. Don't take shortcuts. And don't give up too early. Major career changes are normal today and may prove desirable or essential tomorrow.

---

*Ruth made a great mistake when he gave up pitching. Working once a week, he might have lasted a long time and become a great star.*

Tris Speaker, manager of the Cleveland Indians, commenting on Babe Ruth's plans to change from a pitcher to an outfielder, spring 1921

# Career Makeovers: Four Who Did It

*Fortune sides with him who dares.*

Virgil, *Aeneid*

The following stories on career changers were written by Patricia Kitchen, a staff writer for *Newsday,* a large New York newspaper. The Five O'Clock Club worked with Patricia to provide this valuable information for their readers. Although these are *New York* stories, the approach can work in your town, too.

A variety of people wrote to *Newsday* telling them that they wanted to make a career change. The newspaper chose nine who represented goals or situations common to many readers. I worked with them weekly, in a group, to help them refine their goals and develop plans to make their career dreams come true.

As Patricia said in her introductory article: "While the recareering process is similar for most, each person profiled has a different plan and is starting from a different place. One man had been laid off and several feared it."

Read how these regular, everyday folks made their dreams come true. The process worked for them. It can work for you. All of them are starting out in their careers, and so are you.

# Case Study: Making a Winning Move to Sports

By Patricia Kitchen, Staff Writer for *Newsday*

*If you really want to advise me, do it on Saturday afternoon between 1 and 4 o'clock. And you've got 25 seconds to do it, between plays. Not on Monday. I know the right thing to do on Monday.*

Alex Agase, Northwestern football coach

Rich Kier caught baseball fever when he was seven years old, watching the World Series with his dad and his grandfather, who were both rooting for the Brooklyn Dodgers. For Kier, it was the beginning of his lifelong worship of Mickey Mantle and, like many boys, he started dreaming of playing centerfield for the New York Yankees. "Rock and roll was in its infancy, Mickey was our hero and the Yankees were on top. You couldn't ask for more than that," says Kier.

At age 35, he knows he's never going to play centerfield. But after logging 10 years in the credit and collection business—and, like many others, laid off from his job—Kier is resurrecting his dream of working in the sports industry. He's one of a group of readers chosen by this newspaper to work with counselor Kate Wendleton, director of The Five O'Clock Club, a national career coaching and outplacement firm, to refine their career goals and embark on short- and long-term plans to make them happen.

"The process is the same, no matter what your level. People need a plan. Without one, they're not successful," Wendleton told the group at their first meeting last fall. She helped each person list, analyze, and prioritize the seven most satisfying paid, or unpaid, experiences of their lives, to help guarantee their vision of a new profession is realistic, not just based on glamorized media images or pressures from society.

**Richard Kier, a career-makeover participant, has always dreamed of working for the New York Yankees in their business or legal operations.**

She also asked each to write a Forty-Year Vision, imagining where they would be and what they would be doing at 10-year intervals. After a little thought, it only took most people a couple of hours to actually write their plans. This long-range view will help them break down their pursuit into the small steps that will comprise a campaign. This way they don't feel intimidated at the thought of making a giant leap right away. "People with a longer perspective are more successful. Plus, you can keep your pay up if you look for ways to segue into a new career," Wendleton says.

Members of the group helped one another brainstorm ideas for careers, companies, or agencies to approach in doing research to further test the feasibility of their dream careers. Wendleton emphasized the need to define their targets, and for research. This way they can avoid the "I don't know what it is, but I'll know it when I see it" approach.

As for Kier, he's well into his research of the sports industry, and where he might fit in. After he was laid off, he took another job in the collection industry, but hated it. His wife encouraged him to go back to school to become a paralegal. Going into this career makeover project, his dream job was to work in the business operations or legal area of a professional baseball team, preferably the Yankees. Here's how he refined that dream, and a sketch of his game plan now.

## Major Lesson Learned

One team, or even one sport, is just too narrow a target. Without even going into the woes of professional baseball, it's not realistic to hitch your wagon to only one star. "The numbers have to be on your side," says Wendleton, who suggests targeting enough employers to represent 200 appropriate positions, even if they may be filled at this time. As she points out, "Sports is a huge industry."

So, with the help of the other group members, Kier brainstormed the possibilities to broaden his horizons. He's now researching football, hockey, and minor league affiliates, law firms with sports specialties, college athletic departments, sporting arenas like Madison Square Garden and the Nassau Coliseum, as well as organizations like the New York Mets, the National Football League, and USA Baseball, the group that governs amateur baseball. One member of the group tossed out the idea of the media end of the business and gave him a contact at *Golf* magazine. But when someone suggested sports equipment and manufacturing companies, Kier nixed that idea. "It just doesn't appeal to me. A baseball glove is just a baseball glove. It's a thing. There's no interaction."

## Wrong Turn

When Kier started his research, he jumped the gun. At the second counseling session, he told the group he had sent résumés to the people he was calling. "Wrong," said Wendleton. "That's the activity of a sprinter. This is a long-distance run."

Kier is still an outsider, and as such, getting a job so soon in his campaign is a long shot. His goal now is to gather information on how things work. "You need to get to know a critical mass of people and get to the point where you give as much information as you take away. That makes you a contributor, an insider, and at that stage, getting a job is more realistic," says Wendleton, who is also the author of The Five O'Clock Club series of career books.

## Resources and Research

So Kier adjusted his approach. "I'm finding out the value of research," he told the group. Now when he calls contacts, he says he is a career changer who wants to combine his legal experience with a sports career and just wants information on that process. "I let them know I have a definite idea about what I want. If you sound like you have no plan, they just say, 'Send a résumé,' and that's that. So far, no one has been discouraging."

Now when he reads publications like *Sporting News* and *Baseball America,* he sees them through the eyes not just of a fan, but of a career changer, looking for names, sources, and organizations. And he plans to attend an upcoming conference at Hofstra University on Babe Ruth. "I can make some good contacts there," he says.

## Short-Term Plan

"I anticipate it takes about a year to establish contacts and figure out what you want to do, can do, and won't do," says Kier. So, as he continues his research, he's now looking for a full-time paralegal job that hopefully will take him in the direction of his goal. He's completed an internship at a Garden City law firm and is now working part-time. As for salary, he anticipates taking a financial hit from the $41,000 he was making before he was laid off. Entry-level paralegals start out as low as $25,000, but he says there's potential to double that in two to three years. Fortunately, he has a supportive wife who works full-time as a nurse.

## Smart Move

Going into this project, Kier knew to build on the skills he's developing as a paralegal. It's unrealistic to plunge into a new industry cold, saying you'll take just anything. As Wendleton says, "The goal is to capitalize on skills you already have so you don't have to start at the bottom getting coffee for people. It's a way to keep your salary up."

## What Sports Experts Say

"Kier is definitely on the right track," says David Sussman, general counsel for the Yankees. "You can't look at it as one move [into the sports industry], but as two or three. You need to look for businesses that overlap."

To help flesh out his résumé, Kier can volunteer at corporate and nonprofit sports events, says Sylvia Allen, who's teaching an upcoming seminar at New York University called "Starting a Career in Sports and Special Events. "

As for job targets, Kier's smartest route is to pursue those major law firms that handle cases for teams, leagues, college athletic departments, or individual players, says David M. Carter, author of *You Can't Play the Game If You Don't Know the Rules — Career Opportunities in Sports Management* (Impact, Manassas Park, VA). Kier should also delve into more technical sports journals and specialized newsletters. "What he's reading now is great for fans, but not for practitioners. He needs meatier information beyond who's hit the most home runs," Carter says.

One concern Carter has is Kier's age. It's easier to break into an industry when you are 25 years old by taking an entry-level job, such as season ticket sales. Kier knows that's true, but as he says, "I'm not going to let it stop me. It's only a deterrent if you let it be." And, as he says, a lightbulb went off in his head when Wendleton told the group, "So what if you'll be 40 by the time you make your new career happen? You're going to be 40 anyway."

"That was a wake-up call. I don't want to be stuck in a position someday of saying 'I coulda, shoulda, woulda,'" says Kier.

# Case Study: Working with Animals Was Her First Love

By Patricia Kitchen, Staff Writer for *Newsday*

*If a cat spoke, it might say things like "Hey, I don't see the problem here."*

Roy Blount Jr.

Diane Murray has nursed baby mice with an eyedropper. She's rushed a wounded seagull to the vet. She hangs "Baby Geese Crossing" signs in nesting areas. She rescued a lost Yorkshire Terrier one Christmas and had him over for a filet mignon dinner. She's taken two dream vacations—one a photo safari to Kenya, the other to swim with dolphins in the Florida Keys. Plus, at her home in Seaford, Long Island, she has four cats, a dog, and two birds.

So why is Murray working as a manager at a travel agency instead of with animals? Back in 11th grade, "My guidance counselor talked me out of it. He guaranteed me I would never find a job in that career. He swayed me from animal-related fields, and I ended up going in for art education [in college]," she said.

Like many people, Murray, 37, was derailed at an early age from her true calling. She is one of a group of readers chosen to work with Kate Wendleton, director of The Five O'Clock Club, who is helping them get back on the right career track. As part of the process, Wendleton asked each person to list his or her 7 most satisfying life experiences—either paid or unpaid. Plus, everyone wrote a Forty-Year Vision, outlining at 10-year intervals how they would like to see their futures develop.

"I have been told countless times by the people I work with that I'm in the wrong profession. This is due to the fact that my 'first love' is so obvious," Murray wrote in a letter to this newspaper. So, with counsel from Wendleton and encouragement from the rest of the group, here's how she is plotting her career change into wildlife management or marine biology.

## It's a Process

Like many people with an eye on a different career, Murray was afraid of taking one big, dramatic leap. "That thought was overwhelming," she said. But Wendleton took the pressure off when she told the group: "You can do everything. You just can't do it all at once. That's why it's important to have a long-term plan, so you can fit it all in."

Murray's first stage is to research jobs that involve animals, make contact with people in the field, scout out volunteer opportunities, and collect information on degree programs. Stage two: to be volunteering by the spring and to start a degree program by the summer. In no way is she actually looking for a job at this point. She wouldn't be ready, said Wendleton. People need time to adjust—both emotionally and financially—to the idea of such a big change.

**Diane Murray got a kiss from Winston, a beluga whale, during her dream career day at the New York Aquarium.**

Murray does welcome the time to put her finances in order. She recently bought a new car, had an apartment built in her parents' home, and bought some furniture. Those bills are manageable given her present salary of about $30,000. But a career change could well mean a cut, so she wants to whittle down her financial obligations before she makes a move. As for taking a lower salary, she says, "Personal satisfaction for me is more important than the money."

## What about the Degree?

When Murray had fantasized about working with animals, one roadblock always loomed—she had no related degree. But, she now says, "It's a roadblock I can detour around." Several people she's spoken with had no formal education in the field. One woman at an aquarium answered an ad in the paper, another was hired right out of high school, and a dolphin trainer in Florida had been an air traffic controller.

Yet she knows education is important, so she's researching programs at Adelphi University, State College at Old Westbury, Hofstra University, Dowling College, and Nassau Community College, with an eye to taking one evening class each semester while she keeps her job at the travel agency. But she's not going to wait for the degree itself before moving into her new career. Her plan is to start looking for a new job two years from now, even if her degree is still in progress.

## Love and Marriage

Murray's career is not the only factor in her life equation. She would like to get married and start a family over the next five years, so that needs to be part of her written plan. Though Murray says she's skeptical, Wendleton told her she should use the same approach to find the right relationship that she's using to find the right career. "You have to intentionally and methodically make yourself run into the kind of people you want to meet. Most people, though, don't want to admit to the effort they put into finding a mate," Wendleton said.

Murray, a diehard romantic, maintains that "love is a little luck. The guy I'll probably fall in love with is the hunter I'm trying to stop [from killing animals]."

## Research

Once she saw she could make her dream job happen, Murray plunged into research. She read books such as *Opportunities in Animal and Pet Care Careers, Careers for Nature Lovers and Other Outdoor Types* and *Careers for Animal Lovers and Other Zoological Types.* She rejected the idea of being a veterinarian or vet technician—"I just couldn't see myself putting animals to sleep," she said.

To find volunteer opportunities, she called the Okeanos Ocean Research Foundation in Hampton Bays, the Aquarium for Wildlife Conservation in Coney Island, Volunteers for Wildlife in Huntington, and the Nature Conservancy in Cold Spring Harbor.

And she really got her nickel's worth out of those phone calls. Besides asking for literature to be mailed to her, she grilled everyone she spoke to about their jobs and workplaces. A night watchman talked to her for half an hour about how his daughter got a degree in zoology, found her job, and met her husband in a diving class. He also gave her names of other places to call. "That really broke the ice," Murray said. "It was so easy after that. So many people ended up telling me their personal stories."

Wendleton, who also is the author of The Five O'Clock Club series of career books, says the keys to this kind of research are discipline and enthusiasm. "You want to get people on your side—and not just people you see as high-level. Secretaries, receptionists—and night watchmen—can be tremendous sources of information."

## Expert Advice

Murray's approach—to volunteer while she's taking courses—is a good one, says

Kevin M. Walsh, director of marine mammal training at the Aquarium for Wildlife Conservation. Too often when he's hiring, he sees people with experience and no education or with education and no experience. He also says it's important to have a view of the job that is grounded in reality: "It looks glamorous, especially when you're feeding the dolphins in mid-July in your shorts. But it can be grueling, repetitious, and subject to the weather. Last February we had to shovel our way to the whales—and our hands were frozen!"

**If there's one thing she's learned, she says, it's that "Anyone can reroute their future. It's never too late."**

For people interested in training animals, he suggests studying biology and psychology to learn conditioning techniques. Entry-level jobs as animal keepers pay about $24,000 in the New York area but can pay half that in places like Florida, where the cost of living is lower. As further resources, he suggests two associations, the American Zoo and Aquarium Association in Wheeling, WV, and the International Marine Animal Trainers Association, 1720 South Shores Road, San Diego, CA.

*"My intern has worked out wonderfully. You really should consider getting one."*

Walsh says there are relatively few positions available, so a job search can be frustrating. But Murray is not discouraged. If there's one thing she's learned, she says, it's that "Anyone can reroute their future. It's never too late."

# Case Study: Looking to Make Up a World of Opportunity

By Patricia Kitchen, Staff Writer for *Newsday*

*They laughed at Joan of Arc,*
*but she went right ahead and built it.*
Gracie Allen

Colleen McFarlane is one of those people you could call an adventurer. Not just because she picked up and moved to Australia for a year, crewed on a yacht in the Caribbean, and has an orange belt in karate.

But like many creative people, when it comes to committing to one career, she sees all the possibilities and—until recently—couldn't throw all her enthusiasm behind one thing. She had considered working for an advertising agency, for a fashion magazine, and in retail management. "I was scared I would miss out on something else, and end up being bored," said McFarlane, 34, from Medford, Long Island.

She's one of a group of readers chosen for a career makeover with counselor Kate Wendleton, director of The Five O'Clock Club, a national career coaching and outplacement firm. To pinpoint their true interests, Wendleton asked each participant to list and prioritize their 7 most rewarding life experiences—whether paid or unpaid. Plus, each had to write a Forty-Year Vision, describing at 10-year intervals how they would like their lives and careers to develop.

**Colleen McFarlane went to Revlon for an information interview to learn about cosmetics.**

"I am absolutely desperate! I'm in the process of job hunting and don't want to get railroaded back into my old career," wrote McFarlane in a letter to this newspaper. Encouraged at an early age by her parents to go into medicine, she majored in biology in college but discovered through several internships that she wasn't crazy about the idea of "looking at slide sections of the brain and grinding up people's livers." "I found it sad," she said of her experience working for the Suffolk County medical examiner. So, as she finished college, she took a job in retailing, an industry she's been in for the past eight years, while yearning to do something more entrepreneurial.

Her goal now? To start a small business marketing cosmetics, clothing, crafts, and home products to women of color in South Africa, Latin America, and Australia. As she says, when you run your own shop, there's "freedom and creativity. There may be more pressure, but nobody else blows it for you. If you blow it, you blow it yourself."

Here's how she came to settle on her new career plan.

## The Power of the Pen

"I had dreams and a ton of ideas, but it was a mixing bowl of things. By writing the Forty-Year Vision, those dreams and ideas came together," she says. She discovered that committing to one direction did not make her feel closed in. "Expansive thinkers worry they're going to get bored or miss something, but they really miss something else if they don't focus—that is, they just don't get very far," Wendleton told the group. Her advice? Write down your ideas, decide which ones have the major elements that will make you most satisfied, know that there's not just one perfect career, and then "just shut up and pick something." You can always switch if you find out through research that it really isn't going to meet your needs after all.

Having your goals in writing can also keep you focused when temptations come your way. You may be seduced by other opportunities and end up doing "someone else's thing instead of your own," says Wendleton. "But if your plan is written—in so much detail you can taste it—it's easier to stay on track."

*Unless one travels to completely new territories, one can expect merely a long wearing away of oneself and an eventual extinction.*

Jean Dubuffet, quoted in *The New York Times*, obituary, May 15, 1985

## Finding the Time

McFarlane didn't have just a 9-to-5 job. During this makeover project, she worked as a personal shopper for Bergdorf Goodman's—during the holiday season, yet. Her days started at 10 A.M. and lasted until 7 or 8 P.M. She worked 6 or 7 days a week, and as for lunch break time, "What's that?" she asked.

This means it was just about impossible for her to log in the 15 hours a week Wendleton said career changers who are employed full-time should spend researching their new careers. But even though people are pressed for time, they still should struggle to make some progress—even if it's just thinking about their goal and jotting down notes, says Wendleton. It's easy to take the *all-or-nothing* approach and say, "Well, I'm too busy now. I'll start researching once this spurt of work is over." If you do that, you lose momentum and forget what it is you were planning to do.

So, at the very least, you can subscribe to trade journals. "They just arrive under your door," says Wendleton. You can also call companies to have them send you their promotional material. And you can do something simple that McFarlane caught on to—she just started talking to people about her dream. "I used to keep ideas close to the vest, but I got a lot less paranoid," she says. Simply through articulating her career wish, she learned that one friend in the restaurant business had done considerable research into the cosmetics industry, and another is a friend of a woman who is starting a new fashion magazine.

## Wrong Turn

McFarlane did find time to send letters to six huge cosmetics companies, asking for information interviews so she could learn more about doing business globally. But she addressed the letters to the human resources manager, which was a big mistake. Her follow-up calls generally led her to voice mail. And she ended up getting a flurry of rejection letters because they thought she was looking for a job. "I should have done research to find out who runs the appropriate department or found a contact through a friend," she says.

## Short-Term Plan

Unlike a business that is easier to get into—like a franchise, consulting in your own industry, or buying a business that already exists, McFarlane's idea is a big one—to start a company from scratch that's global in scope. So she knows it's going to take her two years of research and planning before she's ready to take the plunge. She has a lot to learn during that time—marketing, distribution, pricing, finance, profitability. And it's especially important for her to do her homework because starting a business that's successful is no piece of cake. More than 50 percent of new businesses fail within four years, according to the Small Business Administration.

So Wendleton suggested McFarlane get some relevant experience under her belt by working for a small- to medium-sized company where she can learn about the many facets of running a smaller firm. "Learning finance in a big company like General Motors does not translate into finance for a small business," said Wendleton. So the first step in McFarlane's plan is to find a sales or marketing job with a company that sells cosmetics in the new-business markets overseas.

Her next step will be to sign up for courses at the American Woman's Economic Development Corp., a nonprofit group in Manhattan that helps women entrepreneurs set up and manage their own businesses.

**She went to the career research section of her local library.**

## Good Research Sources

So, now that her gig at Bergdorf Goodman's is over, she has her days free to target prospective employers, which she's doing at the job information center of the mid-Manhattan branch of the New York Public Library. Her goal is an ambitious one—to find a job by the time the career makeover group meets again in early March.

Among the sources she's finding helpful: *Research Your Way to Your Next Job;* InfoTrac, a CD-ROM indexing magazine and newspaper articles; *The Million Dollar Directory* published by Dun & Bradstreet; *Standard and Poor's Register of Companies; Hoover's Handbook of American Businesses;* and *The International Business Woman* by Marlene Rossman.

## Role Models

McFarlane already looks up to Anita Roddick, founder of the Body Shop, as well as an African American executive she heard speak at a teleconference conducted by the National Association for Female Executives. She also has developed a mentor relationship with a woman who runs a public relations firm—and a retail operation in St. Thomas. "I'm learning from them that the odds aren't so insurmountable—the key is just to keep going."

And sometimes role models can show you what not to do. Because so much can go wrong in a new business, Wendleton says McFarlane should read magazines like *Success* and *Entrepreneur* with an eye to learning what mistakes others have made so she can avoid them.

## What Experts Say

So far, so good, says Tina Lassiter, director of training at the American Woman's Economic Development Corp. McFarlane has a clear concept of what she wants to do and is taking the right steps to get there. "That's 95 percent of the game."

***"I know you've been waiting for that promotion to V.P., Roberts, but I've decided to give it to my son Timmy. You understand, don't you?"***

One suggestion: After she's settled in a new job, she should attend functions given by groups outside her specialty—and comfort level. That means she needs to network with groups of bankers and investors, says Lassiter.

And this advice from Cindy Melk, 32, founder and creative director of H2O Plus, which sells skin, bath, and bodycare products: Because doing business globally is so complex, McFarlane should consider opening a pilot store in her own backyard, one that she can "watch, nurture, and manipulate," before she ventures overseas. Doing business abroad means bilingual labels, customs clearances, government and safety regulations. McFarlane will be better off if she "defines her unique point of difference" on a smaller, close-to-home scale first.

And as for any negative feedback she'll be getting, Melk advises her to view it as a signal she needs to become better educated in that area. "Negativism can actually be quite motivating. It all depends on how you process it," she says. "Tell her to stick to her guns."

---

*All changes, even the most longed for, have their melancholy; for what we leave behind is part of ourselves; we must die to one life before we can enter into another.*

Anatole France

# Case Study: Trading Aviation Tools for Teaching

By Patricia Kitchen, Staff Writer for *Newsday*

*The first principle of ethical power is Purpose. . . . By purpose, I mean your objective or intention—something toward which you are always striving. Purpose is something bigger. It is the picture you have of yourself—the kind of person you want to be or the kind of life you want to lead.*

Kenneth Blanchard and Norman Vincent Peale, *The Power of Ethical Management*

Five years ago, Angel Perez, 35, of Queens, New York, thought he was living the American Dream. He had a good job as a flight mechanic with Eastern Airlines, earning $42,000 a year. He got to travel, work outdoors, and have the leeway to decide whether or not a plane was fit to take off. But Eastern—and the airline industry—took a nosedive, and along with it went Perez's dream. In 10 years, he's worked for five airlines and expects to be laid off any day from his job at USAir. "I have 15 years' experience, but I keep slipping further and further back," says Perez, who has seen his salary drop by 20 percent.

But sometimes disappointment in one career forces people to look for another—one they end up liking even better. And that was Perez's thinking when he wrote to this newspaper asking to be part of a career makeover project. Nine readers worked as a group with Kate Wendleton, director of The Five O'Clock Club, a national career coaching and outplacement firm. As a preliminary step, each had to identify and prioritize his or her seven most satisfying life experiences, either paid or unpaid. All of them also had to write Forty-Year Plans describing how they want to see their lives and careers develop.

Perez had been dreaming of becoming a high school history teacher. When he was in college, he worked summers as a youth counselor, taking young people on field trips. And more recently, he has been spending time at his neighborhood baseball diamond, coaching young people in playing techniques as well as life skills. "These kids don't have a lot to look forward to. They see guns, crime, and AIDS and ask 'What's the use?'" says Perez. So he talks to them about the merits of getting a steady job instead of going for drugs, which he tells them "have a heavy price tag—fear, running, hiding, and death." Perez says he's living proof to kids that they can take control of their lives. Here's how he's planning to take control of his career change.

## A Bridge Job

A move from aviation mechanic to history teacher is a big leap. Perez could chuck his aviation experience, go back to school, and start all over again from scratch. But, as Wendleton asked, "Why toss away a whole industry?" She suggested he play off his strength by teaching aviation at a vocational high school. That puts him in the teaching arena, and he's then in a position to work toward a degree in history.

## A Move South

By writing out his Forty-Year Vision, Perez and his wife realized part of their dream was to live in Florida, where he had spent nine years working for Eastern. They knew their first step should be a move south, so when his wife, a mortgage banker, heard of an opening at her company's Miami office, she jumped at it. She'll be starting her new job next month, and Perez will follow in April. His plan is to try to find a job in aviation mechanics at the same time he's looking into teaching opportunities.

Wendleton says this two-prong job search is a must. Career changers who are relocating have a tendency to get a job in the old field first, telling themselves they'll start looking for something they really want to do after they're settled in. "Well, you know about inertia," says Wendleton. "It's hard to pick up again once the trail is cold." Perez is better off doing research and making contacts in the two industries at once. This way, if he does take a job as a mechanic, he already has a few "ins" with the teaching profession, so he won't have to start from square one.

So he's talking to some of his buddies in Florida, plus picking up the Miami *Herald* every day—not newsstand copies but discarded ones left on planes that come up daily from Miami. He looks at the help-wanted ads, but Wendleton says he also needs to be reading up on the airline industry in general, as well as issues and activities at high schools, vocational schools, youth organizations, and boys' clubs in the Miami area.

## Learning to Brag

Like many people, Perez is not comfortable tooting his own horn. Wendleton dragged out of him the fact that he routinely had been selected by his companies to attend special training programs and in turn train other mechanics. "Some people don't want to admit how special they are—they take that for granted," says Wendleton. Perez, like many people, needs to become more comfortable identifying and talking about his strengths. As Wendleton says, it's not the brightest and most competent people who get ahead. Often it's the most feisty—the ones who are just dying to get hired and who aren't shy about sharing their accomplishments.

## "Yes, But"

Perez's wife and family support his goal to become a teacher. But some friends and colleagues have pointed out all the potential obstacles to making a career change. Wendleton's response: "Some people have not seen a lot of success in their lives. When they hear about opportunities, their heads are programmed to say, 'Yes, but what about?'" She says the key is to replace "Yes, but" with "How can I get this to work?" And generally, it's best to share your goals only with people who give encouragement and constructive suggestions.

## Wrong Turn

Last year Perez called the New York City Board of Education to find out how to make a move into teaching. But he wasn't specific about his specialty and was given the brush. He wishes now he had done more networking with people who specialize in aviation education. He recently spoke with the assistant principal of Aviation High School, who told Perez he would be an ideal candidate to teach there, given his experience and fluency in Spanish. "I was just barking up the wrong tree first," he says.

## Research

Perez went to the Mid-Manhattan Library job information center, where a librarian helped him find names of Washington, DC–based education associations. He wrote away for pamphlets and received useful information from the American Association for Adult and Continuing Education and the National Council for Accreditation of Teacher Education.

## Expert Advice

According to Ruby Jones, an assistant principal at the George T. Baker Aviation Maintenance Technician School in Miami, Perez already meets the basic requirements to teach airplane mechanics. He has plenty of hands-on experience, plus he has the appropriate licenses required by the FAA. And his experience as a trainer is a definite plus. Perez's first step should be to get an application for employment from the Dade County Public Schools. He also can look into career days at her school and others, because volunteering to speak is a good way to get to know teachers and principals, who can be valuable contacts.

---

*We make a living by what we get,*
*but we make a life by what we give.*

Winston Churchill

# Selecting Internships and Part-Time Jobs

*Our doubts are traitors,*
*And make us lose the good we oft might win*
*By fearing to attempt.*
William Shakespeare,
*Measure for Measure*

## Get Experience

When you were a kid, you could earn money by raking leaves or babysitting. When you were in high school, you could work at the local sandwich shop, the bowling alley, or summer camps. But you're older, and the world has different expectations of you. It's time to move away from the bowling alley—unless your plan is to own your own alley someday. Continue working at the Gap only if you think your future career will be in retail.

Even college juniors and seniors must show *real* work experience on their résumés to land terrific jobs. Whether you want to work in administration or finance, public relations or health care, employers want to see relevant experience.

When you do graduate, having a degree is not enough. If you have not been able to work in your field of interest during your college years, you may be forced to take a job outside your field after graduation. The Bureau of Labor Statistics found that, while in the 1980s *one in five* college graduates worked in jobs that required only a high school diploma, now *one in three* graduates entering the market will be underemployed.

You will need to market yourself aggressively. You are competing with thousands of other graduates who have the same degree and perhaps even went to the same or similar schools. In addition, you are competing with experienced people who have been downsized.

For starters, get whatever job you can. When you are very young, employers just want to see that you've worked *somewhere.* They don't want to be the first one to teach you how to dress for work, come in on time, not squabble with your coworkers as if they were siblings, and not give your boss a hard time as if she were your mother. Sometimes it takes a little experience to remember that you're at *work.* These other people are not your family or students in your dorm. Relationships at work are supposed to be *professional.*

But if your first jobs do not fit in with your career direction, get on track as soon as you can. When I was in college, I cleaned tables in the cafeteria, worked in the dietitian's office in a hospital, was a telephone operator, and *eventually* started my career in computer programming. I stayed in computer technology for the next 10 years and loved it.

## Making the Most of Your Internship

Most students don't take internships seriously enough and get stuck running the copier and getting doughnuts for the staff. Be sure to *read* what you're copying. Ask to help on projects.

Make yourself valuable. Help wherever they need things to be done, and do a great job. In addition, read the company literature and find out about the organization. Build relationships so you can contact people later for references and referrals to other employers or even so you can work there again.

## Getting Paid or Not

Some internships are paid; some are unpaid. Most students cannot afford to work for free. They need paid internships or part-time jobs. Be careful about companies that promise a stipend at the end of the assignment. They don't always pay what they promised. Before starting, ask other students who have worked there.

Internships tend not to be paid in glamor and highly competitive fields such as broadcasting, film production, fashion, and even some aspects of health care. However, companies that want the best interns often have to pay for them.

## Stay a While or Go?

Internships tend to last for three months in the summer or require only one or two days a week during the school year. If you stay a short while, employers can rarely give you anything meaningful to do. You learn what you can and then move on. It takes three months just to get settled into *any* job.

If you stay longer than three months in one place, you are more likely to get actual experience. For example, if you take a short-term public relations internship, your job will be to make copies of press releases and send them out, while you absorb the action around you. However, if a company knows that you're going to stick around, they're more likely to invest the time in training you to actually write press releases, let you telephone the media, and start to grow your career. If you return to that same company summer after summer or even work there during the school year, by the time you graduate, you will already have significant experience and will not be considered an entry-level person.

## Finding Work

Although your school may help you find an internship or part-time job, the responsibility is yours. The Julie case study later in this book shows what she did to land a part-time job (actually, the firm called it an *internship* since they expected to train her, but they paid her very well). The Internet has plenty of websites devoted to specialized internships, such as those in Washington, DC. Just go to Yahoo, and key in *internships*. Also be sure to look at *www.internships.com.*

Trade associations are another good source of contacts. Using the public relations example, you could join the student chapter of the Public Relations Society of America. You could also try to meet people at the professional chapter in your local area. People there will tell you what is happening in their firms and may even put in a good word for you. Associations are powerful.

## Start Looking Early

Don't wait until three weeks before summer break. Start in January to look for summer work. Start in your junior year to look for work for after graduation.

If you know you want to work for a certain organization, start early to try to land an internship or part-time job. Try to meet as many people as you can; let them know how much you want to work there and which semester you would like to start. Stay in touch with them.

Yes, it's true: You can't get a job without experience, and you can't get experience without a job. But if you start early and are diligent, you can graduate with a lot of experience under your belt. You may even get a job offer from an employer you worked for while in school.

## Select Specific Organizations for Which You Want to Work

If you work for larger employers, you will have a brand name to put on your résumé. If you work for a smaller employer, you are more likely to get hands-on experience. If you don't know which environment you are most likely to prefer, try working at one of each. If you think you will want to work for a large employer after graduation, get that kind of experience during your school years. Large employers like to see the names of *other* large employers on your résumé, and small employers want to see that you know what it's like to work for a small employer.

Send out cover letters and résumés, and be sure to follow up with the companies in which you are really interested. Some organizations may require writing or other samples for certain jobs, so keep some of the best examples from your classes.

## How to Turn an Internship into a Job Offer

Some organizations, large or small, have a policy of selecting talent from the interns who have worked there. They try you out, and you try them out.

On the other hand, other companies use interns as a source of cheap labor. You get experience, but they'd rather replace you with other interns than hire someone full-time on payroll.

Once you come on payroll, the cost to your employer skyrockets. They now must pay you a base salary and give you full benefits. If you are now earning, say, $12 an hour as a student, the company pays you only for the actual time you work. Even if you worked 40 hours a week, every week, that would amount to $25,000 a year. But if the company brought you on at a $25,000 salary, you would now get paid holidays and vacation time, health insurance, and other benefits. Your employer may spend 30 percent more than the $25,000 base, and you would have paid time off.

If you're hoping that great internship will turn into a job offer after graduation, ask employers what their policy is: Do they hire interns or not?

Perhaps you're shy about asking to stay. But if you've done well and they seem to like you, say something after you've been there a while. Don't mention it casually. Ask for a meeting with your boss, and say that you really enjoy working for them and would like to continue after graduation. "I know you can't promise me anything, but what do you think the chances are? Do you ever hire interns after they graduate?"

Ask about their history and their policy. Perhaps they make offers to half of the interns. Perhaps they have in the past but don't see it happening this year. Perhaps they didn't know that you were even interested in working there after graduation.

Get experience. Develop references you can use later. Learn about the world and learn about yourself.

# PART THREE

# How to Select Your Job Targets

## BRAINSTORMING POSSIBLE JOBS

# Brainstorming Possible Jobs

*But when the family continued to struggle, and when Steve Ross was a teenager, he was summoned to his father's deathbed to learn that his sole inheritance consisted of this advice: There are those who work all day, those who dream all day, and those who spend an hour dreaming before setting to work to fulfill those dreams. "Go into the third category," his father said, "because there's virtually no competition."*

Obituary of Steven J. Ross, creator of Time Warner, *The New York Times,* December 21, 1992

You've done a lot of thinking about yourself: what you enjoy doing and also do well, your interests, values, education, work experience, and long-range vision. Even if you aren't sure where you are going, keep pushing ahead in The Five O'Clock Club process. No matter how young or old you are, you may have to *reexamine* your Seven Stories, for example, as you go through your job search. It takes time to get to know yourself, and it takes time to get to know the world. For now, it's time to start exploring job possibilities.

Use the worksheet in this chapter to help you brainstorm possible jobs that you can then explore.

1. **Across the top of the page,** list the following elements as they apply to you. Use as many columns as you need for each category.

- Your basic personality
- Interests
- Values
- Specialized skills
- From the Seven Stories Exercise:
  - The role you played
  - The environment in which you worked
  - The various subject matters in your stories
- Long-range goals
- Education
- Work experience
- Areas of expertise

Here is one person's list of column headings across the top:

- Personality: *outgoing*
- Interests: *environment, computers, world travel* (three different interests—takes three columns)
- Values: *a decent wage* so I can support a family
- Specialized Skills: *use of PC*
- From the Seven Stories Exercise:
  - being *part of a research group*
  - enjoy *Third-World countries* (takes two columns);
- Goals from the Forty-Year Vision: *head up not-for-profit organization*
- Education: *master's in public policy*
- Work experience: *three years' marketing experience.*

This takes a total of 11 columns across the top.

*It is never too late to be what you might have been.*

George Eliot

2. **Down the side of the page, list possible jobs, fields, or functions** that rely on one or more of these elements. For example, combine marketing with environment, or computers with research and Third-World countries.

   At this point, do not eliminate anything. Write down whatever ideas occur to you. Ask your friends and family. Do library research and talk to lots of people. Open your eyes and your mind when you read or walk down the street. Be observant and generate lots of ideas. Write down whatever anyone suggests. A particular suggestion may not be exactly right for you, but may help you think of other things that *are* right.

---

CHARLEY: *Yeah. He was a happy man with a batch of cement.*
LINDA: *He was so wonderful with his hands.*
BIFF: *He had the wrong dreams. All, all, wrong.*
HAPPY, almost ready to fight Biff: *Don't say that!*
BIFF: *He never knew who he was.*

Arthur Miller, *Death of a Salesman*

3. **Analyze each job possibility**. Check off across the page the elements that apply to the first job. For example, if the job fits your basic personality, put a checkmark in that column. If it uses your education or relies on your work experience, put checkmarks in those columns. If it fits in with your long-range goals, put a checkmark there.

   Do the same for every job listed in the left column.

4. **Add up the checkmarks for each job, and write the total in the right-hand column**. Any job that relies on only one or two elements is probably not appropriate for you. Pay attention to ones with the most checkmarks. Certain elements are more important to you than others, so you must weight those more heavily. In fact, there are probably some elements that *must* be present so you will be satisfied, such as a job that meshes with your values.

   Those jobs that seem to satisfy your most important elements are the ones you will list as some of the targets to explore on the preliminary target investigation worksheet (in this book). Also list positions that would be logical next steps for you in light of your background.

---

*You must have long-range goals to keep you from being frustrated by short-range failures.*

Charles C. Noble, Major general

## CASE STUDY *Agnes*
## Broadening Her Targets

Agnes had been a marketing/merchandising major in college. Her only love was retail, and her dream job was working for one specific, famous fashion house. Perhaps she could actually get a job with that fashion house, but what kind of job could she go for after that? The retail and fashion industries were both retrenching at the time of her search, although she could probably get a job in one of them. She needed more targets and preferably some targets in growing industries so she would have a more reasonable career path.

In addition to the retail and fashion industries, what other industries could Agnes consider? In the banking industry, where she had been for only three years, some of the products she promoted had been computerized. In combining *computers* with *retail,* we came up with *computerized shopping"* a new field that was threatening the retail industry. Computerized shopping and related areas were good fields for Agnes to investigate. What about something having to do with debit cards and credit cards or Prodigy—all computer-base systems aimed at retail? Or what about selling herself to banks that were handling the bankrupt retail companies that she was so familiar with?

She came up with 20 areas to explore. Agnes's next step is to conduct a preliminary target investigation (which you will read about soon) to determine which fields may be worth pursuing in that they hold some interest for her and there is some possibility of finding a job in them. At this point she has an exciting search lined up—one with lots of fields to explore and one that offers her a future instead of just a job.

Remember that the search process is a process of exploration. As you go out and explore, you will uncover other possibilities that could not possibly be on your target list at the beginning of your search. Explore. Try to have fun while doing it. You will learn a lot about the world, what it has to offer, and where you fit in.

Don't think that this exploration process is only for those just starting out. Even those who have worked 20 or 30 years have to explore to find out where they now fit in.

---

*I've got peace like a river ina my soul.*

African American spiritual

# Brainstorming Possible Jobs Worksheet

| **Assessment Results →**<br><br>**Possible Jobs** | | | | | | | | | | | | | | | | | | | | | **Total Check-marks Across** |
|---|---|---|---|---|---|---|---|---|---|---|---|---|---|---|---|---|---|---|---|---|---|
| | | | | | | | | | | | | | | | | | | | | | |
| | | | | | | | | | | | | | | | | | | | | | |
| | | | | | | | | | | | | | | | | | | | | | |
| | | | | | | | | | | | | | | | | | | | | | |
| | | | | | | | | | | | | | | | | | | | | | |
| | | | | | | | | | | | | | | | | | | | | | |
| | | | | | | | | | | | | | | | | | | | | | |
| | | | | | | | | | | | | | | | | | | | | | |
| | | | | | | | | | | | | | | | | | | | | | |
| | | | | | | | | | | | | | | | | | | | | | |
| | | | | | | | | | | | | | | | | | | | | | |
| | | | | | | | | | | | | | | | | | | | | | |
| | | | | | | | | | | | | | | | | | | | | | |
| | | | | | | | | | | | | | | | | | | | | | |
| | | | | | | | | | | | | | | | | | | | | | |
| | | | | | | | | | | | | | | | | | | | | | |
| | | | | | | | | | | | | | | | | | | | | | |
| | | | | | | | | | | | | | | | | | | | | | |
| | | | | | | | | | | | | | | | | | | | | | |
| | | | | | | | | | | | | | | | | | | | | | |
| | | | | | | | | | | | | | | | | | | | | | |
| | | | | | | | | | | | | | | | | | | | | | |
| | | | | | | | | | | | | | | | | | | | | | |
| | | | | | | | | | | | | | | | | | | | | | |
| | | | | | | | | | | | | | | | | | | | | | |
| | | | | | | | | | | | | | | | | | | | | | |

# How to Target the Job You Want

*I always wanted to be somebody, but I should have been more specific.*

Lily Tomlin

You are on your way to finding your place in the world. Using the Seven Stories and other exercises, you made a list of your motivated skills and what you want in a job, and then you brainstormed a number of possible job targets that might fit in with your enjoyable accomplishments and/or your vision of your future. Some of these targets may be very long term. Then you thought about what you would be willing to offer. (You took it an extra step by stating these as accomplishments.)

Now we will work on firming up your job targets. You will do some preliminary research on each target through the Internet and by talking to people to see if these areas still interest you and are practical. Next you will *focus* by selecting two, three, or four areas on which to concentrate, based on what appeals to you and what you think you have that is marketable. Then you will conduct a thorough campaign aimed at each area. Because each campaign takes a lot of work, it is best if we spend some time refining your targets.

## Selecting Job Targets—Your Key to Job-Hunting Success

Selecting a job target means choosing: a specific geographic area, a specific industry or organization size, and a specific position within that industry. A job target must have all three.

Select your targets. Using the book, conduct a campaign to get meetings in each target. Concentrate your energies, and you increase your chances for success.

Approach each target with an open mind. Commit to a target, but only as long as it makes sense. You can change your mind after you find out more about it. It makes no sense to strive to be a ballerina after you find you have absolutely no ability as a dancer. Commitment to a target lets you discover your real possibilities and increases your chances of landing a job of your choice. The unsuccessful ballet student may have something else of great value to offer the world of dance—such as the ability to raise funds or run a ballet company.

## The Results of Commitment

Commitment increases the chance that you will come across clearly and enthusiastically about the industry and the position you seek; it will help you do a thorough job of networking in the chosen area, of investigating and being knowledgeable about the area, of conducting a thorough search, and of being successful in that search.

If the result of your initial commitment is that you realize a job target is not what you thought it would be, you have resolved the issue and can move on.

Sean thought he wanted to work in accounting. He lined up a number of accounting interviews, learned a lot about the field, and decided the last thing he wanted to do was accounting. It was only after a brief but committed job search that Sean found the accounting area was not for him: The people in it were different from what he had expected. He would not be able to do the things he had imagined he would do there. That target no longer interested him. Sean then researched his second target, which was market analysis, and found that it was very exciting to him. He found a good match for himself.

Commitment to a target means you'll give that target your best shot—and results in a better job hunt than if you had no target at all.

## Target a Geographic Area

Targeting a geographic area is usually the easiest part of the targeting process. Some people decide that they want to work near their present homes, while others decide that they would be willing to move where the jobs are. Are you willing to move anywhere? Are a small town and a big city the same to you? Would you move to the coast? To Arizona? Would you rather be near your family? If you want to stay where you are now, target that area as your first selection—and you'll have a better chance of getting offers there. If you really care about where you live, *target it.*

Think about where you stand on this. You will be assigning yourself an impossible task if, for example, you want to be an export manager but want to work only in a geographic area where there are no export-management positions. If you must live in a particular area, be realistic about the kinds of jobs open to you there.

Resolve this issue. Then you will know if you'd be willing to change your target industry so you can live where you want, or change your geographic area so you can work in the industry or function that interests you.

*I even thought about getting transferred down there, but, you know, Atlanta's not where it's happening as far as banking goes. If I want to keep being successful and move up I have to keep current, and Boston is where it's all going down.*

Bruce Faulk, *You Still Got to Come Home to That*

## Target an Industry and a Function in That Industry

Many people say they don't care what industry they work in. When pressed, they usually have stronger opinions than they thought.

If you think *any* industry would be okay for you, let's find out. Would you work in the not-for-profit sector? If so, where? In education? A hospital? How about government? A community organization? Does it matter to you?

Would you work for a magazine? A chemical company? The garment industry? How about a company that makes cardboard boxes? Or cheese? Does it matter to you?

Does it matter if the organization has 40 employees? What about 40,000? Or 400,000? Does it matter to you?

## You've Selected a Target If . . .

. . . you can clearly state the industry or organization size in which you'd be interested, your position within each industry, and some guidelines regarding geographic location.

For example, if you're a junior accountant, you may already know that you want to advance in the accounting field. You may know that you want to work for a small service organization as an assistant controller in the geographic area where you are now living.

If you have clearly selected your targets, then you can get on with finding interviews in your target area. To do that, you would conduct a campaign in your target area. (Job-hunting campaigns are covered in this book.)

Here is one person's target list.

By geographic area:

- Washington, DC
- New York City

By industry:

- Book publishing
- Magazine publishing
- Advertising
- College administration (weak interest)
- Administration of professional firms (weak interest)
- Nonprofit associations
- Direct-marketing organizations

By function:

- Business assistant
- International accounting or control
- Corporate-level financial planning analysis
- Finance—nonprofit organizations

## Other Issues You May Want to Consider Even If You Have a Target

Does the style of the organization matter to you? Would you rather be in a fast-paced, dynamic organization with lots of headaches or one that's more stable and slow-paced, with routine work as the norm? Which would you prefer?

What kind of people do you want to work with? Friendly people? Sharp, challenging people? People interested in making a fast buck? People who want to make the world a better place? Think about it. You may have said before that you just want a job—any job—but is anything still okay with you?

If you want to be in sales, for example, would it matter if you were selling lingerie or used cars or computers or large office building space? What if you were selling cats? Rugs? Butter? Saying you want to be in "sales" is not enough.

Let's take it a step further. If what appeals to you about being a salesman is that you like to convince people, why not be a politician? Or a clergyman? Or a doctor? If what appeals to you is money, why not become a trader? Or a partner in a law firm? Remind yourself where your heart lies.

---

*It is therefore vital that each of us examine the values by which he lives, to decide what is truly important and what will ultimately give him feelings of fulfillment and well-being.*

Michael Lynberg, *The Path with Heart*

## CASE STUDY *William*

## Finally—An Organized Search

William wanted a job—just about any job he saw in the want ads. He spent months answering those ads. He thought he was job hunting, but he wasn't. He was simply answering ads for positions for which he was unqualified. William didn't stand a chance.

After a long time, William gave up and agreed to follow The Five O'Clock Club system. At first he resisted because, like so many job hunters, he did not want to "restrict" himself. William thought that focusing on only two or three job targets would limit his opportunities and lengthen his search. He wanted to be open to whatever job came his way.

Many job hunters, like William, simply want a job. But William needed to put himself in the position of the hiring manager: Why would he want to hire William? In his cover letters, William took the "trust me" approach. He did nothing to prove his interest in the industry, the organization, or even the position for which he was applying. His credentials matched the ad requirements only by the greatest stretch of the imagination.

A shotgun approach like William's may lead to a job offer, but it may also lead your career in a direction that is not what you would have preferred. Later, you may find yourself back in the same boat again—wondering what to do with your life, wanting to do almost anything but what you are doing, hoping your next job will miraculously be in a field that will satisfy you.

William's basic problem was that he didn't know what he wanted to do. He was willing to do anything—anything except focus on a specific area and go after it.

William eventually narrowed himself to two targets in which he was truly interested. Then he worked to find out his chances for getting jobs in those fields. William did the exercises in this book and came up with this list to focus his search.

What I want in a job:

- A challenge in meeting new situations/variety
- Something I believe in
- A chance to express creativity through communication
- A highly visible position
- An opportunity to develop my leadership and motivational skills

What I have to offer (that I also want to offer):

- Enthusiasm for organization's basic mission/purpose
- Penetrating analysis that finds the *answer*
- An ability and desire to be in new/untested situations
- Effectiveness in dealing with many kinds of people
- Strong oral and written communication skills

Goal: A small- or medium-sized organization where I can feel my impact:

- Service
- Health care
- Human care
- Science
- Academia and learning
- Human understanding

Description of targeted areas.

- Targeted geographic areas:
  - Major East Coast cities or locales:
  - New York
  - Philadelphia
  - Boston
  - Baltimore
  - Washington
- Targeted industries:
  - First priority is health care:
  - Pharmaceuticals companies
  - Biotechnology companies
  - Hospitals
  - Maybe research labs
- Second priority is not-for-profit community organizations
- Targeted positions:
  - Marketing/competitive analysis
  - Brand positioning
  - Operations analysis

William's first campaign was aimed at pharmaceuticals companies. He discovered what they looked for in new hires, and how he could get a position. In addition, he pursued his second objective: not-for-profit community organizations.

The result: William discovered he could make a transition into the pharmaceuticals industry but decided it no longer interested him. He learned of a job being created in a not-for-profit organization. Although he was not qualified for this position, he knew he could handle it, and it matched the list of what he wanted.

William went through the steps described in the chapter *How to Change Careers* to convince his prospective employer he could indeed handle the job and was eager to have the chance to do it. This was difficult because the other candidates were better qualified than William—they had had this kind of job before. For William, it was a new field.

William decided to write a number of proposals. To write them, he first needed to do research, which would not be easy. After some library research, he called the heads of development at six major not-for-profits. He told them he was hoping to get a position at a certain organization and wanted some ideas of how he could write a proposal of what he would do if he were hired.

Amazingly, his sincerity won the day. All six gave him information over the phone. Because he had done library research, William was able to ask intelligent questions. He wrote a proposal, stating in his cover letter that he had spoken with the heads of development at major not-for-profits, and asked for another interview. It would be nice if that were all it took: William got another interview but was rejected a *number* of times. Yet he continued to do research, and eventually showed enough fortitude and learned enough that he was hired.

The position was just what he wanted: a brand-new entry-level marketing research position at a major not-for-profit organization. He would head his career in a different direction and satisfy his motivated skills. His career was back on track, under his own control. And he's still with the organization today.

On the other hand, if you must find a job quickly, concentrate first on the area where you stand the best chance of getting a job—perhaps the field you are now in. After you are settled in your new job, you can develop yourself in the area that interests you in the long run. Remember, it's okay to take something less than your ideal job; just keep working toward your dreams.

If you are targeting a geographic area different from where you are now, be sure to conduct a serious, complete campaign aimed at that target. For example, you will want to contact search firms in that area, do library research, perhaps conduct a direct-mail campaign, and network. For in-depth information on all of these topics, read those sections in this book. Use the worksheets on the following pages to plan your targets.

*Let not my thinking become confused by listening to too many opinions, but let me consider each one individually, to see if it can be of help to me. To make good choices, I must develop a mature and prudent understanding of myself that will reveal to me my real motives and intentions.*

Paraphrased from Thomas Merton,
*No Man Is an Island*

## Select *Your* Targets

*The only difference between caprice and a lifelong passion is that the caprice lasts a little longer.*

Oscar Wilde

List your targets in the order in which you will conduct your search. List first the one you will focus on in your first campaign. If you are currently employed and have time to explore, you may want to select as your first target the most unlikely one. (Job hunters sometimes want to target areas they had only dreamed about before.) Concentrate on it and find out for sure whether you are truly interested and what your prospects are. If it doesn't work, you can become more realistic.

## Measuring Your Targets

You've selected one to five targets on which to focus. Will they be enough to get you an appropriate job?

Let's say, for example, that your first target aims at a small industry (10 organizations) having only a few positions that would be appropriate for you. Chances are those jobs are filled right now. In fact, chances are there may be no opening for a year or two. The numbers are working against you. But if you have targeted 20 small industries, each of which has 10 organizations with a few positions appropriate for you, the numbers are more in your favor. On the other hand, if one of your targets is large and has a lot of positions that may be right for you, the numbers are again on your side.

## A Rule of Thumb

A target list of 200 positions (positions, not job openings) results in 7 interviews, which result in 1 job offer. Therefore, if there are fewer than 200 potential positions in your targets, develop additional targets or expand the ones you already have. Remember that when aiming at a target of less than 200, concentrated effort will be required.

However, sometimes one organization by itself may be enough. What if a very qualified administrative assistant wanted to work for a large regional telephone company? What are the chances she would find a job there? A regional telephone company may have *thousands* of administrative assistants, and a qualified person would certainly be able to find a job there within a reasonable time frame.

In a tight job market, however, you will probably need to *expand your job-hunting targets.* If you are searching only in Chicago or only in the immediate area where you live, think of other geographic areas. If you are looking only in large public corporations, consider small or private companies or the not-for-profit area. If you are looking for a certain kind of position, what other kinds of work can you do? Think of additional targets for your search, and focus on each target in depth.

Later, you will learn how to position yourself for each of these targets. That way, when you go after a target, you will have a better chance of seeming appropriate to the people in each target area.

# Target Selection

After you have done some preliminary research, select the targets that you think deserve a full campaign. List first the one you will focus on in your first campaign. If you are currently employed and have time to explore, you may want to select as your first target the most unlikely one, but the one that is the job of your dreams. Then you can concentrate on it and find out for sure whether you are still interested and what your prospects are.

On the other hand, if you must find a job quickly, you will first want to concentrate on the area where you stand the best chance of getting a job—probably the area where you are now working. After you get that job, you can explore your other targets. (To expand your targets quickly, consider broadening your search geographically.)

If you are targeting a geographic area different from where you are now, be sure to conduct a serious, complete campaign aimed at that target. For example, you will want to contact search firms in that area, do Internet or library research, perhaps conduct a direct-mail campaign, and network.

Target 1: Industry or organization size: ____________________
Position/function: ____________________
Geographic area: ____________________

Target 2: Industry or organization size: ____________________
Position/function: ____________________
Geographic area: ____________________

Target 3: Industry or organization size: ____________________
Position/function: ____________________
Geographic area: ____________________

Target 4: Industry or organization size: ____________________
Position/function: ____________________
Geographic area: ____________________

Target 5: Industry or organization size: ____________________
Position/function: ____________________
Geographic area: ____________________

# Measuring Your Targets

You've selected one to five (or more) targets on which to focus. Will this be enough to get you an appropriate job?

Let's say, for example, that your first target aims at a small industry (10 organizations) having only a few positions that would be appropriate for you.

Chances are, those jobs are filled right now. In fact, chances are there may be no opening for a year or two. The numbers are working against you. Now, if you have targeted 20 small industries, each of which has 10 organizations with a few positions appropriate for you, the numbers are more in your favor.

On the other hand, if one of your targets is large and has a lot of positions that may be right for you, the numbers are again on your side.

Let's analyze your search and see whether the numbers are working for you or against you.

Fill out the following on your own target markets. You will probably have to make an educated guess about the number. A ballpark figure is all you need to get a feel for where you stand.

**Target 1:** Industry or organization size: ______________________
Position/function: ______________________
Geographic area: ______________________

How big is the market for my "product" in this target?
A. Number of organizations in this target market: ________
B. Number of probable positions suitable for me in the average organization in this target: ________
A x B = Total number of probable positions appropriate for me in this target market: ________

**For Target 2:** Industry or organization size: ______________________
Position/function: ______________________
Geographic area: ______________________

How big is the market for my "product" in this target?
A. Number of organizations in this target market: ________
B. Number of probable positions suitable for me in the average organization in this target: ________
A x B = Total number of probable positions appropriate for me in this target market: ________

**For Target 3:** Industry or organization size: ______________________
Position/function: ______________________
Geographic area: ______________________

How big is the market for my "product" in this target?
A. Number of organizations in this target market: ________
B. Number of probable positions suitable for me in the average organization in this target: ________
A x B = Total number of probable positions appropriate for me in this target market: ________

**Rule of thumb:**
A target list of 200 positions in a healthy market results in 7 interviews, which result in 1 job offer. Therefore, if there are fewer than 200 potential positions in your targets, develop additional targets or expand the ones you already have. Remember that when aiming at a target of less than 200 potential positions, a more concentrated effort is required.

# Developing Your A-List, B-List, C-List

*Every man is born into the world to do something unique and something distinctive and if he or she does not do it, it will never be done.*

Benjamin E. Mays, "I Knew Carter G. Woodson," *Negro History Bulletin*, January–March 1981

Again, what is a job target? A job target consists of:

- an industry or organization size where you think you'd like to work, such as banking
- a specific position within those industries you are targeting, such as marketing
- a geographic area, such as St. Louis

Once you've thought of a few *tentative* job targets, you are ready to work on your personal marketing plan. This plan will guide you throughout your entire job search.

In my small group, I often ask someone to name something that he or she is targeting and the group helps that person brainstorm how to go after that target. Let's say Joe is targeting *investment advisory*—a job that involves giving investment advice. Jim and his group might start brainstorming where a person could do investment advisory work: perhaps commercial banks, investment banks, hedge funds, insurance companies, mutual funds.

So far, Joe is targeting a position (investment advisory) and the industries (that we just named). Finally, the formula is complete when he names the geographic area. Joe said he was interested in both New York and Chicago.

*The price one pays for pursuing any profession or calling it an intimate knowledge of its ugly side.*

James Baldwin, *Nobody Knows My Name*

## Segmenting Your Targets

If a person says that she wants to work in the not-for-profit area, *not-for-profit* is *not* a target. That's because it's too broad.

Not-for-profit could include associations, hospitals, universities, the government—and each of those subtargets is huge!

Breaking your targets into manageable subtargets is called *segmenting your targets.*

### Develop *Your* Personal Marketing Plan

**The position:**

"Investment advisory"—a job where I would give investment advice

**The industries:**

commercial banks
investment banks
hedge funds
insurance companies
mutual funds

**The geographic areas**

New York and Chicago

*Not-for-profit* **is too broad to be useful.**

**It could include:**
- **associations**
- **hospitals**
- **universities**
- **the government—and all of those subtargets are huge!**

What if a person wants to target health care? Health care is huge! It could include, for example, hospitals, home health care, HMOs, pharmaceutical companies, nursing homes, hospice care, health insurance companies, crisis intervention programs, congregate care facilities, medical billing, health care consulting firms, and medical device manufacturers and distributors (Who makes the catheters? And who makes the beds?).

You could go on and on. Health care could be anything having to do with the aging of America, for example. You could brainstorm lots of other job targets having to do with health care itself.

Let's go back to our investment advisory example. I would say to Joe, "How many commercial banks would you say are appropriate for you to consider? Name a number, any number." (Of course, job hunters don't really know, but I want them to name *some*thing.) And Joe would give me a rough guess. "Let's say there are approximately 24 commercial banks," he would say, "24 investment banks, 20 hedge funds—all within my targeted geographic areas. Let's also say there are 6 insurance companies, 8 mutual funds, and so on."

So Joe, our investment advisor, has a lot of targets: commercial banks, investment banks, hedge funds. It's just too much. In addition to segmenting his targets, he also has to *rank* his targets. If he doesn't rank, he will be scattered and ineffective. His list is too big and too unwieldy.

Joe must organize his work. My next question is: "What is your target #1?" Joe says his target #1, the place where he would most like to work, is commercial banking. So I respond, "Let's analyze commercial banks. How many positions would a typical commercial bank have that would be appropriate for you?" Joe doesn't really know the answer. Would there be 1 position or 10? We're talking about *positions,* not job openings. Positions.

**Break your targets down into subtargets.**

**Health care, for example, could include:**
- **hospitals**
- **home health care**
- **HMOs**
- **pharmaceutical companies**
- **nursing homes**
- **hospice care**
- **health insurance companies**
- **crisis intervention programs**
- **congregate care facilities**
- **medical billing**
- **health care consulting firms**
- **medical device manufacturers**
- **distributors**

**Health care could also include:**

- **Anything having to do with the aging of America**
- **Vitamin companies**
- **Health care publishing**
- **Lots of other subcategories, depending on your interests**

**Subtargets For Uur Investment Advisory Example**

**"How many commercial banks are appropriate for you to consider? Name a number, any number."**

**Approximately:**
- **24 commercial banks**
- **24 investment banks**
- **20 hedge funds**
- **6 insurance companies**
- **8 mutual funds**
- **and so on, all within your targeted geogrpahic areas.**

Joe doesn't really know the answer, but I push him to guess. Joe says, "Well, out of 24 commercial banks that I'm targeting, I think each one might have an average of 10 positions that are appropriate for me" (*positions,* not openings). So Joe is targeting 240 positions at just those 24 banks. That is a lot of positions!

In fact, we say to be successful in your search in a reasonable time frame, you must target 200 positions. So you can see that Joe is going after 240 positions in just this one target area, increasing the likelihood of a successful search. So if you are targeting a *smaller* number of positions, you will have a longer search. Chances are, you can come up with targets with totaling at least 200.

**Target #1: Commercial Banks**

**"How many *positions* would a typical commercial bank have that would be appropriate for you?"**

So rank your targets. Decide which targets you want to go after first, second, third, and fourth. It may be, if you are desperate, you'll focus first on the target where you are most likely to get a job. If you are not desperate and have time to explore—maybe you're employed right now—then maybe your first target is your dream job, the thing you've always wanted to explore. So first rank your targets.

Then measure your targets. If the total number of positions you're going after is fewer than 200, that's not good.

Remember that we are not measuring job openings but positions. And it does not matter if the positions are filled right now. You are trying to avoid targets that are just too small. Those searches are doomed from the start.

**Target #1: 24 Commercial Banks**

**An average of 10 positions at each bank Joe is targeting 240 positions at just these 24 banks. That is a lot of positions!**

As a separate but very relevant issue, think about the state of the market within each of those targets. Some markets are growing, and some markets are retrenching. If your target market is retrenching, you'll need to go after even more positions.

On the other hand, if it's growing and they need to hire people, you may be able to get away with targeting fewer positions.

**Measure *positions,* not job openings. It doesn't matter if the positions are filled right now.**

Now, take a look at Joe's targets in more detail. Let's say he's targeting commercial banks as Target #1. And investment banks as his Target #2. He's targeting two dozen companies in each of these targets.

**Most people start out with targets that are just too small. Their searches are doomed.**

But Joe needs to divide up his list of commercial banks: The A-list includes companies he would die to work for, those that are okay go into the B-list, and the C-list companies actually are of no interest.

Joe should contact his C-list companies first to get his feet wet and practice on them. Because he does not care that much about them, he will probably be more relaxed and confident and will interview better. He is *practicing.* He will also be testing his market to see if he gets a good response from these C-list companies.

**To get a job within a reasonable time frame, target 200 positions—not *openings, positions.***

If the companies on Joe's C-list are *not* interested in him, that's important for him to know. And he needs to talk to the people in his small group to find out what he is doing wrong. However, if he is well received by the companies on his C-list, then Joe can contact the companies on his B-list. He could say something like, "I am already talking to a number of companies in our industry [which is true], but I didn't want to accept a job with any of them [which is also true] until I had a chance to talk with you." This is just a suggestion. Talk to your small group about the right things for you to say to those on your B-list.

- **Your A-list: You'd love to work there.**
- **Your B-list: They're okay.**
- **Your C-list: They don't interest you.**

Your search will have more impact if it is focused by segments and targets. For example, if you are going after the health care market, talking to all of the hospitals on your list within a certain time frame gives you credibility. You can say, "Oh, I talked to . . ." and name the hospital that you talked to yesterday, "and what is happening there is this. And I am really interested in working for a hospital." It makes you sound believable.

- **Contact C-list companies first.**

Remember what we said above about segmenting your targets. The pitch that you use with one of these targets, say, hospitals, will be very different from the pitch you would use with a different target, say, health care manufacturers.

Your approach cannot be casual—even in the initial stages of your search. You might claim, "I don't care whether I work for a hospital or a manufacturer, so long as I have some connection to health care. I can do what I want to do just about anywhere." *You* may not care, but your prospective employers care. They want to know that you understand—and care about—their industry.

**If you are well received by organizations on your C-list, move on to your B-list.**

*There's a lot of talk about self-esteem these days. It seems pretty basic to me. If you want to feel proud of yourself, you've got to do things you can be proud of. Feelings follow actions.*

Oseola McCarty, a washerwoman who gave her life savings of $150,000 to help complete strangers get a college education

# Preliminary Target Investigation: Jobs/Industries Worth Exploring

*Until you know that life is interesting—*
*and find it so—you haven't found your soul.*
Geoffrey Fisher, Archbishop of Canterbury

Although it takes up only a few paragraphs in this book, preliminary target investigation is essential. Your preliminary target investigation could take only a few weeks if you are high in energy and can devote your full time to it. You have to test your ideas for targets in the marketplace to see which ones are worth pursuing. As you research at the library, on the web, and by meeting with people in your fields of choice, you will refine those targets and perhaps develop others. Then you will know where to focus your job search, and the search will be completed much more quickly than if you had skipped this important step.

People who conduct a preliminary target investigation while employed or in school sometimes take a year to explore various fields while they continue in their old jobs. If you are not at all familiar with some of the job targets you have selected, do some preliminary target investigation *now* through the web, library research (be sure to read *Researching Your Job Targets* in this book), and networking. You will find that some targets are not right for you. Eliminate them and conduct a full campaign in those areas that seem right for you and that offer some reasonable hope of success.

Whether you are in school, employed, or between jobs, preliminary target investigation is well worth your time and a lot of fun. It is the difference between blindly going after something because it is the only idea you have and finding out what is really happening in the world so you can latch on to a field that may carry you forward for many, many years. This is a wonderful time to explore—to find out what the world offers. Most job hunters narrow their targets down too quickly and wind up later with not much to go after. It is better for you emotionally as well as practically to develop more targets *now* than you need so you will have them when you are actively campaigning. If, on the other hand, you do not have the inclination or time to explore, you can move on. *Just remember, you can come back to this point if your search dries up and you need more targets.*

Most job hunters target only one job type or industry, take a very long time to find out that this target is not working, get depressed, try to think of other things they can do with their lives, pick themselves up, and start on one more target.

Instead, **brainstorm as many targets as possible *before* you begin your real job search**. Then you can overlap your campaigns, and go after a number of targets at once. If some targets do not seem to be working as well for you as others, you can drop the targets in which you are no longer interested. And when things don't seem to be going well, you will have other targets to fall back on.

1. **List below all of the jobs/industries that interest you at this point.**
2. If you are not at all familiar with some of the targets you have selected, do some preliminary

target investigation *now* through library research or networking. Eliminate the targets that are not right for you, and conduct a full campaign in those areas that *do* seem right for you and seem to offer you some reasonable hope of success.

As you find out what is happening in the world, new fields will open up for you. Things are changing so fast that if you conduct a serious search without some exploration, you are probably missing the most exciting developments in an area.

Spend some time exploring. Don't narrow your targets too quickly; you will wind up later with not much to go after. It is better for you emotionally, as well as practically, to develop *now* more targets than you need so you will have them when you are actively campaigning. If, on the other hand, you do not have the time or inclination to explore, you can move on to the next step. **Just remember: you can come back to this point if your search dries up and you need more targets.**

## Jobs and Industries That Interest Me at This Point

Conduct a preliminary target investigation to determine what is really going on in each of them.

_______________________________________

_______________________________________

_______________________________________

_______________________________________

_______________________________________

_______________________________________

_______________________________________

_______________________________________

_______________________________________

_______________________________________

_______________________________________

_______________________________________

*Dream. Dream* big *dreams! Others may deprive you of your material wealth and cheat you in a thousand ways, but no man can deprive you of the control and use of your imagination. Men may deal with you unfairly, as men often do; they may deprive you of your liberty; but they cannot take from you the privilege of using your imagination. In your imagination, you always win!*

Jesse Jackson

## Targeting: The Start of an Organized Search

To organize your targeting

1. Brainstorm as many job targets as possible. You will not conduct a campaign aimed at all of them, but will have backup targets in case certain ones do not work out.
2. Identify a number of targets worthy of preliminary research. (If they are large targets and represent a lot of job possibilities for you, you will need fewer targets.)
3. Research each one enough—through the Internet, the library, and a few networking meetings—to determine whether it is worth a full job-search campaign. This is your preliminary target investigation.
4. If your research shows that a target now seems inappropriate, cross it off your list, and concentrate on the remaining targets. **As you continue to network and research, keep open to other possibilities that may be targets for you. Add those to your list of targets to research**.

As you add new targets, reprioritize your list so you are concentrating first on the targets that should be explored first. Do *not* haphazardly go after everything that comes your way.

5. If you decide the target is worth pursuing, conduct a full campaign to get interviews in that area.
   - Develop your pitch.

- Develop your résumé.
- Develop a list of all the organizations in the target area and the name of the person you want to contact in each company.

6. Then contact each organization through networking, direct contact, ads, or search firms.

## Serendipitous Leads

Make a methodical approach the basis of your search, but also keep yourself open to those serendipitous "*lucky leads* outside your target areas that may come your way. In general, it is a waste of your energy to go after single serendipitous leads. It is better to ask yourself if this lead warrants a new target. If it does, then decide where it should be ranked in your list of targets, and research it as you would any serious target.

*Life is God's novel. Let him write it.*

Isaac Bashevis Singer

*Counterbalance sources of stress in your life with sources of harmony. Develop closer ties to the people you love. Set up dependable routines in your schedule to which you can look forward during times of stress: a few moments each evening in a hot bath, regular nights to eat out, one day per month in bed, seasonal vacations. Create environments around you that are physically and emotionally restorative: a peaceful workspace, a blossom-filled window box you can see from where you eat, a permanent exercise nook. Regularly perform simple tasks that you can be certain will give you a sense of accomplishment.*

Jack Maguire, *Care and Feeding of the Brain*

# Ready for the Next Step

*This is the true joy in life, the being used for a purpose recognized by yourself as a mighty one, the being thoroughly worn out before you are thrown on the scrap heap; the being a force of nature instead of a feverish selfish little clod of ailments and grievances complaining that the world will not devote itself to making you happy.*

George Bernard Shaw

By selecting and ranking your targets, you have completed a very important task. If your targets are wrong, the campaigns you aim at those targets are wrong. Maintain an exploratory mind-set—assessing the targets you are pursuing and being open to others.

Next, you will start to develop your tentative résumé, which you will need if you are going to contact anyone in any target area. Contacting people is part of your research to help you understand a target area. In addition, this book will help you conduct research through the library, the Internet, or your college guidance office.

Make an organized search the basis for your campaign. Some lucky job hunters know lots of important people and just happen onto their next jobs. Sometimes those jobs are even satisfying. If that has happened to you in the past, count your blessings, but do not rely on that approach to work for you in the future. The world has changed, and organizations are more serious about whom they hire. In addition, you probably got those leads through people who are not thinking about what might be best for you but instead are telling you of the places they happen to know. These leads may be appropriate for you, or they may not be.

**Do not think that you have to complete your research before you develop your résumé. The job-search process *is* largely a research process. You will continually refer tothe research portions of this book throughout your campaign.**

*Out of every crisis comes the chance to be reborn. . . .*

Nena O'Neill

*True commitment transforms you. You really know where you stand. You have a base on which to build your life. You're not in shifting sand anymore.*

Christopher Reeve, former star of *Superman,* in an interview with Barbara Walters. Reeve became a quadriplegiac after a horseback-riding accident.

*We will make the best possible life out of this life that we now have and there's no question that he will continue to be a leader and continue to be a strong person and a funny person and a lively person.*

Mrs. Christopher Reeve (Dana), in that same interview

*We must not be afraid of the future. We must not be afraid of man. It is no accident that we are here. Each and every human person has been created in the "image and likeness" of the One who is the origin of all that is. We have within us the capacities for wisdom and virtue. With these gifts, and with the help of God's grace, we can build in the next century and the next millennium a civilization worthy of the human person, a true culture of freedom. We can and must see that the tears of this century have prepared the ground for a new springtime of the human spirit.*

Pope John Paul II, speech to the United Nations General Assembly, October 5, 1995

# PART FOUR

# Building A Great Résumé

# Case Study: Julie
# Before and after Résumé

*Words have weight, sound and appearance; it is only by considering these that you can write a sentence that is good to look at and good to listen to.*

W. Somerset Maugham

*The successful person has the habit of doing things failures don't like to do. They don't like doing them either necessarily. But their disliking is subordinated to the strength of their purpose.*

E. M. Gray, *The Common Denominator of Success*

Julie, a college sophomore majoring in architecture, wanted summer employment. Although she had some relevant job experience, her résumé was a cookie-cutter version: It looked like everyone else's and started out with her education.

Most of the 24,000 undergraduates attending the University of Michigan will have résumés that start out exactly the same: Bachelor's degree, Major, University of Michigan, 20XX.

If she wants a job with an architectural firm, Julie must make sure the reader sees her as quite a find for summer help at an architectural firm. The average résumé is looked at for only 10 seconds. Julie needed to make it easier for the employer to see what she had to offer and to distinguish herself from her competition: all of the undergrads in her geographic area. The way to do that, most often, is to highlight your work experience, not your education.

Under *Work Experience,* highlight the jobs that would be of most interest to your target market. Julie had listed first her work as a library aide—certainly not something that would make architectural firms sit up and take notice. Julie's relevant experience was buried in the middle of her résumé.

## The Start of a Good Résumé

So Julie did what every Five O'Clock Clubber does: She didn't skip the assessment. She took time to do her Seven Stories Exercise as well as her Forty-Year Vision. Through the Seven Stories, she uncovered those things she *enjoyed doing and also did well*. The results would help confirm whether architecture was the right path and give her accomplishments to talk about on her résumé and cover letter, as well as in the interviewing process.

Here are the results of Julie's Seven Stories Exercise:

1. editor of yearbook
2. soloist in 7th and 8th grades
3. played Gwendolyn in 11th grade play
4. built chair for design class this year
5. built igloo with family
6. trained my dog
7. built stand for cinderblock; it held
8. learned AutoCAD—fast & accurately
9. organized binders at work
10. wrote poems that got published

11. helped establish a cappella group
12. won *best science and math student* in my high school (of 40 students)
13. created dance with friends for talent show and won!

Here's Julie's ranked list:

1. editor of yearbook
2. built stand for cinderblock; it held
3. built chair for design class this year
4. wrote poems that got published
5. helped establish a cappella group
6. built igloo with family
7. learned AutoCAD—fast & accurately

Julie's Seven Stories results contain elements that support her interest in architecture. At age 11, she was interested in building the igloo. She enjoyed her architecture courses and did well in them. She worked in a civil engineering firm using AutoCAD, a tool that architects use. She enjoyed doing it and did it well. She even enjoyed editing her high school yearbook, which included extensive design work, albeit of another kind.

## Julie's Forty-Year Vision

### At Age 29

Because Julie had not worked on her Forty-Year Vision before we met, we did a quick version together. Julie imagined herself 10 years from now—at age 29—working for a small architecture firm with about 20 employees. Although Julie was interested in building museums, very few museums get built—as compared with other structures. So she imagined herself in a firm that built family houses, schools, and new business owners' offices.

By age 29, Julie did not want to be working on the nitty-gritty everyday work but wanted to be more involved in planning and have client contact.

*People cannot let others limit their imagination of what is they want to do or can do. Otherwise, we would never have discoveries or advance.*

Mae C. Jemison, physician, chemical engineer, and America's first black woman astronaut

### At Age 39

"I'll have my architect's license and would be able to start my own firm if I wanted to. However, 39 may be young to start my own firm, but I would be the person others go to in my present firm."

So, Julie's Forty-Year Vision fits in nicely with the results of her Seven Stories Exercise. **What kind of summer job should Julie aim for now at age 19?**

Julie wanted hands-on experience as much as possible, and she was more likely to get that at a smaller firm. She was afraid of getting assigned to doing AutoCAD all day long and actually preferred administrative work, perhaps as an assistant to a busy architect, lining up meetings, putting proposals together, and so on. She could see herself doing a variety of computer work.

## Her Résumé

So Julie's new résumé emphasized her administrative expertise over her AutoCAD experience. Most often, a student will have a brief summary and list accomplishments under each job. But in Julie's case, we wanted to keep all of her AutoCAD experience together, so we had to put all of it in her summary.

In addition, Julie was hoping to have some client contact. She had no related experience (unless you count talking to customers in a grocery store!), so at the end of her summary, we have listed some personality traits. Perhaps the hiring team will consider Julie for client contact work.

Wherever possible, we quantified Julie's accomplishments. Details can show substance and attract attention!

On the following pages are Julie's "before" and "after" résumés. After that, you will see a few other sample résumés for college kids and recent grads.

---

*I know you are asking today, "How long will it take?" I come to say to you this afternoon, however difficult the moment, however frustrating the hour, it will not be long, because truth pressed to earth will rise again. How long? Not long, because no lie can live forever. How long? Not long, because you still reap what you sow. How long? Not long, because the arm of the moral universe is long but it bends towards justice. How long? Not long, 'cause mine eyes have seen the glory of the coming of the Lord, trampling out the vineyards where the grapes of wrath are stored. He has loosed the fateful lightning of his terrible swift sword. His truth is marching on. He has sounded forth the trumpets that shall never call retreat. He is lifting up the hearts of man before His judgment seat. Oh, be swift, my soul, to answer Him. Be jubilant, my feet. Our God is marching on.*

Rev. Martin Luther King Jr.

*Dear sir, Be patient toward all that is unsolved in your heart and try to love the* questions themselves *like locked rooms and like books that are written in a very foreign tongue. Do not now seek the answers, which cannot be given you because you would not be able to live them. And the point is, to live everything.* Live *the questions now. Perhaps you will then gradually, without noticing it, live along some distant day into the answer. Perhaps you do carry within yourself the possibility of shaping and forming as a particularly happy and pure way of living; train yourself to it—but take whatever comes with trust, and if only it comes out of your own will, out of some need of your inmost being, take it upon yourself and hate nothing.*

Rainer Maria Rilke
*Letters to a Young Poet*

## "Before" Résumé

**JULIE ANGELO**
julieangelo@umich.edu
angelo555@hotmail.com
76 North Churchill Rd.
Brewster MI 99945

**EDUCATION**

University of Michigan — 1999–2003
BA, Architecture — Current GPA: 3.42

The Curtis School — 1995–1999
Graduated Salutatorian, with Highest Honors

**WORK EXPERIENCE**

Library Aide — 1999–2001
*University of Michigan Blain Library*
- Answered customer questions
- Shelved and checked out books

Assistant Office Manager — 1999–2001
*Engineering Firm: J. Robert Folchetti and Associates, L.L.C.*
- Ran office when needed
- Typed and formatted Correspondence
- Answered 8 line phone

Assistant Cad Operator — Summer 2000
*Engineering Firm: J. Robert Folchetti and Associates, L.L.C.*
- Corrected and Revised Details
- Convert drawings to CAD 2000 format

Produce Manager, Assistant — Summer 1998
*Kobakers Grocery Store*
- Organize and Layout Produce
- Answer customer questions

**SKILLS**

*Computer*: AutoCAD 2000, Adobe PageMaker, PowerPoint, Word, WordPerfect, Excel, Adobe Photoshop, QuarkExpress

*Languages*: proficient in German, knowledgeable in Spanish

## JULIE ANGELO

julieangelo@umich.edu
76 North Churchill Rd.
Brewster, MI 99945

863 Erie Avenue
Ann Arbor, MI 99999
555-666-4693

**Assistant Office Manager / Assistant AutoCAD Operator
with Civil Engineering Firm**

- **A strong administrator**
  - Organized 90-page client proposals.
  - Organized all forms used in office. Put together 7 binders of forms.
  - Reshelved 400 catalogs.
  - Ran office when needed; answered 8 phone lines; typed and formatted correspondence.
- **AutoCAD experience**
  - Took intensive 40-hour AutoCAD course.
  - Routinely handled small AutoCAD assignments for engineers, saving them hours.
  - Converted drawings to CAD 2000 format.
  - Put together 70-page AutoCAD Manual with drawings.
  - Offered full-time AutoCAD job.
- In **Architecture** class, **won contests**: "most structurally sound design," "most pleasing to eye."
- Computer experience: AutoCAD 2000, Adobe PageMaker, Quark Express, Adobe Photoshop, PowerPoint, Excel, Word, WordPerfect
- Languages: proficient in German, knowledgeable in Spanish

***Strong working relationships at all levels.
Known for getting the job done efficiently and correctly, and putting in the hours needed.***

### Work History

Assistant Office Manager / Assistant AutoCAD Operator — Summer, 2000 & 1999 to present
Engineering Firm: J. Robert Folchetti and Associates, L.L.C.

Library Aide — 1999 to present
University of Michigan Blain Library
- Answer customer questions; shelve and check out books

Produce Manager, Assistant — Summer 1998
Kobakers Grocery Store
- Organized and laid out produce; answered customer questions

### EDUCATION

BA, Architecture, University of Michigan pending (Current GPA: 3.42) — 1999–2003
- Helped to develop and create a new a cappella group.

The Curtis School — 1995–1999
- Graduated Salutatorian, with Highest Honors
- Yearbook Editor: Developed 250-page book celebrating school's 150th anniversary
- Wrote poem for national publication; selected as one of ten for audiocassette

# Additional In-Depth Résumé Case Studies

by Mark Gonska

*Start where you are with what you have, knowing that what you have is plenty enough.*

Booker T. Washington

## Targets for an Attorney: Sarah Moghal

Sarah Moghal came from a family of professionals. Her father, a general surgeon, had built up a strong practice through 40 years of hard work. With that same kind of work ethic and determination, Sarah completed her undergraduate degree.

For Sarah, entering law school brought with it excitement and dreams of righting the wrongs of society. Her summers were filled with law clerk positions at local firms. Graduating from law school meant more grueling hours of study for Sarah to pass the bar exam and become admitted to the state bar.

Then the realities of supply and demand came into focus. There are lots of attorneys. More are graduating every semester. However, the demand for legal services does not seem to be growing as quickly.

Sarah selected prime opportunities posted at her law school placement office. She sent out résumés and hoped for the best. She subscribed to the *Ohio Bar Association Report (OBAR)*, which serves as a clearinghouse for classified ads for admitted attorneys. She answered ads.

Most advertisements failed to result in even a rejection letter, let alone an offer. She worked harder and answered more ads, even for positions that she felt were beneath her.

Sarah finally landed a part-time job with a small firm. Much of the work she received seemed to be at the law clerk level, similar to the summer jobs she had held for the last three years. The pay was not significantly better.

Sarah became part of the *underground* of underemployed professionals. Many capable people in every market have settled for part-time jobs, sometimes outside their chosen fields. They are stuck and unsure of what to do next.

The Five O'Clock Club approach is an important tool job searchers can use to get unstuck. Sarah went through the assessment exercises in *Targeting a Great Career* and identified three job targets. She had not received any significant offers while playing the generalist role. Yet, the idea of focusing on specific targets seemed like wishful thinking to Sarah, at least initially. She was concerned that "pigeonholing" her approach would limit her options even further.

Despite her concerns, The Five O'Clock Club approach eventually came to make sense to her. Anything productive would be an improvement.

Sarah's initial résumé was designed using the format recommended by her law school. It looked nearly identical to those of hundreds of other newly graduated lawyers—a juris doctor degree, summer clerk experience, and little else.

Sarah identified three targets:

Target 1:

| | |
|---|---|
| Industry: | Public Sector |
| Position: | Municipal Law |
| Geographic area: | Cleveland |

Target 2:

| | |
|---|---|
| Industry: | Local Firm |
| Position: | Staff Attorney Specializing in Municipal Law |
| Geographic area: | Cleveland |

Target 3:

| | |
|---|---|
| Industry: | Public Sector |
| Position: | Municipal Law |
| Geographic area: | Chicago |

Discussions with Sarah revealed that she had had a fair amount of experience with municipal law. In fact, the firm where she had clerked and now worked as an attorney had served as a kind of law department for five city governments. The significance of the firm had to be highlighted on her résumé. Also, an accurate description of the types of municipal casework she had done was essential.

Sarah's "before" and "after" résumés follow.

**SARAH N. MOGHAL**
6662 Gates Mills Blvd.
Gates Mills, OH 44040
(216) 555-0820

EDUCATION:

**Cleveland-Marshall College of Law**
Cleveland, Ohio
J.D., 1998
Business Law Classes: Commecial [*sic*] Law; Secured Transactions; Real Estate; Small Business Enterprises; Antitrust
GPA: 3.43/4.00

**Ohio State University**
Columbus, Ohio
B. S. in Business Administration, 1995
Major: Finance
GPA: 3.80/4.0

WORK EXPERIENCE:

January 1999–Present

**Robert J. Dobbs Jr. & Associates**
(AV-Rated) Cleveland, Ohio (216) 555-1567

Attorney. Handle cases in the areas of *commercial contracts, business, municipal, labor and personal injury law.* Perform research, drafting of briefs, pleadings and interrogatories; debtor's exams, depositions, litigation support, court appearances.

February 1998–May 1998

**Chadbourne & Lewis**
Cleveland, Ohio (216) 999-5500
Law Clerk. Performed legal research and wrote memoranda in the areas of *consumer sales* and *personal injury;* drafted pleadings.

Summer 1997

**Jerome and Zoller**
Cleveland, Ohio (216) 533-2200
Law Clerk. Conducted legal research and wrote memoranda in the areas of *business law* and *contracts;* filed pleadings.

Summer 1996

**Uhlinger and Keis**
Cleveland, Ohio (216) 681-4100
Law Clerk. Provided legal research in the areas of *torts, contracts* and *insurance subrogation;* prepared complaints; wrote legal memoranda.

BAR ADMISSION:

State Bar of Ohio, 1998; Member, American Bar Association; Member, Ohio State Bar Association; Member, Cleveland Bar Association.

PERSONAL:

Proficient with LEXIS, WESTLAW, and numerous word processing programs. Knowledge of Lotus. Enjoy basketball and reading.

**SARAH N. MOGHAL, ESQ.**
6662 Gates Mills Boulevard
Gates Mills, Ohio 44040
(216) 555-0820[H]; (216) 555-6800[O]

---

**MUNICIPAL LAW ATTORNEY**

**with the research, analytical and writing skills required to provide timely opinions and interpretations. Accustomed to meeting stringent deadlines. Experience includes:**

- Legislative Analysis
- Tort Liability/Sovereign Immunity
- Contract/Liability Issues
- Zoning Interpretation
- Employment Litigation
- Land Usage

---

**Employment History**

**Attorney** *1999 to Present*
ROBERT J. DOBBS, JR. & ASSOCIATES, Cleveland, Ohio
[An AV-Rated firm serving as legal department/prosecutor for five municipalities.]
- Support litigation involving all aspects of municipal law.
- Assist with complex cases; gained broad experience with labor and commercial contract disputes.
- Participated in successful litigation of a major suit involving vindication of employee's rights.
- Research, prepare and draft pleadings, motions briefs and memoranda of law; execute all phases of discovery.
- Completed research and wrote opinions on municipal legislation, zoning variances, traffic law, taxation and land usage cases.

**Law Clerk** 1996 –1998
CHADBOURNE & LEWIS (1998)
- Conducted research, organized and wrote legal memoranda, drafted complaints and briefs involving the Ohio Consumer Sales Practices Act and personal injury cases.

JEROME AND ZOLLER (1997)
- Provided legal research and drafted memoranda regarding business organizations, anti-competitive practices and contracts.

UHLINGER AND KEIS (Summer, 1996)
- Researched, wrote memoranda and drafted pleadings on personal injury and insurance subrogation issues.

**Education and Training**

**JD, Cleveland-Marshall College of Law**, 1998
**BS, Business Administration**, The Ohio State University, 1995 (Major: Finance)
Proficient with LEXIS, WESTLAW, word processing and spreadsheet applications.

**Bar Admission**

**State Bar of Ohio**, 1998
Member: American Bar Association, Ohio State Bar Association, Cleveland Bar Association

## What Sarah Did Next

### Target 1, a Position in Her Local City's Law Department

Like most public sector situations, the hiring process for Sarah's first target was mired in red tape, multiple gatekeepers, and delays. But Sarah was persistent. She found a decision maker and arranged for a personal interview. During the meeting, she positioned herself in light of her updated pitch for municipal law. She also identified two "influencers" in the prosecutor's office and met with them for advice. Unfortunately, the meeting with the law director was delayed twice.

In the process, Target 3, a position in Chicago's law department, came into play. Sarah contacted The Five O'Clock Club affiliate in Chicago for some help with local firms that specialized in municipal law. One of the leads she got resulted in a job offer with an attorney who was planning to leave an established firm. The soon-to-be entrepreneur needed a young attorney to help him hit the ground running. The stories of how the initial long hours of work would turn to gold were music to Sarah's ears.

However, Sarah declined the offer. She really needed structure, training, and a mentor, none of which this start-up opportunity would provide. While she was in Chicago, Sarah did the unthinkable. She walked into the city's law offices and asked to meet with the law director, with no appointment and no previous résumé, letter, or contact of any kind. She claimed that she had only one afternoon in Chicago and needed only a few minutes to meet with the director. She asked for help.

After a 40-minute wait, Sarah was ushered into the office. She had rehearsed the questions she needed to ask. During a short but cordial reception, Sarah met the director, presented her pitch and received important advice on how to navigate through the departmental bureaucracy.

She felt that prospects were encouraging enough to study for the Illinois Bar Exam. After careful consideration, she feels that relocating to Chicago is the preferred option. Despite an abundance of law schools and a plethora of attorneys there, Sarah sees greater opportunity in the Chicago market. Currently, Sarah is spending most of her waking hours studying for the Illinois Bar. Despite this decision, she is still pursuing Targets 1 and 2.

---

*Whenever you can, shorten a sentence. And one always can. . . . Caress your sentence tenderly; it will end by smiling at you.*

Anatole France

## Accounting for All of Your Skills: Ismail Daod

While capturing a job when you have limited experience is difficult under the best circumstances, additional issues like age, disability, gender, and national origin can present further challenges. Regardless of the Equal Employment Opportunity Commission, these biases persist. While some of these differences can actually be an asset in certain environments, they need to be handled carefully.

Concerned about his Middle Eastern accent, Ismail Daod wondered if his lack of interviews was due to discrimination. Were his first words on the telephone revealing his ethnic background and immediately disqualifying him? His frustration led him to do the worst thing any job seeker can do: nothing. Ismail stopped making follow-up phone calls and started feeling sorry for himself. He wondered if the thousands of dollars and hundreds of hours he had invested in his accounting degree had all been a waste.

In a desperate frame of mind, he met with his Five O'Clock Club coach. The coach recommended a different approach: to think of the accent as an asset rather than as a liability. The idea sounded ridiculous to Ismail. He developed 30-second and Two-Minute Pitches that actually emphasized Ismail's ethnic background. Ismail was skeptical, but he felt that his situation couldn't get any worse.

**ISMAIL A. DAOD**
1120 Revere Drive
Glenfield, Ohio 44113
(216) 888-4160

OBJECTIVE

Desire to positively contribute my diverse entrepreneurial skills to an accounting establishment that needs an analytical, hardworking, and resourceful person.

SUMMARY

Strong background in purchasing, supply, and negotiations. Experience with Lotus. Excellent customer service skills; an accomplished entrepreneur. Bilingual (English and Arabic) and enjoy traveling.

EMPLOYMENT

CAVANAGH ACCOUNTING, Cleveland, Ohio (11/98–Present)
Accounting Staff
Prepare payroll
Prepare sales taxes and returns
Check compliance with local and federal regulations

A & I INC., Cleveland, Ohio (1996–Present)
President
Oversee all bookkeeping matters
Ensure compliance with all relevant tax regulations
Increase net worth of corporation from $2,000 to $100,000 in 3 years

3M, Cleveland, Ohio (2/93–3/96)
Salesman
Conducted 50-60% of division sales

MIKE DISCOUNTS, Cleveland, Ohio (1990–1993)
Section Manager, Dairy & Frozen Section
Department Manager
Managed a chain of 10 stores
Ordered and stocked commodities

EDUCATION

Cleveland State University, Cleveland, Ohio
Bachelor's of Business Administration, March 1998
Major: Accounting
Major GPA: 3.38/4.0
CPA Candidate

Amman Community College
Diploma, 1989
Major: Business and Office Practice
Took Jordan Comprehensive Professional Examination and was rated fifth best candidate in the country.

ACTIVITIES

Member, Cleveland State University Accounting Association.
Running, swimming, travel.

*References will be provided upon request.*

**"After" Résumé**

**ISMAIL A. DAOD**

1120 Revere Drive, Glenfield, Ohio 44113 (216) 888-4160

---

**ACCOUNTING PROFESSIONAL**

Diverse analytical skills, proven business sense, and technical expertise.

- Financial analysis
- Efficiency enhancements
- Multiple software packages
- Operational controls
- Cash management
- Tax preparation and filing

**Summary of Related Experience:**

**Productivity:** Established a reputation for effectiveness and efficiency; able to complete assignments on time and within budget. Demonstrated an exceptional energy level and strong negotiating skills. Managed multiple projects and departmental responsibility.

**Financial Analysis:** Gained experience in business analysis, valuation, and acquisition.

**System Enhancements:** Provided more effective internal management reporting. Constructed and analyzed financial reports using Lotus 1-2-3 spreadsheets, TurboTax, QuickBooks, Quicken and many others. Understand Windows 98 and XP operating systems.

***An aggressive professional who has demonstrated determination to reach ambitious goals. Skilled in general accounting, auditing, and tax planning. Passed the CPA exam in May 1995.***

---

Staff Accountant, CAVANAGH ACCOUNTING SERVICES, Cleveland, Ohio 1998 to Present

- Prepare payroll and sales tax filings for more than 50 businesses. File corporate taxes.
- Construct financial reports. Provide full-charge bookkeeping through financial statements.
- Assure compliance with tax regulations.
- Advise clients on investment options, performance enhancement, asset allocation strategies, and risk management.

Principal, A & I INC., Cleveland, Ohio 1996 to 1998

- Established a successful business. Starting with an undergraduate class project, recognized a real-world opportunity, and now participate in a business with a six-figure net worth.
- Created, constructed, and implemented all financial reporting and operational controls.
- Learned, hands-on, how to manage inventory and maximize cash flow.

Sales Representative, 3M Distribution Company, Cleveland, Ohio 1993 to 1996

- Ranked as top sales producer among six sales representatives. Negotiated sales agreements.

Department Manager, Mike Discounts, Cleveland, Ohio 1990 to 1993

- Managed a chain of 10 stores.

**EDUCATION AND PROFESSIONAL TRAINING**

BBA, Accounting, Cleveland State University, 1998 (GPA: 3.38/4.0 in major); CPA candidate

**Jordan Comprehensive Professional Examination**

Rated as the country's fifth best accounting candidate.

**Proud U.S. citizen; Open to travel**

Target 1 was small to mid-size public accounting firms that served local businesses owned by Arab Americans. The Five O'Clock Club coach recommended that he contact a high-profile city councilman of Arab descent. The councilman told Ismail about two professional organizations made up of Target 1 businesses. He also provided Ismail with current membership rosters of each association.

Ismail scripted out a 30-second pitch and then contacted these business owners by telephone. The pitch went something like this:

> I am an Arab American with proven business start-up and management experience. I have built on this hands-on experience by completing accounting and CPA training. My lifelong goal has been to better serve the Arab American business community. Specifically, I want to join an accounting firm that has demonstrated a commitment to this growing ethnic group. I am willing to start at a lower position and work toward using my business skills and accounting training to help others overcome the obstacles I have faced in obtaining financing, implementing prudent financial controls, and reducing unnecessary taxation. Further, I bring a personal understanding of cross-cultural challenges as well as multiple language skills.

More than once, Ismail delivered his 30-second pitch in Arabic. Each contact could prove to be an important resource. For Target 2, Ismail hoped to join an Arab American–owned company as an accountant or financial manager.

Five O'Clock Club research indicates that follow-up phone calls require an average of eight attempts to actually reach the desired contact. Therefore, to reach his 40 targeted companies, Ismail might need to make more than 300 telephone calls. So far, the hard work has paid off handsomely. In two months, he has already generated seven face-to-face interviews.

Ismail also learned about three smaller accounting firms that cater to Arab American clients, and he has received additional requests to help with year-end financial reporting. Most important, when Ismail put the accent on his strengths and began marketing himself more effectively, he found a much more receptive audience. His pitch worked, not because of any clever trick or technique, but because he used The Five O'Clock Club method to determine what he really wanted to do. His sincerity would have come through in any language.

---

*To feel that one has a place in life solves half the problem of contentment.*

George Edward Woodberry, American poet, critic, and educator

## A Professional Track—Instead of a Job in Fast Food: Shelley

Many young people feel stuck in the fast-food jungle and are unsure of how to prevent the phrase "would you like fries with your order" from being permanently etched into their memories. Real-world experience would sure be an improvement over hokey uniforms and busing tables. Yet, how does a young person acquire real-world experience, and is it possible to get *before* completing a degree program? Can young people be pre-positioned, that is, put on their career track before completing their degree, in a technical field that requires professional licensing? With rapid, profound change affecting so many professions, how can anyone identify a career path that offers sustained growth?

Shelley Mulligan, a high school student from Ohio, wanted to pursue a career in nursing. Her friends and family thought Shelley had overlooked the headlines. The local hospital market was consolidating. Two of the area's largest hospitals had merged, and experienced nurses were let go in the ensuing *streamlining* and downsizing. Rumors that other hospitals would be closing became reality as major health care consortiums swallowed up the strongest remaining facilities. What would a national health care plan mean for nurses? What would the job market look like when Shelley finished her degree?

Despite these valid concerns, Shelley insisted that nursing was her calling. She worked with a Five O'Clock Club counselor to devise a flexible career development plan to better position her for the future. The assumptions made in this plan were debatable but seemed to make sense:

- Health care delivery systems will continue to consolidate and change at an accelerated pace.
- Regardless of the changes, more services will be delivered on an outpatient basis.
- Home health care options will expand and continue to displace traditional hospital employment opportunities.
- Lower level technicians will perform more support work and further reduce the demand for traditional RN staffing.
- Specialization and advanced training will be a requirement for the professional nurse in the United States.
- People will live longer; older people will make up a larger percentage of the U.S. population. All aspects of elder care and geriatrics will be in greater demand in the future.
- Developing countries will have an unfilled demand and will lack funding for health care professionals.

This was serious analysis for a teenager, but then again Shelley was serious. She developed a career plan that focused on obtaining real experience in the hotter areas of health care , which would better weather the storms of change.

At age 17, Shelley left the fast-food crew behind and looked at food service or dietary positions in the area's upscale assisted living center. Far more than a nursing home, this facility offered many different opportunities for health care professionals. However, the most critical need at the retirement community was not for dietitians' assistants but for nurses' aides. This often thankless job is on the lowest rung of the staff hierarchy, and consequently many health care facilities suffer from a high rate of turnover among their nurses' aides. Shelley found that a $100 bonus was offered for candidates who joined the staff and completed state certification requirements. After she completed the training program—at full pay—she received an hourly increase and a shift differential bonus. Additional training and certification in CPR was also provided. Because reliable employees were so hard to find, Shelley was soon called on to work as much overtime as she was willing to take. She worked closely with the staff nurses and demonstrated a positive, enthusiastic outlook.

Before joining the staff at the retirement community, Shelley's favorite nurse had worked with a home health care service. The nurse explained that the service was always looking for nurses' aides. Shelley found that although the service did not offer benefits, they did pay two dollars more per hour. She liked getting out of the confines of the assisted living center and enjoyed spending more time with each patient.

In her spare time, Shelley volunteered to work at the office of her family physician. She worked there only a few hours a week, but she gained a working knowledge of the ICD-9 codes and CPT codes required for every insurance company claim. That isn't all she hoped to gain. Ever the strategist, Shelley thought that working in a physician's practice adjacent to the hospital might eventually give her a leg up on support positions within the hospital.

The next summer, Shelley put all her work responsibilities on hold for a three-week visit to Quito, Ecuador. She wanted to know what living in another culture was like, and she hoped to get a glimpse of health care outside the comforts of the United States. The Ecuador experience gave her real inspiration and a dream to practice cross-cultural nursing.

Within 18 months of leaving her fast-food job, Shelley acquired legitimate experience. More important, she has begun to learn how to develop contacts within her chosen field. In three years, she intends to graduate as a registered nurse with her first degree. Although she can do nothing to guarantee job security, she is building not only her résumé but also her employability security. She is working hard, at times to the detriment of her social life, but she is moving forward toward her goals.

---

*1. Never use a long word where a short one will do.*
*2. If it is possible to cut out a word, always cut it out.*
*3. Never use the passive where you can use the active.*
*4. Never use a foreign phrase, a scientific word or a jargon word if you can think of an everyday English equivalent.*
*5. Break any of these rules sooner than say anything barbarous.*

George Orwell, "Politics and the English Language"

*The man who makes no mistakes does not usually make anything.*

Edward John Phelps, American lawyer and diplomat

**SHELLEY MARIE MULLIGAN**
2053 Aldersgate Drive
Fairstead Village, Ohio 44124
(216) 777-6804

OBJECTIVE

Entry-level position in health care leading to a position in **Nursing**.

PROFILE

Hardworking, enthusiastic individual with excellent communication skills.

EDUCATION

CUYAHOGA COMMUNITY COLLEGE, Cleveland, Ohio Pursuing Associate Degree—1999
Dean's List Spring, 1998

THE KING'S ACADEMY, Elyria, Ohio Graduate—1997
Received Varsity Letter in fast-pitch softball.
Toured three states with the drama group, "The Ambassadors."
Actively participated in local political campaigns, SADD (Students Against Drunk Driving) and Student Council.
Proficient with WordPerfect and Microsoft Office products.

EXPERIENCE

BURGER DELIGHT, Cleveland, Ohio
Crew Leader—1996
Crew Person 1996 to 1997 (part-time)
As Crew Leader, directed a busy shift of customer service associates in a busy suburban location. Gained thorough understanding of sanitation and cash-control procedures.

- Received "Crew Leader of the Month" award for three consecutive months.
- Assist manager with staff scheduling and training of newly hired associates.

THE GAP, Cleveland, Ohio

Sales Associate—1996 to 1997 (part-time)
Enjoyed the challenge of delivering excellent service to discriminating customers. Encouraged repeat business and maintained excellent cash controls.

VISION QUEST, INTERNATIONAL, Cleveland, Ohio

Software Duplication Assistant—1995 to 1997 (part-time)
Duplicated a high volume of "shareware software" for wholesale distribution.

LANGUAGE PROFICIENCIES
Able to read, write, and speak Spanish.

**Shelley Marie Mulligan**
2053 Aldersgate Drive
Fairstead Village, Ohio 44124
(216) 777-6804

---

**Health Care Professional**

Experience working in skilled nursing facilities, a physician's office, and on home health care assignments.
Certified Nurse's Aide, State of Ohio. Trained in CPR and Infant CPR.
Hardworking and enthusiastic.

---

**Related Experience**

THE GEORGIAN RETIREMENT COMMUNITY, ASSISTED LIVING CENTER
**State-Certified Nurse's Aide**—1997 to present
Assist professional nursing staff with direct patient care and encouragement. Work with a variety of residents with special needs, including: Alzheimer's/dementia patients, orthopedics, and short- and long-term care. Work well with demanding residents, assist them with basic needs, hygiene, and companionship.

- Manage the challenges of working alternating shifts and working productively with changing support staffs and nurses.
- Received attendance incentive award. Worked overtime as requested.

EVERGREEN HOME HEALTH SERVICES
**Caregiver**—1998 (part-time)

- Traveled to patients requiring basic care. Interfaced with family members and prepared detailed records for review by staff nurses or physicians.

DR. KORNELIA BRATTON
**Volunteer Office Assistant**—1997 to present (part-time)

- Gained an understanding of office practices and procedures in this growing family practice.

**CREDENTIALS AND TRAINING**

Certified Nurse's Aide—State of Ohio. Trained in CPR and Infant CPR.

**EDUCATION**

CUYAHOGA COMMUNITY COLLEGE, Cleveland, Ohio
Dean's List Spring, 1998
Pursuing Associate Degree—1999

THE KING'S ACADEMY, Elyria, Ohio—Graduate 1997
Received Varsity Letter in fast-pitch softball.
Toured three states with the drama group, "The Ambassadors."
Actively participated in local political campaigns, SADD (Students Against Drunk Driving) and Student Council.

**COMPUTER AND LANGUAGE PROFICIENCIES**

Proficient with WordPerfect and Microsoft Office products. Able to read, write, and speak Spanish.

# Additional Résumés for College Students, Recent Grads, and Others

There is no one standard approach for those who are starting out in their careers. For some people, it will be best to have a long summary and highlight accomplishments from various parts of your background, as Julie did. Others, who have strong recent experience, should have a very small summary so that the most recent job will stand out.

No *objective* is needed if the job you want next is a logical extension of your experience. You will need to have an objective, however, if you want to change directions or start on a career after simply having had job after job in the past, or if your direction may not be so obvious to the reader.

The case studies in this section show examples of all of the above.

## CASE STUDY *Richard and Angie*

### Summary or No Summary?

The average résumé is looked at for only 10 seconds. Julie needed a large summary on her résumé because she wanted to bring together all of her autoCAD experience. If you want the reader to see more than your most recent job or education in those first 10 seconds, you will need to include more in your summary, as Julie did.

After Julie does well in her architectural internship, she can then have a very small summary: Her most recent job will be the most important thing for the reader to see and will encompass all the relevant experience she had before then.

If you have *no* summary, you are positioned by your most recent job. You can have a very *small* summary on your résumé if, like Richard and Angie, your most recent job is the best one you've ever had, it's the one you want the reader to focus on, and it positions you for the kind of job you want to have next.

If you have no summary, the reader's eye will go immediately to your most recent job. Because Richard and Angie's most recent jobs were so great, the hiring managers in their target markets are likely to want to see them because of it.

## CASE STUDY *Jacqueline*

### Using an *Objective* on Her Résumé

If you have essentially no direct experience in the field or industry in which you are interested, stating an objective on your résumé shows your interest in that area. Jacqueline has never worked for a hotel, but she is very interested in that industry. So stating "Objective: Front Office within the Hotel Industry" shows her commitment to that industry.

In addition, in her summary, Jacqueline lists accomplishments that she thinks may qualify her for a front office position in a hotel, including a training program that she completed having to do with hotel management.

## CASE STUDY *Marva*

## Move from a Job to a Career

Marva wants a career in customer service, although she has held only administrative positions in the past. When Marva did her Seven Stories Exercise, she realized that she had turned most of her administrative jobs into customer service jobs. So her résumé now emphasizes the customer service aspects of those jobs. How can Marva move into a customer service career when she has had no direct experience in customer service?

First, Marva's summary repositions her for customer service. Furthermore, she lists no job titles for any of the jobs on her résumé. If she listed her job titles, she would be stereotyped in the administrative jobs she has held in the past. Finally, she lists accomplishments that are related more to customer service than they are to administration and highlights those she wants the reader to notice.

It's time for Marva to get a career in customer service, and her résumé helps her to do that.

**Richard K. Sims**

2035 Seventh Avenue #61
Politboro, IL 55555

Phone: (312) 222-3094
E-mail: RichardSims555@msn.com

---

**PUBLICIST**

***Develops campaigns from concept through execution.***
***Quickly absorbs organization's PR needs.***
***A team player who works independently.***

**PUBLIC RELATIONS ASSISTANT** January 2003– Present

**The Bear Club International**

- Report directly to company president and company chief operating officer.
- Generate a minimum of **two media placements per week** including many new relationships:
  - "Hits" include ***PEOPLE*** magazine, **TIME** magazine, AP, Reuters, MSNBC, PBS, CNN-fn, *Smart Money,* the *Economist, Wall Street Journal, Chicago Tribune.*
  - Maintain over 350 journalist relationships.
- Manage and **train new public relations staff**.
  - Designed effective methods for press release distribution and follow-up procedures.
- **Write and edit press releases** and pitch letters.
  - Research and compile lists of targeted journalists for specific press releases.
- Successfully **place articles in nationwide trade journals.**
  - Researched targets, prepared press kits with promotional cover letter, completed follow-up. For example: ***Healthcare Executive, Journal of Accountancy,*** HR.COM.

**OXYGEN MEDIA** (Cable Network, Internet Portal)

**Internship in Public Relations** September 2002–January 2003

- Reported to Director of Corporate Communications; supported entire PR Staff.
- Prepared company press kits.
- Executed mass mailings.
- Prepared press clippings.

**EDUCATION**

MARYMOUNT COLLEGE 9/01–Present

BA, English expected May 2003.

- Three-time recipient of college's **COMPETITIVE SCHOLARSHIP IN ENGLISH**.
- Working to open an MC branch of the **Public Relations Student Society of America**.

**Angie Cayo**

1806 Voorhies Ave, Unit #1D
Elvira, Texas 55555

Phone: (847) 555-1409
E-mail: ac628@yahoo.com

## ACCOUNTING ASSISTANT

***For a small but complex organization.***
***Quickly absorb organization's needs. Accurate.***
***An independent worker who gets along well with others.***

**ACCOUNTING ASSISTANT** May 2001–present

**Melissa Healthcare, Inc.** (with 6 profit centers and one not-for-profit)

- Report directly to company president and chief operating officer.
- Maintain the books for all **six profit centers**.
  - Started up and maintain books for **non-profit** arm of the organization.
  - Manage general ledger, accounts receivable, accounts payable, bank reconciliation.
- **Audit monthly P&L** submitted by four branches.
  - Calculate complicated **monthly commission** payments.
- Project weekly **cash flow**, recommending items to be paid.
  - Maintain excellent vendor relationships.
- Close books at **year end** including preparation of all 1099s, reports for tax accountants, and year-end adjustments.

## OFFICE ASSISTANT

***For one of the departments within New York University.***
***Quickly adapt to frequent changes. Fast paced.***
***Work under little supervision in a demanding environment.***

**Texas State University, School of Continuing and Professional Studies**
**Information Services Assistant** February 2000–present

- **Receive and screen inquiries** via phone, electronic mail, and fax.
  - Log inquiries in database and maintain database files.
  - Follow up outstanding inquiries by telephone and/or electronic mail; forward referrals to research area to resolve for further assessment.
- Promote **customer service efforts** including delivering courteous and efficient service.
- Assist in the preparation of weekly and monthly **statistical & analytical** reports.
- Assist with other **clerical duties** such as screen calls, take messages, photocopy, collate and fax materials, mail distribution, maintaining files and archives.

## EDUCATION

**Texas State University** 9/99–Present
BA in Finance and Accounting expected May 2003.
AA in Liberal Arts
- Three-time recipient of Texas State University Academic Scholarship.

**JACQUELINE D. MERCATOR**

410 St. Barts Avenue, Phoenix, AZ 55555 Residence: (555) 555-6437; jacqmerc999@aol.com

---

**OBJECTIVE**

***Front office position within the hotel industry.***

**SUMMARY OF QUALIFICATIONS**

- 12 years successful experience in handling customer complaints. Handle heavy phone load.
- Sharp, personable. Convey a warm yet professional image.
- Phoenix Food and Hotel Management School:
  completed front office management program.

---

**Information Services Representative** 1998–Present
**THE REUTERS MUSEUM**

- Advise visitors, offering cultural information; describe museum offerings.
- Meet with 150+ visitors a day (many are foreign customers).

**Receptionist** 1997–1999
**Kleiner Corporation**

- Managed front desk.
  - Meet and greet, offer hospitality to over 25 visitors per day.
- Scheduled appointments for 8 recruiters.
- Organized and maintained filing system for office.
- Answered over 250 phone inquiries per day.
- Handled all mailing and outgoing correspondence.

**Telephone Operator** 1993 –1995
**Blarney's**

- Handled all internal and domestic calls from customers and buyers.
- Answered over 1,500 calls per day.
- Paged executives and security personnel as needed.

**File Clerk** 1990–1993
**Bank Netherland**

- Microfilmed 300 or more cables for research purposes.
- Filed cables and other related documents.
- Arranged yearly inventory of more than 2,600 files.
- Prepared files for warehouse storage.

**EDUCATION**

**Phoenix Food and Hotel Management** **1998**

Completed comprehensive front office management program: front office procedures, accounting, and practical application on the Hotel Management System

**MARVA SCULLY**
62 Park Street
Kingston, GA 55111
Residence: (555) 555-6186
E-mail mascot333@hotmail.com

---

**Customer Service / Inside Sales Experience**

**Over 12 years' experience with major employers including Georgia Telephone and U.S. Steel.**
**Computer literate, dependable, punctual, good with figures.**

---

WORK EXPERIENCE

A variety of temporary positions within governmental, service and retail industries. 2000–Present

BATTEN BROTHERS, INC. 1995–2000

- Provided **sales staff support**. **Increased market share** of petroleum product line **by 25%.**
- Built long term relationships with buyers resulting in over **50% increase** in company's return business.
- Received **commendations** for assisting customers to make better buying decisions on products.

U.S. STEEL CORP., New York, NY 1978–1994

- Served as liaison between customers and management.
  - Noted for the highest rate of customer request for repeat business in 200-person organization.
- **Managed division office**.
  - Initiated new program allowing sales personnel to conduct more field calls.
  - Resulted in **20% increase in sales**.
- **Saved over $225,000** annually by developing new product tracking system.

**GEORGIA TELEPHONE** 1976–1978

**EDUCATION**

CDY, Atlanta Certificate, **Computer Training Course** 2001
Allright University, Atlanta **B.B.A.**, Marketing/Management 1993

**APPLICATIONS SOFTWARE KNOWLEDGE**

Excel, PowerPoint, Pagemaker, WordPerfect, Lotus, dBase 111+

# Résumé Checklist: How Good Is Your Résumé?

1. **Positioning:**

- If I spend just **10 seconds** glancing at my résumé, what are the ideas/words that pop out? (specific job titles, my degrees, specific company names)
- This is how I am *positioned* by my résumé. Is this how I want to be positioned for this target area? Or is this positioning a handicap for the area I am targeting?

2. **Level:**

- What *level* do I appear to be at? Is it easy for the reader to guess in 10 seconds what my level is? (For example, if I say I "install computer systems," I could be making anywhere from $15,000 a year to $200,000 a year.)

3. **Summary Statement:**

- If I have no summary statement, I am being positioned by the most recent job on my résumé. Is that how I want to be positioned?
- If I have a summary, does the very first line position me for the kind of job I want next?
  - Is this followed by a statement that elaborates on the first statement?
  - Is this followed by statements that prove how good I am or differentiate me from my likely competitors?
  - Have I included a statement or two that give the reader an indication of my personality or my approach to my job?

4. **Accomplishments:**

- Within each job, did I merely list historically what I had done, or did I state my accomplishments with an eye to what would interest the reader in my target area?
- Are the accomplishments easy to read?
  - Bulleted rather than long paragraphs.
  - No extraneous words.
  - Action-oriented.
  - Measurable and specific.
  - Relevant. Would be of interest to the readers in my target area. Either the accomplishment is something they would want me to do for them, or it shows the breadth of my experience.

5. **Overall Appearance:**

- Is there plenty of white space? Or is the information squeezed so I can get it on one or two pages?
- Is it laid out nicely so it can serve as my marketing brochure?

6. **Miscellaneous:**

- Length: Is the résumé as short as it can be and still be readable?
- Writing style: Can the reader understand the point I am trying to make in each statement?
- Clarity: Am I just hoping the reader will draw the right conclusion from what I've said? Or do I take the trouble to state things so clearly that there is no doubt that the reader will come away with the right message?
- Completeness: Is all important information included? Have all dates been accounted for?
- Typos: Is my résumé error-free?

# Your Two-Minute Pitch: The Keystone of Your Search

*Fortune favors the brave.*

Terence, *Phormio*

**If your pitch—the way you position yourself—is wrong, everything else about your search is wrong.**

Your Two-Minute Pitch is the backbone of your search. You'll use it in job and networking interviews and in your cover letters. You'll be ready when someone calls and says, "So tell me about yourself."

Your résumé summary statement could serve as the starting point for your pitch. Keep in mind

- to whom you are pitching
- what they are interested in
- who your likely competitors are
- and what you bring to the party that your competitors do not

In your pitch, you are *not* trying to tell your life story. Instead,

- Let this person know that you are competent and interested in the area in which he or she is interested.
- Say things that are relevant.
- Come across at the right level.

Think about your target audience and what you want to say to them. Examine your background to find things that fit.

## CASE STUDY *Julie*

### Starting with Her Résumé

The summary in your résumé is your written pitch. Your *Two-Minute Pitch* is your verbal pitch. If you have a good Five O'Clock Club résumé, you should be able to develop your verbal pitch directly from it. Let's use Julie's résumé as a example. She is targeting architectural firms.

If a hiring manager (or anyone else) says to Julie, "So, Julie, tell me about yourself," Julie could answer like this (taken mostly from her résumé ):

> I've been an assistant office manager and an assistant AutoCAD operator at a civil engineering firm. I worked there for two summers, but now I want to move on to an architectural firm.
>
> While at the engineering firm, I developed strong administrative skills. I answered the phones, developed excellent client relationships, organized forms, files, catalogues ,and client proposals. In the absence of the office mangier, I was the one who ran the office.
>
> In addition, I have developed some experience in AutoCAD. I took an intensive 40-hour AutoCAD course, and routinely helped the engineers at the engineering firm by handling small AutoCAD projects. *[She would then give the examples that appear in her résumé].*
>
> I'm devoted to architecture, and want to be in this field for life. I'm very interested in your company because I want a small firm where I can learn a lot and contribute a lot.

Julie can memorize her pitch ahead of time, or she can have her résumé in front of her during the interview and use the résumé as a prop. As she moves along in her pitch, she can point out to the manager items in her résumé.

## What's Wrong with This Pitch?

Take a look at the beginning of another client's pitch, and see if you can tell what's wrong.

> I have five years' experience in education and training: in helping develop training programs, in administering training centers [etc.].

What's wrong with this pitch? We can't know until we know to whom he is talking. It turns out that the pitch was wrong because the interviewer was not interested in training but in personal computers. How much did my client know about PCs? A lot. "Why, I can make PCs dance," he said. "The only problem is that the hiring manager would probably want someone who could network them together, and I've never done that."

"*Can* you do that?" I asked.

"Of course I can do it," he replied.

"Then go *do* it," I said, "so you can tell her you have already done it. Network together the computers you have at home. And join a group that specializes in that. Ask one of the people if you can go along and help him or her network computers together."

Here's the pitch one week later:

> I have five years' experience in computers, specializing in PCs. I have built PCs from scratch, and I've done software and applications programming on PCs. I also understand how important networking is. I've even networked together the PCs I have at home, and I belong to a group of PC experts, so I always know whom to talk to when tricky things come up. I can do anything that needs to be done with PCs. I can make PCs dance!
>
> I'm excited about talking to you because I know your shop relies on PCs.

Do you see how a pitch has to be tailored to each specific situation?

## Know Something about Them

When you go for an interview, and they immediately say: "Tell me about yourself," how will you know how to position yourself? You don't want to bound into a standard Two-Minute Pitch unless you feel that you know something about them.

If you don't know anything at all about them or the job, you may say: "I'd be happy to tell you about myself, but could you first tell me a little about the kind of job we're talking about?"

## They Won't *Get It* So Just Tell Them

Most job hunters think: I'll just tell them my background, and they'll see how it fits in with their needs. But they probably won't see.

**Don't expect the hiring team to figure out something about you. If you have a conclusion you'd like them to reach about you, *tell* them what it is.**

If you want them to see how all of your jobs have been involved in international, say, "All of my jobs have been involved in international." Isn't that easy?

If you want them to know that you have done things in finance that people at your age rarely do, then tell them that.

Do you want them to know that FORTRAN is your favorite language? Then don't just say, "I have three years of FORTRAN experience." That's not your point. Do you want them to know that you can make computers dance? Tell them. Don't make them figure it out for themselves.

Make your message so clear that if someone says to them, "Tell me about John," they will know what to tell the other person about you.

## Communicating Your Pitch

Many job hunters try to cram everything they can into their Two-Minute Pitch, but then people can't hear it. Think about those who are considered great communicators.

Today, our standards are based on the medium of TV. The best communicators speak on a personal level—the way people talk on TV. Whether you are addressing a big audience or are on a job interview, cultivate a TV style—a friendly, one-on-one conversational style—not a "listing of what I've done" style.

The interviewer is assessing what it would be like to work with you. Make your pitch understandable. Before people go on TV, they decide the three major points they want to make—what they want the audience to remember.

What do you want your *audience* to remember about you? Polish both your Two-Minute Pitch and the two or three accomplishments that would interest this person. Prepare your pitch about each accomplishment the same way you prepared your Two-Minute Pitch. For example, don't say, "I started out in this job in program support, where I traveled to *x* and *y* and worked on special projects, etc."—if what you *really* want them to know is: "That was a great assignment. I helped arrange the details for 9 speeches given by my department head. I organized the handouts, arranged for delivery, and sold our company's books at the meetings. I sold more books than any assistant they ever had, and I enjoyed every minute of it. This has convinced me that sales is the field for me."

Use a conversational tone. Speak the way you would normally speak.

## Two Minutes Is a Long Time; Show Enthusiasm

In this TV society, people are used to 15-second sound bites on the news. As the communicator, you have to engage the listener. If you are a boring person, the very least you can do is sit forward in your chair. Reinforce your main points. Don't say too many things. Sound enthusiastic.

I once did a magazine article on who gets jobs and who gets to keep them. In my research, I talked to deans of business and engineering schools.

I learned that the person most likely to get the job is the one who sounds enthusiastic. And the one who gets to keep the job is the enthusiastic one—even over people who are more qualified. Employers keep people who are willing to pitch in and do anything to help the company.

Display enthusiasm. If you really want this job, act like it. It does not hurt your salary negotiation prospects.

# Summary of What I Have/Want to Offer—Target 1

## *To Help Me Develop My Pitch to That Target*

(Use a duplicate of this sheet for your other targets.)

You must know:

- to whom you are pitching; you have to know something about them
- what they ideally would want in a candidate
- what they are interested in
- who your likely competitors are
- what you bring to the party that they do not

***For Target 1:***

Geographic area: ______________________________

Industry or company size: ______________________________

Position/Function: ______________________________

1. What is the most important thing I want this target to know about me? (This is where you position yourself. If they know nothing else about you, this is what you want them to know.)

   ______________________________

2. What is the second most important thing I want this target to know about me? (This could support and/or broaden your introductory statement.)

   ______________________________

   ______________________________

3. Key selling points: statements/accomplishments that support/**prove** the first two statements:
   1. ______________________________
   2. ______________________________
   3. ______________________________
   4. ______________________________
   5. ______________________________

Statement of why they should be interested in me/what separates me from my competition:

______________________________

______________________________

______________________________

______________________________

Other key selling points that may apply even indirectly to this industry or position:

______________________________

Any objection I'm afraid the interviewer may bring up, and how I will handle it:

______________________________

PART FIVE

# Knowing the Right People

## HOW TO GET INTERVIEWS IN YOUR TARGET AREAS

# Conducting a Campaign to Get Interviews in Your Target Markets

*The codfish lays ten thousand eggs,*
*The homely hen lays one.*
*The codfish never cackles*
*To tell you what she's done.*
*And so we scorn the codfish,*
*While the humble hen we prize,*
*Which only goes to show you*
*That it pays to advertise.*

Anonymous

**Do not expect to get a job through:**

- **On-Campus Recruiters**
- **Internships**
- **College Career Placement Offices**
- **Contacting Companies Directly**
- **Search Firms / Employment Agencies**
- **Ads (even on the Internet)**

**These are techniques for getting *meetings*, not jobs.**

**After you get the meeting, you can think about what to do next to *perhaps* turn it into a job. (See the chapters on Follow-Up)**

## An Overview of the Strategy for Your First Campaign

*If the only tool you have is a hammer, you tend to see every problem as a nail.*

Abraham Maslow

By now, you have developed preliminary job targets. You've spoken to a few people to find out whether those targets make sense: Are these fields right for you? And what are these fields really like?

Once you've talked to a few people to find out whether these targets are worth your while, you are ready to start your campaign to get meetings in these target areas. Your goal is to contact every organization in your target areas.

1. **Research to develop a list of all the organizations,** if you have not already done so. Find out—through networking, or research—the names of the people you should contact in the appropriate departments in each of those organizations.
2. **Develop your cover letter.** Paragraph 1 is the opening; Paragraph 2 is a summary about yourself appropriate for this target; Paragraph 3 contains your bulleted accomplishments ("You may be interested in some of the things I've done"); Paragraph 4 is the close. (Many sample letters appear later in this book.)
3. **Develop your plan for getting a large number of meetings in this target.** There are four

basic techniques for meeting people in each of the areas you have targeted for a full campaign. In the following chapters, you will learn more about them. They are:

- networking
- direct contact (direct mail, targeted mail, walk-in, cold call)
- search firms (not very helpful for *career starters*)
- ads (print, online, and through your college placement office).

Do not think of these as techniques for getting *jobs* but as techniques for getting *meetings*. After the meeting, think about what to do next to keep the relationship going or perhaps to turn the interview into a job offer.

Organize the names of the people you want to contact, and develop strategies for contacting them.

Only 5 to 10 percent of all job leads are through ads. Furthermore, search firms and employment agencies are unlikely to be very helpful for you. You do not have much control over these leads: You have to *wait* for an ad to appear and *wait* for a search firm to send you on an interview.

On the other hand, both networking and direct contact are *proactive* techniques you can use to get meetings in your target market. In networking, you contact someone simply by using someone else's name. In direct contact, you contact someone directly—usually after you have done some research and know something about him or her. Networking and direct contact complement each other and gain added effectiveness when used together. You may start your campaign either with direct contact (if you know your target area very well) or with networking (to research an area you don't know well or to find a way to contact people) and introduce the other technique as your campaign progresses.

Consider every technique for getting meetings, but spend most of your energy and brainpower on networking and direct contact.

*Opportunities are multiplied as they are seized.*

Sun Tzu, *The Art of War*

## Selecting the Techniques

*Do not be too timid and squeamish about your actions. All life is an experiment.*

Ralph Waldo Emerson

Select the techniques most appropriate for the industry or profession you are targeting, as well as for your own personality. Each technique can work, but the strength of your campaign lies in your ability to use what is best for your particular situation. Contact as many potential employers as possible and then *campaign* to keep your name in front of them.

Use all of the techniques to

- Learn more about your target area.
- Test what you are offering.
- Let people know you are looking.
- Contact people in a position to hire you.

## Using Search Firms

If you are a few years out of school, have good experience in a field or industry, and are looking for a position that naturally follows your most recent one, you can immediately contact search firms. However, only about 5 to 10 percent of all professional and managerial positions are filled by search firms, so it would seem logical to spend only 5 percent of your effort on them. However, certain professions use search firms more than others do.

Contact reputable search firms that tend to handle positions in your target area. If you don't already have relationships with search firms, find the good ones through networking by asking managers which search firms they use or recommend. Remember, search firms are rarely able to help career changers or those with little or no experience.

## Answering Ads

Five to 10 percent of all jobs are filled through ads—print ads, ads on the Internet, and ads in your college placement office. The odds are against you, so don't spend too much thought or energy on them. And don't sit home hoping for a response. Just answer the ad—so long as it sounds close to what you have to offer—and get on with your search. Maybe you'll hear from them—maybe you won't. (See the chapter *How to Answer Ads.*)

## Networking

*You must call each thing by its proper name, or that which must get done will not.*

A. Harvey Block, President, Bokenon Systems

Studies show that about 60 to 70 percent of all positions are filled through networking. This is partly because it is an effective technique and partly because most job hunters mistakenly refer to talking to people as *networking,* no matter *how* they wound up talking to them. For example, Pete just found a job. I asked how he got the initial meeting. He said, "Through networking." When I asked him to tell me more, he said, "I'm an accountant, originally from Australia. There is an association here of accountants from Australia. I sent for a list of all the members and wrote to all of them. That's how I got the job.

**Pete got the job lead through a direct-mail compaign, not through networking**. That's why the survey numbers are off, and that's why you should consider using every technique for getting meetings in your target market. You never know where your leads will come from.

*The beginning of wisdom is to call things by their right names.*

Chinese proverb

Networking simply means getting to see someone by *using another person's name.* You are using a contact to get in. You want to see the person *whether or not he or she has a job for you.* This technique is essential if you want to change careers, because you can get in to see people even if you are not qualified in the traditional sense. To stay in the same field, you can network to get information on which organizations are hiring, which are the best ones to work for, and so on.

Networking can lead you in directions you had not thought of and can open up new targets to pursue. You can network to explore even if you are not sure you want to change jobs right now. What's more, it's a technique you can use *after* you land that new job, whenever you get stuck and need advice.

Networking is more popular today than ever before, and it is effective when used properly. But, depending on your target, it is not always the most *efficient* way to get meetings. Furthermore, it is getting a bad name because although people are constantly networking, they are doing it incorrectly. Learn how to network correctly (see the chapters on networking), but combine targeted mailings (a direct-contact technique) with your networking when you are aiming at small organizations or ones that have very few jobs appropriate for you. Networking your way into all of them could take forever. Also, contact other people directly when you would have great trouble getting a networking contact. If the direct contact doesn't work, you can always network in later.

When you combine direct mailing with networking, you can cover the market with a direct-mail campaign and then network certain sections of that market. Or you can network in to see someone and then perhaps get a list of names you can use for further networking or a direct-mail campaign.

If you do not cover your market, you risk losing out. You may find later that they "just filled a job a few months ago. Too bad we didn't know you were looking." Be thorough. Let *everyone* in your target market know that you are looking.

---

*If I had eight hours to chop down a tree, I'd spend six sharpening my ax.*

Abraham Lincoln

## Direct-Contact Campaigns

Writing directly to executives is a consistently effective technique for generating meetings. At least 20 percent of all jobs are found this way, and more jobs would result from this technique if more job hunters knew about it. You can write to lots of organizations (direct mail) or a few (targeted mail). The techniques are quite different.

Direct contact can save time. You can quickly test your target to see if there are job possibilities for someone like you. If you are familiar with your target area, you can develop your list, compose your letter, send it out, and start on your next target, all within a matter of weeks. Most job hunters contact larger corporations, ignoring smaller firms. Yet new jobs are being created in smaller organizations, so don't overlook them.

Direct contact is also the only technique that allows you to quickly contact *every* employer in the area that interests you. You are essentially blanketing the market. Networking, on the other hand, is spotty by nature: You get to see only those organizations where your network knows someone. Direct contact is effective for an out-of-town job search. And this technique works whether you are employed or unemployed. It works for all job levels.

This technique is an effective one for career changers. You can state all the things that are positive about what you are offering, and leave out anything that does not help your case. Those things can be handled at the meeting.

Direct contact can help you get in to see someone you know you cannot network in to see. Shelli, for example, wanted to see someone very senior in an industry in which she had no experience. But she knew the field would be a good fit for her; she researched the industry and figured out how her background could fit in. She targeted six organizations and was able to network into two of them. She knew she would not be able to network into the other four organizations within a reasonable time frame: It would take her months to find someone who could only *possibly* help her get in to see the people she'd need to see.

Instead of networking, she researched each of the four organizations, wrote to the senior people she was targeting at each one, and followed up with a phone call. Because of her presentation, three of the executives agreed to see her. This saved her many months in her search. Sometimes a targeted mailing can be *more* effective than networking in getting in to see important people. It takes more brainpower than networking, but you already have that.

Direct contact primarily involves targeted and direct mailing, but a junior person can also go from organization to organization to talk to personnel departments or store managers. So long as job hunters follow up, this technique can work. A client of mine used this technique effectively, by walking into a small, privately owned, prestigious store, speaking with the store manager to find out the name of the president, and then calling the president. It led to a marketing position with that company. This was "direct contact" because he did not use someone's name to get in to see the store manager or the president. Even when I was very young, I used direct contact to get in to see virtually anyone I wanted.

Sometimes I had trouble getting in, but people eventually saw me because I usually had a good reason, did my homework, didn't waste their time, was sincere about why I wanted to see them, and was gently persistent. It suits my personality because I am shy about using someone else's name for the core of my effort, I am comfortable about putting my effort into research and writing, and I don't have the time it takes to see a lot of people who may not be right on target for me. As I go along, I network when appropriate.

Direct contact also includes cold calls, which can work for some personalities in some industries.

We will now focus on targeted mail and direct mail:

A **targeted mailing** is similar to networking. You target a relatively small number of people (say, fewer than 20 or 30) and try to see all of them, *whether or not they have a job for you.*

Instead of having a human contact, you *establish* your own contact through the research you do. The meeting is handled exactly the same as a networking meeting.

**Direct mail** is used when you have a large number of organizations to contact (such as 200 or more). You would mail a brilliant package to all of them and expect seven or eight meetings from the mailing.

## Using All of the Techniques

A good campaign usually relies on more than one technique to get meetings. Think of how you can divide up your target list. For example, if you have a list of 200 organizations in your target area, you may decide you can network into 20 of them, do a targeted mailing (with follow-up phone calls) to another 20 or 30, and do a direct-mail campaign to the rest. That way you have both blanketed your market and used the most appropriate technique to reach each organization in your target area. In addition, you could also contact search firms and answer ads.

## Networking versus Direct Mail

Let's use the banking industry as an example.

You could easily network your way into a large bank. You could find someone who knew someone at a number of them. Each contact you'd make at a large bank could refer you to other people within that same bank—and that increases your chances of getting a job there. Because one person knows others within that organization, networking is efficient. You can meet many potential hiring managers within one organization.

On the other hand, it may be difficult to network into smaller banks. Fewer of your friends are likely to know someone there, because each small bank has far fewer employees. Each networking meeting would represent fewer jobs and fewer referrals within each bank. Referrals to other small banks would also generally represent fewer jobs than the larger banks have. It could take forever to network to the same number of potential jobs at hundreds of small banks that could easily be covered by networking at large banks. Networking can be inefficient with smaller organizations, and you may find that you can't put a dent in the market.

You could contact smaller banks directly. They do not expect you to know someone who works there, so they are more open to intelligent mailings. They tend to get fewer contacts from job hunters. You could categorize the smaller banks in a way that makes sense to you—those strong in international banking, for example, or those strong in lending. Or you could categorize banks by nationality—grouping the Japanese banks, European banks, South American banks, and so on. Then you could *target each segment* with a cover letter customized for that market.

Decide which techniques are best for you. Think about how people tend to get hired within your target industry and profession. Also consider your own circumstances, such as whether you are currently employed, how much freedom you have to go to networking meetings, how much use you can make of the phone, and so on. You can always network your way into a few specific organizations, but a great number is sometimes not possible.

Remember, networking requires a great deal of time and travel. Direct mail is often appealing to those who are working and must ration their meeting and travel time.

*Things which matter most must never be at the mercy of things which matter least.*

Goethe

## In Summary

Have a list of all the people you should meet in *each* of your target areas or, at the very least, have a list of all the organizations in your target areas. Intend to contact all of them. Get meetings with people in your target area through networking, direct contact, search firms, and ads (print as well as online). Do not think of these as techniques for getting *jobs,* but as techniques for getting *meetings.* Plan how you can contact or meet the *right* people in *every* organization in each of your target areas—as quickly as possible.

After the meeting, either keep in touch with networking types of contacts (regardless of how you met them) or think about what you can do next to *perhaps* turn the interview into a job offer.

## Getting Polished for a Full Campaign

Before the meeting, be prepared: Know exactly what you want and what you have to offer. Prepare your verbal "pitch" to organizations. Have your pitch ready even *before* you contact anyone—just so you are prepared. Read the chapters on interviewing, and *practice.* Be a polished interviewer. Remember the cliché: "You don't get a second chance to make a good first impression."

After you have practiced interviewing, contact the people on your *hit list.* Start with those who are less important to you, so you can practice and learn more about your target area. You will want to know, for example, your chances in that market and how you should position yourself.

After you have met with someone, follow up. This method works. Read the chapters on following up. Once you have contacted a target area, contact it again a few months later. Keep following up on the people you meet.

Read magazines and newspapers. Attend organizational meetings. Keep abreast of what is happening in the field. Keep on networking.

## A Promotional Campaign to Get Meetings

Sometimes I say to a client who is shy "So far, you and I are the only ones who know you are looking for a job." Get your name out there. Get on the inside track. You must conduct a promotional campaign to contact as many potential employers as possible. *Campaign* to make sure they remember you.

Make a lot of contacts with people in a position to hire or recommend you. If there are sparks between you, and if you help them remember you, you will be the one they call when a job comes up. Or they can give you the names of others to contact. They may even create a job for you, if it makes sense.

The goal of your promotional campaign is to let the *right* people know what you are looking for. Some discussions will become job interviews, which will lead to offers. Get a lot of meetings so you will have a number of offers to consider. You want options.

Focus on getting *meetings* in your target area. People who focus on *getting a job* can get uptight when they have a meeting. They do not think of themselves as *looking around* or *finding out what is out there.* They act as if they are in a display case, hoping someone will buy them. They may accept the first offer that comes along—even when they know it is inappropriate—because they think they will never get another one.

If you aim to make lots of contacts and get lots of meetings, you are more likely to keep your perspective. If you are an inexperienced job hunter, talk to some people who are not in a position to hire you. Practice your lines and your techniques. Get experience in talking about yourself, and learn more about your target market. Then you will be more relaxed in important meetings and will be able to let your personality come through.

## You Are the Manager of This Campaign

You are in control of this promotional campaign. After reading this book, you will know what to say, how to say it, and to whom. You will select the promotional techniques to use and when, and learn how to measure the effectiveness of your campaign.

You will also decide on your image. You can present any picture of yourself that you like. You present your image and credentials in your written communications—résumé, cover letters, and follow-up notes. You have *complete* control over what you put in them and how you present yourself.

How you act and dress also importantly affects your image. Look like you're worth the money you would like. Watch your posture—sit up straight. *Smile!* Decide to feel good and to feel confident. Smile some more. Smile again. Smiling makes you look confident and competent and gives you extra energy. It is difficult to smile and continue being down. Even when you are at home working on your search, smile every once in a while to give yourself energy and the right attitude to help you move ahead. This is true no matter what your level. Even executives are better off doing this as they go through their searches. The ones who cannot tend to do less well than those who can.

Whether direct contact or networking, search firms or ads, choose techniques most likely to result in a good response from your target—techniques appropriate to your situation. When you become expert, change a technique to suit yourself.

Modify your approach, or even abandon an effort that is ineffective. You want a good response from your promotional efforts. A *response* is a meeting. A polite rejection letter does not count as a response. Some organizations have a policy of sending letters, and some have a policy against them. Rejection letters have nothing to do with you. They do not count. Only meetings count.

This is a campaign to generate meetings. Your competition is likely to have polished presentations. Decide on the message you want to get across in the meeting, and practice it. There are two kinds of meetings: information-gathering (*networking*) meetings and actual job interviews. Do not try to turn every meeting into a job interview. You will turn people off—and lessen the chances of getting a job. *In the beginning, you are aiming for contact, or networking, meetings.* (See the chapters on networking meetings, as well as information on handling the job interview.)

When things do not work, there is a reason. Be aware and correct the situation. There is no point in continuing an unsuccessful campaign. Remember, when things go wrong—as they will—it is not personal. This is strictly business. It is a project. With experience, you will become better at managing your promotional campaigns to get meetings.

In the chapter, *Case Study: Julie—Getting and Doing Well in Interviews,* you will read about Julie's campaign using direct contact. She ended up with lots of job offers and a 50 percent pay increase. Whether you are in college, a recent grad, or finally deciding to have a career instead of a job, Julie's efforts should inspire you.

---

*Begin at the beginning . . . and go on till you come to the end: then stop.*

Lewis Carroll

## What You Can Do Next

- Talk to people in the fields in which you are interested. Ask them:
  - What is your background? Where did you go to school? What was your major?
  - What kind of work do you do?
  - How do you spend your day?
  - What do you like most about your job?
  - What do you like least?
  - What kind of person do you think is right for this kind of work?
  - How can I learn more about this field? (trade journals, associations)
  - How can I meet others in this field?
  - What is the best way to get started?

- Look up the fields that interest you in the newspaper or on the Internet.
- Read about people in the newspaper.
- When you have the chance to work, try lots of different things. Observe what you like and why you like it.
- If you have the opportunity, observe people while they are working so you can learn what their jobs are about.

# Researching Your Job Targets

*Natural talent, intelligence, a wonderful education—none of these guarantees success. Something else is needed: the sensitivity to understand what other people want and the willingness to give it to them. Worldly success depends on pleasing others. No one is going to win fame, recognition, or advancement just because he or she thinks it's deserved. Someone else has to think so too.*

John Luther

## Why Is Research Important?

Research can help you decide which fields and industries you want to work in. In our book *Shortcut Your Job Search,* we'll tell you how to research those targets, eliminate some, add others, and develop a detailed list of organizations to contact, and contact them. But for right now, you simply want a list of *tentative* targets. You need to explore what kinds of positions *may* be appropriate for you. Which industries? Which geographic areas?

During the course of your research, look for the following about each industry in your tentative target list:

1. trends and future prospects in a particular industry
2. areas of growth and decline in that industry
3. the kinds of challenges the industry faces that could use your skills
4. the culture of the industry
5. the major-league organizations in the industry, of course, but also the second- and third-tier firms as well

In the bibliography at the back of our *Shortcut Your Job Search* book, you will find many sources for exploring these issues and concerns. Having a *lot* of information will help you determine whether you are in sync with a particular industry and whether there is a place for you. It generally requires only a small amount of information to decide that an industry should go on your tentative target list. You will continue to research throughout your search because, as you will see, the entire job-search process is a *research* process. You will continue to refine your targets and your list of organizations as you go forward.

## Library Research

Find a university or big city library that's conveniently located and has an extensive business collection. The great thing about libraries is that you will not be on your own: Librarians are usually experts at helping job hunters, so plan to spend some time with the business reference librarian. Be specific. Tell the librarian what you want to accomplish. I have always said, "The librarian is your friend." I personally love libraries (although I now do most of my research on the Internet). I was a librarian in both high school and college. Get comfortable with the environment. Spend time using the reference books. Photocopy articles you can read at home.

If electronic information at the library is a new frontier for you, do not be intimidated. Ask for assistance. Computer-aided research will make your work immeasurably faster, easier, and more accurate. Let it work for you. If you are of a certain age or inclination and *don't like computers,* the best advice I can give you is *get over it*. In about any field I can think of, information sharing is now done by computer. You *will* need to adapt.

---

*There are going to be no survivors.*
*Only big winners and the dead.*
*No one is going to just squeak by.*

Ronald Compton,
CEO, Aetna Insurance Company

## Basic Research

For most job hunts, you should **set aside at least two full days strictly for library or Internet research**. If you are not sure of the industry you want to pursue, you can spend two days just researching industries (or professions). One of my favorite tools is the *Encyclopedia of Business Information Sources*. It lists topics, such as *oil, clubs, finance,* and *real estate*. Under each topic, it lists the most important sources of information on that topic: periodicals, books, and associations. Using this resource, you can quickly research any field in depth. You also may want to read the U.S. Department of Labor's reports on various industries or professions (www.bls.gov/emp and www.bls.gov).

**Two important Internet resources on careers are www.Vault.com and www.Wetfeet.com.**

**Vault.com** provides information on more than 1,200 organizations. If you click on *fashion*, for example, it will bring up links to articles about the fashion industry and its leading players. You can click on health care, investment banking, and many other major industries. Vault.com doesn't offer information on minor industries, but its goal is to provide you with the inside scoop on key industries from a job hunter's point of view. There are plenty of sites out there where you can find out about an industry from the financial investor's point of view, but vault.com offers the employee perspective.

**Vault.com** covers the following industries: accounting, advertising and PR, consulting, entertainment, fashion, government, health/biotech/pharmaceutical, investment banking, investment management, law, media and marketing, nonprofit, real estate, technology, television, and venture capital.

**Wetfeet.com** is a good site to find information about various types of careers, the latest industry news, and the key players in each area. Wet Feet covers the following industries and professions: accounting, advertising, biotech and pharmaceuticals, brand management and marketing, consulting, entertainment, financial services, health care, human resources, law, manufacturing, information technology, nonprofit and government, oil and gas, and real estate.

Once you have selected tentative industries, you will network to find out issues, trends, and buzzwords, and all this will help you refine your pitch. In addition, networking at this point may uncover other tentative targets to add to your list of targets or research right away.

While networking, you may find someone who will give you a list of people in a targeted field—perhaps an association membership list. Or someone may invite you to an association meeting and you can find lists and newsletters there. You may need to spend time in the library to gather the list of organizations. You can use an industry directory or local business publications that provide listings of organizations.

If you think you can work in many industries, get a sense of those that are growing and also fit your needs.

---

*Few executives yet know how to ask:*
*What information do I need to do my job?*
*When do I need it?*
*And from whom should I be getting it?*

Peter F. Drucker, "Be Data Literate—
Know What to Know,"
*The Wall Street Journal*

## Where Else Can You Find Information?

- **Associations.** Almost every profession imaginable has an association—sometimes several—and these are important sources of information. If you don't know anything at all about an industry or field, these groups are often the place to start. They tend to be very helpful and will assist you in mastering the jargon so you can use the language of the trade. *The Encyclopedia of Associations* is a massive list of professional groups. If you are interested in the rug business, there's a related association. You may also try the Internet. To zero in on key associations, go to Google or Yahoo and key in the field or industry in which you are interested plus the word *association.* For example, key in the words *accounting association,* and you'll get a listing of 25 or so. Or try www.business.com, which includes links to hundreds of associations.

  Just by their very nature, associations are welcoming—so call them. If they have lots of local chapters, chances are there's one near you, and it will be a great place to network. Contact the headquarters, and ask for information and the name of the person to contact in your area. Then call that person, and say you are interested in the association and would like to attend its next meeting. If there is no local chapter in your area, associations can still send you information.

- **The press.** Read newspapers *with your target in mind,* and you will notice all kinds of things you would not otherwise have seen. Contact the author of an article in a trade magazine. Tell him or her how much you enjoyed the article and what you are trying to do, and ask to get together just to chat. I've made many friends this way.

- **Chambers of commerce.** If you are doing an out-of-town job search, call the chamber of commerce in your targeted area. Ask for a list of industries and organizations in their area.

- **Universities** have libraries or research centers on fields of interest. A professor may be an expert in a field you are interested in. Contact him or her.

- **Networking** is a great research tool. At the beginning of your search, network with peers to find out about a field or industry. When you are in full job search, network with people two levels higher than you are.

- **The Yellow Pages** are a useful source of organizations in your local area. This is so obvious that most people overlook it!

---

*Avoid the crowd. Do your own thinking independently. Be the chess player, not the chess piece.*

Ralph Charell

## Get Sophisticated about Using Reference Materials

Research will result in your Personal Marketing Plan, which you will see later in this book and which will guide you through your search. But you'll need more research to construct it.

**Need more help researching your targets? Go to the *Members Only* section of our website: *www.FiveOClockClub.com.* You will see a 40-page bibliography of research sources—the best available. You will also find all of our worksheets, which you may download.**

CASE STUDY *Denise*

## Brainstorming Possible Industries

Developing your list of tentative targets takes creativity as well as research. The Brainstorming

Possible Jobs Worksheet in this book is an important start. Denise was a recent graduate who knew she liked writing and computers and had her undergraduate degree in agriculture. She had no geographical restrictions and would enjoy relocating. Which industries should she target? The question could be put this way: Who employs people to communicate with the agriculture and farming communities? The world is big, and even though the agriculture market is declining in the United States, it's a big market internationally. Who knows where this research could take her? Here are a few ideas for starters:

- The government—local, state, and federal—for example, USDA
- Chemical companies, such as Monsanto
- Financial services companies that specialize in mortgages and loans to farmers
- Publishers that aim at the agriculture or food market, such as Rodale (*Organic Gardening* magazine)
- Advertising agencies and pubic relations firms that aim at that market
- United Nations, AID, World Health Organization, and other governmental and quasi-governmental organizations that help farmers in Third World countries
- Associations such as Future Farmers of America; some may be too small to have paid employees, but other associations are worth exploring
- Agriculturally focused events, such as World Food Day
- Denise can go to **www.About.com**, key in *agriculture* or *farming*, and see what comes up.

Denise will next try to come up with a list of specific employers by industry and subindustry. So, for example, under *government*, she would list all government agencies that are appropriate. Under *chemical companies*, she would list as many as possible and *not* focus only on the big names that make the news every day. If the list contains only *recognized* names that everyone has heard about, Denise did not do a good research job. She must go after the small and midsized firms as well.

If I were Denise, I'd spend *at least* 15 hours researching the market—probably more. We're lucky to have the Internet so we can just sit at home and build the list. Later on, Denise will probably need library research, and she'll also have to actually talk to people to find out what's going on. But right now, she needs to find out how big her universe of potential employers is.

After Denise has a list of tentative targets, she'll conduct a preliminary target exploration aimed at each of the industries to see which industries and subindustries appeal to her the most. She also needs to know where she might stand the *best chance* of starting her agriculture communications career. For example, she may think that the USDA sounds appealing, but after conducting a preliminary exploration, she may find that her preconception was completely wrong. Or Denise may think at this point that a large chemical company would be the best place for her. But after meeting with a few people in that industry, she may change her mind and decide that it is the worst place for her.

## Salary Information

**Salary.com** contains job descriptions and salary ranges for hundreds of professions by geographic area. You can get a brief look at various fields. But remember, you have a unique background and bring specific experience to the situation. So what *others* are paid might not reflect what *you* are worth. Salary negotiations must be based on many factors, not just standard industry ranges.

## Other Sources

Jane Elliott's **50 Cutting-Edge Jobs** (Ferguson, Chicago, 2000) presents information on 50 newer careers, plus how to break into a field, a glimpse at the future of the field, and the specific earnings, responsibilities, and locations of the jobs. This is a potpourri of occupations that have been spurred by changes in technology, business, and the makeup of the population. Some listings are adventure travel specialist, biotechnology patent lawyer, computer and video game designer, forensic psychophysiologist, fuel cell technician, Internet quality assurance specialist, retirement counselor, and wireless service technician.

The **www.business.com/directory/index.asp**. page lists about 25 industries, each broken down into three or more subcategories. For example, financial services is broken down into banking, insurance, and investment. For banking, the subcategories include associations, banking institutions, banking law, certificates of deposits, employment, online banking, small business, and software. A section called popular searches has links to banking for small business, the banking industry, foreign banking, and sweep accounts, plus more.

You can probably pick up the **JobBank** (Adams Media, Avon, MA, www.adamsmedia.com) book for your area at your local bookstore. Just browse through the table of contents and see which industries interest you. Each book contains profiles of local companies in all industries, with up-to-date information on company descriptions, common professional positions, projected number of hires, educational backgrounds sought, internship information, and benefits. The guides are published for *Atlanta, Austin/San Antonio, Boston, the Carolinas, Chicago, Connecticut, Dallas/Fort Worth, Houston, Los Angeles, New York (includes New York City, Long Island, Rockland County, Westchester County, and Northern New Jersey), New Jersey, Ohio, Philadelphia, Phoenix, San Francisco Bay Area, Seattle, Virginia, and Washington, DC.* You'll still need to find the names of people to contact in each organization, but these books are great for developing your Personal Marketing Plan.

**Do you want to work for the government?** Even at the state level, you will find abundant information. For example, if you want a job in Tennessee, try www.tennessee.gov and click on *A to Z Directory*. It's exciting to see the list of departments. Starting with A, the listings include the appellate courts, the department of agriculture, the alcoholic beverage commission, the arts commission, and the attorney general. Review the various departments and see if there are a few that are of interest to you. At the top of the home page is a link to *employment.* You can search for the jobs and submit an application. But you can also target specific agencies that interest you, send your résumé directly to them, call them (that is, a phone call, not an E-mail), and tell them that you are specifically interested in their agency. If you have a specific agency or two in mind, add them to your target list.

---

*The choice of a career, a spouse, a place to live; we make them casually, at times, because we do not know how to articulate the choices. . . . I believe that people often persuade themselves that their decisions do not matter, because they feel powerless to make the* best *decision. Some of us feel that, no matter what we do, our decisions won't matter much. . . . But I believe that we know at heart that decisions do matter.*

Peter Schwartz, *The Art of the Long View*

## A Brief List of Industries To Consider

If you are completely stumped about the industries in which you might like to work, the following list is a starting point. Just say yes or no to each one, selecting the ones that may hold even a slight interest for you. You will investigate them further. Eliminating industries is just as important as selecting industries.

Of course, if there are no companies in your targeted geographic area for the industries you've chosen, you'll have to change the industries or your targeted geographic area.

Also be sure to look at the bibliography at the back of our *Shortcut Your Job Search* book or in the Members Only section of our website.

Academic and Education

Accounting

Advertising, including Graphic Art and Design
Aging Workers
Apparel, Textiles, Fashion, and Beauty
Art and Design
Associations
Automotive
Aviation and Aerospace
Banking, Finance, Investing, Securities, Trading, and Credit
Biotechnology
Communications Equipment and Services, including Telecommunications
Construction and Building
Consulting
Disabled
Diversity and Minorities
Electronics
Energy, Alternative Energy, and Utilities
Engineering
Entertainment, including Media (Broadcasting and Publishing)
Environmental
Food and Beverages
Franchising
Furniture
Government
Health Care and Medicine
Human Resources
Information Technology/High-Tech (Computers, Technology, and e-Commerce)
Insurance
Law
Law Enforcement and Criminal Justice
Library Science
Manufacturing
Nonprofit
Nursing
Public Relations
Publishing (Books, Magazines, Newspapers, Other)
Real Estate
Retailing
Sales and Marketing
Small Business
Transportation (Shipping, Marine, Freight, Express Delivery, Supply Chain)
Travel, Leisure, and Hospitality (including Hotels, Food Service, Travel Agents, Restaurants, and Airlines)
Veterans
Vocational (no Four-Year College Degree)
Volunteering
Wholesaling and Distributing/Importing and Exporting

---

*Hold fast to your dreams*
*For if dreams die*
*Life is a broken-winged bird*
*That cannot fly.*

*Hold fast to dreams*
*For when dreams go*
*Life is a barren field*
*Frozen with snow.*

Langston Hughes (1902–1967)

# Using the Internet as a Job-Search Tool

by Patricia L. Raufer

*Jobholders do not see the organization as a shifting pattern of needs. The only "opportunities" they recognize are the jobs that are currently posted on bulletin boards down at Personnel. And they grumble about how damned few of those there are, failing to note all the while the expanding range of unmet needs all over the organization.*

William Bridges, *JobShift: How to Prosper in a Workplace without Jobs*

**The entire job-search process is a research process. You need research to:**

- **develop your target list of companies to contact,**
- **research a company before the interview, and**
- **figure out what to say to them after your interview.**

When you consider that the Internet is a global network linking individuals, companies, governments, organizations, and academic institutions, it is not surprising that it is a valuable job-search tool. Although the Internet can be considered an electronic version of what already happens in a job search, this format offers the benefits of immediacy, connection, and searchability. The Internet, however, does not provide the benefits of personal contact and valuable perspectives that one-on-one information gathering interviews provide. Consider the Internet as simply another job-search tool to be added to your repertoire of Five O'Clock Club techniques. The following hints will help to make it an effective complement.

## Develop an Internet Plan to Coincide with Your Job-Search Marketing Campaign

With the vast amount of information available online, it's easy to spend hours and hours of good job-search time scrolling through databases, accessing career centers, looking at job postings, or chatting in newsgroups. Be very careful that you do not spend too much time online. The Internet can be interesting, but it can also be somewhat addictive. It may seem like productive time because a few hours online can generate a lot of information. However, the time may be better spent elsewhere. Are you as likely to spend just as many hours on your networking calls?

The best way to develop your Internet plan is to *define specific tasks that you will need to accomplish in your allotted Internet time.* Include the Internet as part of the research component of your target list and then as a further source when obtaining information about specific companies. Consider online job postings in the same way that you would consider ads in periodicals, a great source of open positions but not the only source. Visit the sites sponsored by search firms, but remember, it's your job to find your next position, not theirs.

The Internet has become another means of obtaining interviews to be added to the list: networking, direct mail, search firms, ads, and now the Internet. Also, keep in mind that there may be a lot of hype and media articles about the effectiveness of online campaigns as compared with other job-search methods. However, each ad on the Internet may receive tens of thousands of responses!

## Choose Websites That Are Appropriate for Your Search

Finding the right websites for online postings should be part of your initial campaign as you develop your target list. Just as you want to find the periodicals that the movers and shakers in your industry read, you'll also want to find industry-specific websites. These websites often contain job postings or have links to affiliate job sites. During the course of your information interviews, ask about both industry periodicals and websites. Check the websites of industry organizations and associations. These can be sources for leads through job postings and will mention activities in your field for networking opportunities.

Visit online business periodicals and their affiliated job sites for related business information about your target companies. Current and past editions of these publications contain articles that are often available online for a minimal amount. If the person you're meeting with has been quoted or mentioned in the business press, a good way to find out is through searching the newswire and publications website databases.

Portal sites or search engines such as Yahoo (**www. yahoo.com**) and AOL (**www. aol com**) contain career sections and job postings in their business sections. Career-specific websites such as Monster.com (**www. monster.com**) and CareerCentral.com (**www.careercentral.com**) offer job postings and links to their participating companies. There are even search engines such as Jobhunt (**www. jobhunt. com**) and Dice (**www.dice.com**) that combine a number of career websites, thereby minimizing the number of career sites the job hunter needs to access.

Career sites often contain job postings that are not listed on the firm's own corporate website. If it appears that there are no open positions at a company, it may be because their jobs are listed elsewhere, so check through career sites for company-specific listings of your target firm. Keep in mind that not all open positions are posted to websites and not all of the positions posted to websites are open.

Search firms often have sites that allow users to complete a profile that is then included in the candidate database. Complete the profile if you consider the firm reputable, but make sure there's a notation about privacy so that your résumé is sent out only with your permission.

## Confidentiality

Be sure to use the confidentiality option offered by many job-posting sites. You want to control where your résumé goes and who sees it. You need to be able to block selected companies from receiving your contact information. If your résumé is not posted on a site, you don't have to worry about your current employer's knowledge of your job search. You want to make sure that only those hiring companies that you approve will receive a copy of your résumé.

## Responding to Online Job Postings

Before responding to an online posting, verify whether the format that you're using to send your cover letter and résumé is correct. Some companies want your résumé included in the body of the E-mail with no attachments. Other firms want two attachments, the cover letter and your résumé. Some companies request responses in text format only, so sending a word-processed document is not appropriate. In that case, convert the word-processed document (.doc) into a text format (.txt) before sending. This may seem trivial, but you don't want your response eliminated before it is even reviewed.

When sending your résumé as an attachment, include your last name as part of the document name. For instance, don't call the attachment "My Résumé." If the attachment gets separated from the E-mail or if there is internal E-mail correspondence about a number of candidates, you don't want your documents to be easily confused or misplaced. On the subject line of the E-mail, try to include a notation that will address the topic but also encourage the reader to open the E-mail. For instance, instead of just "My Résumé," include a notation about your area of expertise (from the first line of your Two-Minute Pitch). Try to keep this line to a minimum as this field is not uniform across all Internet service providers.

Consider online job postings in the same way that you would want ads in newspapers and trade periodicals. Position your response by matching your background to their requirements. Your response may be scanned by a computer, so be sure that your résumé contains the appropriate buzzwords for your industry.

Before sending your E-mail response to the company, send it to yourself first. Check the "From" box. If you have a cutesy online name, change it to a more business-appropriate name, even if it means signing onto a new online service or expanding the existing membership with your current Internet service provider. Check your subject line to see if all of the characters that you intended are included in this space.

There's often a tendency to be less formal when sending E-mail than when sending written documents. Remember that this is still a job search, so spell-check your E-mail before it goes out, and use upper and lower case. If your browser does not have a spell-check feature, cut and paste a word-processed document that you've verified off-line into the body of the E-mail. Always add the E-mail address as the last item so that you don't accidentally send an incomplete letter while you're still working on it.

## Posting Your Résumé Online

Many of the Internet career websites provide an area in which job hunters post their résumés for access by potential employers. However, access is not limited to just potential employers. Who else has access to your personal information, credentials, and employment history? Do you want your current boss looking at your résumé online? Would you tack up your résumé on a public bulletin board or hand it out to strangers just because they asked for it? And how can you follow up effectively if you don't know who has viewed your credentials?

There are, however, job hunters who have found posting their credentials helpful in their search, and there are ways to minimize some of these concerns. For instance, you can post only a portion of your personal information, so that interested respondents can call you for further details, which allows you to screen them. Online posting is certainly an option, but it is not recommended. Be aware also that removing or replacing an online résumé is rarely as easy as posting it.

Remember, the Internet is another tool to supplement your Five O'Clock Club techniques. Be sure to check out our website at **www.FiveOClockClub.com.**

# The Truth about Internet Job Searching

## "I Searched the Web and Became a Company President in Under Two Hours!"

That's the kind of story the press likes to report. Even respected journalists call The Five O'Clock Club hunting for odd spectacular stories. If only job search were that simple!

Yet the Internet has revolutionized job searching by removing much of the drudgery and making it a more intelligent process.

One Five O'Clock Clubber uses job-posting sites to find the buzzwords used in his industry. It's more thorough and faster to search Internet ads than newspaper ads for that kind of information.

Another member noticed that at one time there were few job postings in the biotech field—she was "ahead of the market" and took a job in another industry. But now there is a lot of job activity in biotech and it's time for her to network into that field more seriously.

Only a few years ago, we advised job hunters to spend two full days in the library to develop their initial list of companies. Today, most Five O'Clock Clubbers use the Internet to develop their initial lists—their Personal Marketing Plans. In addition, through the Internet you can quickly get you up to speed on virtually any company—and its management.

These uses alone have made the Internet one of the most important job search tools to come along in the past few decades. The Internet saves you time and helps you make better decisions.

**If a technique results in meetings for you, then that technique is working.**

## Answering Ads Online

But what about answering Internet ads? That's what people—and the press—mean when they talk about an Internet job search.

Remember that there are still four basic techniques for getting interviews in your target market: networking, direct contact, answering ads, or contacting search firms. Only 10 percent of all jobs are filled through search firms and 10 percent through ads—whether those appear in print or online. If a technique results in meetings for you, then that technique is working.

The headlines don't scream about common experiences that fizzle. *Fortune* magazine reported that one search firm site attracted 250,000 people, who each spent about three hours filling out a form. Only 70 of them ended up with jobs! Perhaps five times the 70—or 350 people—out of 250,000 got meetings. Those are the odds.

Should you answer ads online? Sure. But if you are really interested in that company, also try to get in through networking or through contacting the company directly. Use ads to learn more about the company, to better position yourself for the industries and fields you are targeting, and to learn the jargon and trends in the field.

Journalists don't talk about what a great research tool the Internet is, but that's the best thing about it!

## When Answering Ads Online

Human resource officers, hiring managers, and search firms have software packages that allow them to search résumé databases for candidates. Your résumé has to make it past the cut in the initial computer search. The computer can't use human judgment. For example, it may search for the *frequency* of a certain word, like JAVA. The résumé that repeats JAVA like a mantra may come up higher in the search than the résumé of a more experienced candidate who uses the word JAVA once or twice in the résumé.

Internet job postings are growing, but they still account for a very small percentage of interviews. Your résumé may be computer-selected, but you still need to do the same old things to separate yourself from your competition.

The Internet is not a magic wand for instant interviews. So do yourself a favor. Use the Internet shrewdly, follow the Five O'Clock Club method for job search—and don't believe everything you read in the newspapers.

# Sample Personal Marketing Plan

## Personal Marketing Plan
## Julie Angelo

**Target Functions: Architectural Assistant**

**Responsibilities:**

- Have some client contact. Actually attend some client meetings.
- Learn how the business operates.
- Do some AutoCAD work and improve my AutoCAD skills. But don't want to do AutoCAD all day long.
- Get some real work to do. Work closely with the architects.

**Target Companies:**

**Attributes**

- People-oriented
- Small, highly professional firm
- Primarily firms with 5 to 15 employees
- Commercial, residential as well as museum work.
- Receptive to new ideas on how to do business or utilize new technologies

**Location**

- Primary—New York City
- Secondary—Westchester, Connecticut suburbs

**Target List:**

New York City:

75 firms (?), some of them rather large

Suburbs:

50 firms (?), all of them small to medium

# Campaign Checklist

Aim for a critical mass of activity that will make things happen, help you determine your true place in this market, and give you a strong bargaining position.

I plan to approach this target using the following techniques:

1. Do research (gather information at the library, through the Internet, or college placement office).
2. Network (gather information through people).
3. Conduct a direct-mail or targeted-mail campaign.
4. Contact selected search firms.
5. Join one or two relevant trade organizations.
6. Regularly read trade magazines and newspapers.
7. Follow up with "influence" notes.
8. Follow up with key contacts on a monthly basis.
9. Answer ads.
10. Aim to give out as much information as I get.

The best techniques for you to use to get meetings depend on your personality and your target market.

For certain targets, search firms may be the most important technique for getting meetings. In other fields—my own, for example—people *rarely* get job leads through search firms. When you are networking in your target market, ask people: "Are there certain search firms that you tend to use? How do you go about hiring people?"

# Current List of Active Stage-1 Contacts

**Networking Contacts With Whom You Want to Keep in Touch**

## *The Beginning of a Search*

**Measure the effectiveness of your search** by listing the number of people with whom you are currently in contact on an ongoing basis, either by phone or mail, who are in a position to hire you or recommend that you be hired. The rule of thumb: If you are seriously job hunting, **you should have 6 to 10 active contacts going at one time. At the beginning of your search, these will simply be networking contacts with whom you want to keep in touch**. You are unlikely to get an offer at this stage. You are gathering information to find out how things work—getting your feet wet. You look like an outsider and outsiders are rarely given a break. Keep adding names to your list because certain people will become inappropriate. Cross their names off. You should probably have some contact once a month with the people who remain on your list.

Because you have already developed targets for your search, please note below the target area for each contact or note that it is serendipitous and does not fit in with any of your organized targets. This will help you see the progress you are making in each target area.

| Name of Contact | Company | Position | Date of Last Contact | Targeted Date of Next Contact | Target Area |
|---|---|---|---|---|---|
| 1. | | | | | |
| 2. | | | | | |
| 3. | | | | | |
| 4. | | | | | |
| 5. | | | | | |
| 6. | | | | | |
| 7. | | | | | |
| 8. | | | | | |
| 9. | | | | | |
| 10. | | | | | |
| 11. | | | | | |
| 12. | | | | | |
| 13. | | | | | |
| 14. | | | | | |
| 15. | | | | | |
| 16. | | | | | |
| 17. | | | | | |
| 18. | | | | | |
| 19. | | | | | |
| 20. | | | | | |

# Current List of Active Stage-2 Contacts

**The Right People at the Right Levels in the Right Organizations**

## *The Middle of a Search*

The nature of your *6 to 10 things in the works* changes over time. Instead of simply finding networking contacts to get your search started, you meet people who are closer to what you want.

Getting a job offer is not the way to test the quality of your campaign. A real test is when people say they'd want you—but not now. Do some people say: **"Boy, I wish I had an opening. I'd sure like to have someone like you here"**? Then you are interviewing well with the right people. All you need now are luck and timing to help you contact (and recontact) the right people when they also have a need.

If people are *not* saying they want you, find out why not. If you think you are in the right targets, talking to people at the right level, and are not early on in your search, you need feedback. Ask: "If you had an opening, would you consider hiring someone like me?" Find out what is wrong.

Become an insider—a competent person who can prove he or she has somehow already done what the interviewer needs. *Prove* you can do the job and that the interviewer is *not* taking a chance on you.

You still need 6 to 10 contacts at this level whom you will recontact later. Keep adding names to your list because certain people will become inappropriate. Cross their names off. You should probably have some contact once a month with the people who remain on your list.

| | Name of Contact | Company | Position | Date of Last Contact | Targeted Date of Next Contact | Target Area |
|---|---|---|---|---|---|---|
| 1. | | | | | | |
| 2. | | | | | | |
| 3. | | | | | | |
| 4. | | | | | | |
| 5. | | | | | | |
| 6. | | | | | | |
| 7. | | | | | | |
| 8. | | | | | | |
| 9. | | | | | | |
| 10. | | | | | | |
| 11. | | | | | | |
| 12. | | | | | | |
| 13. | | | | | | |
| 14. | | | | | | |
| 15. | | | | | | |
| 16. | | | | | | |
| 17. | | | | | | |
| 18. | | | | | | |
| 19. | | | | | | |
| 20. | | | | | | |

# Current List of Active Stage-3 Contacts

**Moving Along Actual Jobs or the Possibility of Creating a Job**

## *The Final Stages of a Search*

In this stage, you **uncover 6 to 10 actual jobs (or the possibility of creating a job) to move along**. These job possibilities could come from *any* of your target areas or from serendipitous leads. Find a *lot* of people who would hire you if they could. If you have only one lead that could turn into an offer, you are likely to try to close too soon. Get more leads. You will be more attractive to the manager, interview better, and not lose momentum if your best lead falls apart. A good number of your job possibilities will fall away through no fault of your own (such as job freezes or major changes in the job requirements).

To get more leads, notice which targets are working and which are not. Make *additional* contacts in the targets that seem to be working, or develop new targets. **Recontact just about everyone you met earlier in your search.** You want to develop more offers.

**Aim for three offers**: This is the stage of your search when you want them. When an offer comes during Stage 1 or Stage 2, you probably have not had a chance to develop momentum so you can get a number of offers. When choosing between offers, **select the job that positions you best for the long term**.

| Name of Contact | Company | Position | Date of Last Contact | Targeted Date of Next Contact | Target Area |
|---|---|---|---|---|---|
| 1. | | | | | |
| 2. | | | | | |
| 3. | | | | | |
| 4. | | | | | |
| 5. | | | | | |
| 6. | | | | | |
| 7. | | | | | |
| 8. | | | | | |
| 9. | | | | | |
| 10. | | | | | |
| 11. | | | | | |
| 12. | | | | | |
| 13. | | | | | |
| 14. | | | | | |
| 15. | | | | | |
| 16. | | | | | |
| 17. | | | | | |
| 18. | | | | | |
| 19. | | | | | |
| 20. | | | | | |

# How to Assess Your Campaign

**Based on Marketing Plan for John Smith**

***Target Functions: Publishing Sales/ Sales Management***

| Stage 1 | Stage 2 | Stage 3 | Current Offers |
|---|---|---|---|
| **Target #1: Consumer Publishing** | **Target #1: Consumer Publishing** | **Target #1: Consumer Publishing** | **Target #1: Consumer Publishing** |
| Time-Warner<br>Condé Nast<br>Hearst<br>Hachette<br>Meredith<br>KIII Holdings<br>Gannett<br>Times-Mirror<br>Bertlesman/G&J<br>Reader's Digest<br>McGraw-Hill<br>Outdoor Services<br>Parade<br>NY Times Corp.<br>Tribune Corp.<br>Contact<br>Perf Arts Network | Time Pathfinder *Inc.* magazine<br>Time Relationship Mktg.<br>*Boston Globe*<br>*Washington Post*<br>Fancy Publications<br>Thirteen-WNET | *USA Today*<br>—Baseball Weekly met w/4 execs<br>Media Vehicles<br>—GE Capital met w/3 execs<br>MAMM and POZ met w/2 execs | Tradewell<br>The Sales Associates<br>—Offered VP, Sales and Head of Internet Sales<br>*Inc.* magazine |
| **Target #2: Trade Publishing** | **Target #2: Trade Publishing** | **Target #2: Trade Publishing** | **Target #2: Trade Publishing** |
| Fairchild Pub.<br>Reed Travel<br>Progressive Grocer<br>James G. Elliot Co. | McFadden<br>M. Shanken<br>Wine and Food<br>BPI<br>Cahners | Supermarket Business<br>Final 2 out of 465 for NE Sales Mgr. | |
| **Target #3: Internet/Computer** | **Target #3: Internet/Computer** | **Target #3: Internet/Computer** | **Target #3: Internet/Computer** |
| CMP<br>Intl Data Mgmt.<br>Ria Group | Preview Travel<br>i33 Communications<br>IDG-Games<br>Mpath-Mplayer | Planet Direct/CMG 2 meetings | Interactive Advertising Net.<br>—One of 10 selected |

# Case Study: Julie
# Getting and Doing Well in Interviews

*He who seizes the right moment, Is the right man.*

Goethe, *Faust*

Most college students and recent grads conduct awful searches. It's not their fault. No one teaches them how to search correctly. And they don't get started early enough. In some respects, students are like our executive job hunters who are employed full-time: When can they possibly find the time to search?

## The Importance of This Next Job

Some savvy students plan ahead. Starting in their freshman or sophomore year, they get summer or part-time jobs where they can learn something and then trade up as they go through school. By the time they graduate, they already have the ingredients for a great résumé to help them land their first job or get into graduate school. (Most people work one full year in their field before grad school.) And they line up their after-graduation job at least six months before they graduate.

The kind of job Julie takes after graduation will have a big impact on Julie's acceptance at graduate school. Some of the best graduate schools will barely consider applicants unless they have at least one full year of work experience, preferably *great* experience.

So a summer or part-time job can be a stepping-stone for the rest of your career.

Students themselves know that they will need real work experience to land a good job after graduation. No more working as a lifeguard unless you're interested in a job in a related field. No more working at the modern equivalent of the local five and dime or soda fountain—unless you're majoring in retail management.

Most students would like some *real* experience, but many don't know how to go about it. Yet they know they have to work, if not for the experience, then for the money, since tuition is so high these days and need-based scholarships are on the decline.

The vast majority of new and prospective graduates have been employed in various capacities, according to the 2001 Graduating Student & Alumni Survey, an annual study conducted by the National Association of Colleges and Employers (NACE). Only 1.3 percent of 985 survey respondents indicated that they had no work experience.

**Julie was planning to work as a camp counselor. Instead, she got four terrific offers at architectural firms.**

Of course, The Five O'Clock Club wants students to get the right kind of work experience. For many, this means trying out a few fields before graduation to see what may be of interest. However, here's the story of one student who was very focused on her long-term goal.

## Targeting Architecture

Julie (not her real name) had just finished her sophomore year at a small college (not the University of Michigan, which we just used for our case study).

Julie was having a problem finding a summer job having to do with her major, which is architecture. If Julie had actually gone to a school such as the University of Michigan, she could have contacted alumni who were in her field, used the job-posting boards on the University of Michigan website, or gone to on-campus job fairs where the employers come to the students.

But those options were not open to her. Julie's school was small and not especially geared to helping students get placed. And even if her school had job fairs, it would have been unlikely to attract many architectural firms, which is where she wanted to work. This article is for those students who have to go beyond school job postings and fairs to get good jobs and for those who want advice on how to interview and then select the best job for their career.

Julie needed to earn money, so she couldn't take an unpaid internship. She was actually planning to take a job as a camp counselor when she started to use The Five O'Clock Club approach. Here's what it took for her to get four terrific concurrent offers.

## Being Specific about Where to Work

The Five O'Clock Club suggests *targeted* searches when you have a clear goal in mind, as Julie did. A target consists of three elements:

- the industry where you want to work
- the position you want to have
- the geographic area

The geographic area is often the easiest to determine. Julie lived in a rural area. So she targeted the major metropolitan area that was closest to her (90 minutes away) because that's where most of the firms were located. She also targeted the suburban areas that were near her home. There were no architectural firms in her town.

Julie decided she would be glad to do administrative work in an architectural firm and also some CAD work, which is a computer program for architects. She had taken a CAD course and worked on CAD a little at a previous job. But she didn't want to get stuck as a CAD operator. Instead, she wanted to learn more about the way small architectural firms work. Doing some administrative work would help her get a feel for the firm. So **Julie had defined her targets The Five O'Clock Club way**:

- Industry: architectural firms
- Position: administration or CAD operator
- Geographic area: large metropolitan area and the suburbs near her home.

---

*You can have anything you want if you want it desperately enough. You must want it with an inner exuberance that erupts through the skin and joins the energy that created the world.*

Sheilah Graham, *The Rest of the Story*

## Even Students Must Target 200 Positions

A basic Five O'Clock Club tenet is that a job hunter must go after 200 job possibilities to get one good offer! This holds true for students as well as for the most senior executives. Now, if you know that a certain company employs 200 students over the summer, then that one company may be enough for your entire search. If you find a company that employs 20 students, then you would need 10 such companies to total 200. **This target of 200 does not mean an organization must have 200 job *openings* but simply *positions* that would be appropriate for you—whether or not they are filled right now.**

Architectural firms are small, perhaps employing only one student per firm, so Julie would probably have to contact 200 of them. How could Julie come up with the names of 200 architectural firms—and quickly? She was only a week away from the end of the term and had not yet tried to contact many firms.

**Julie contacted 200 small firms in less than 10 hours.**

## Using Job Posting Sites for the Beginning of Her Contact *List*

Julie needed to contact 200 firms. First, she went into *Monster.com* and selected job postings for *architects* in the major metropolitan area near her. Then she selected job postings for architects in the nearby suburban areas. Julie selected only architectural jobs at *firms* as opposed to architectural jobs in the government or inside a major organization, such as a hospital or hotel chain.

So Julie clicked on the companies she was interested in—*as if* she were responding to the ad. After all, those organizations were hiring! Her response would go to the person in that small firm who was doing the hiring. (This works for young people who want to work in a small firm. A more senior person would need to contact the department or division head, which can require a phone call for research.)

When ads are answered automatically like this—through a job-posting site—the *subject* line contains the ad number so the organization will know which ad a person is responding to. Julie changed the subject line to read (see example on the next page):

> Administrator/CAD Drafter—Architecture-related—Summer employment for top student.

Julie contacted about 50 firms that way. But that was not enough. She needed to find at least 150 additional firms.

**Julie responded to ads for full-time architects but asked for a summer job instead. Let them know what *you* want.**

## Next Stop: Yahoo

Then Julie went into Yahoo and keyed in the word *architect* and the two geographic areas she was interested in, one at a time. The American Institute of Architects was a good source, but she also found lots of individual architectural firms listed. In most cases, Julie had to go to the company website to get an appropriate E-mail address. One by one, she came up with 155 additional organizations to contact, bringing her total to 205 firms (including the 50 from *Monster.com*).

## Sending Bulk E-Mail

To save time, she stopped e-mailing the firms individually. Instead, she captured the E-mail addresses in a Word document, with one E-mail address per line. After she had gathered 20 or 30 E-mail addresses, Julie sent a *bulk E-mail.* She didn't put the addresses in the *To* space. She copied all the E-mail addresses into the *bcc* space so the recipients would not be able to tell how many firms she had mailed to. Nor would they be able to tell which other firms she had contacted. She put the same *subject* as she had for her earlier e-mails, attached her résumé as before, and addressed the E-mail to herself. She did this until she had sent out all 205 E-mails. Then she took her last final exam.

Julie had spent a total of about 10 hours on her research and e-mailing.

**Using a bulk E-mail technique, Julie was able to contact 20 to 30 firms at a time using the *bcc* line.**

**This is the E-mail Julie sent to 205 architectural firms.**
**Her Five O'Clock Club résumé was an attachment.**

**E-mail**

To: julieangelo@udallas.edu
Subject: **Administrator/CAD Drafter—Architecture-Related—Employment for Top Student.**

May 11, 200x
Dear Sir or Madam:
I am writing to you because yours is a prestigious firm in the architecture industry and I am an architectural student interested in summer work at a firm such as yours. I'd like to meet with you or someone else in your firm to find out more about your company and to tell you about myself. Even if you have no openings right now, you never know when you may need someone like me.

I have 10 months' experience with a civil engineering firm. You may be interested in some of the specific things I have done:

- Served as an **assistant office manager**, organizing client proposals and setting up manuals. I also answered an 8-line phone.
- Because of my **basic AutoCAD experience**, engineers turned to me when they wanted routine things done.

As an Architectural Studies major, I tend to **be among the best in my class**, winning contests and doing excellent work. I would be excellent at client contact, helping architects get ready for meetings, putting proposals together, and assisting with AutoCAD work. I would appreciate a meeting and look forward to hearing from you.

With thanks,

Julie Angelo

**julieangelo@udallas.edu**, University of Dallas Box #3124, 76 North Churchill Rd., Irving, TX 99999, 555 666-4693

**angelo555@hotmail.com**, 863 Erie Avenue, Brewster, TX 99945

**Attachment**: JAngelo résumé

## The Calls Come In

Within two days, Julie received nine calls for meetings. Interestingly, eight of the calls were from the suburban area, and only one call was from the major metropolitan area.

Julie had sent 75 percent of her E-mails to firms in the major metropolitan area—that's where most of the firms were. The major metropolitan area was the obvious place for students and others to look for architectural jobs. That means, of course, that job hunters had far more competitors.

Firms in the suburban area were more responsive because there were few colleges in those areas and fewer students contacting those firms.

The results of *your* search may surprise you. That's why you have to contact so many places. You never know who will respond.

Julie scheduled seven interviews (she immediately ruled out two firms because the travel would have been more than two hours from home, something she would have found acceptable if she had gotten only a few calls).

A well-known Five O'Clock Club maxim is to have 6 to 10 job possibilities in the works. It increases the chances of landing something appropriate for you.

## Chase Companies, Not Jobs

Another Five O'Clock Club maxim is "Don't chase jobs—chase companies." Contact organizations whether or not they have an opening right now. If your search is solely from postings, you will have competition for the jobs you go after. Everyone's chasing those same job openings. So, too, most students target the top-tier firms in major metropolitan areas. If Julie had done that, she would have been discouraged by the results.

**Even though 75 percent of her E-mails went to firms in the major metropolitan area, Julie received almost no response from them.**

Many firms will tell you they have no openings (regardless of your level) but say they would be glad to meet with you anyway. *Meet with them!* Most jobs are created for people, and most companies will hire someone if the right person comes along—even though they have no formal opening and were not looking to hire at the moment. Julie didn't know this and turned down two exploratory meetings because she felt such urgency to get a job.

However, Julie did schedule five interviews over three days' time.

## In a Tight Job Market, See the Employer Immediately

Sometimes the market favors the job seeker, and there are plenty of jobs in your target market; sometimes it favors the employer, and there are more job hunters than jobs. Even an organization as small as The Five O'Clock Club is often in the driver's seat when the economy favors the employer. During those times, we can get 30 résumés from Ivy League schools in just a few days after posting an opening. If a student can't or won't come in for a week or two, the job could be gone.

On the other hand, employers that get little traffic from job hunters may have to wait for the job hunters to show up.

**The Five O'Clock Club wants you to line up 6 to 10 meetings. Julie lined up 7.**

So, if things are going well for you or not well for you, a lot of it may have to do more with the economy and your target areas than with you personally. Don't blame yourself too much—or take too much credit. Just analyze and refine your search.

Julie was lucky, even though she told companies she could not meet with them for 10 days because she had finals. She had contacted many firms that apparently received few inquiries from students, so the companies had to wait. Two of the firms were already preselling her on the phone, telling her the kind of experience she would get, and saying that they thought she would fit in perfectly at their firm—and they hadn't even met her! This would not have happened in a market where there was more competition for jobs.

Before she went on her interviews, Julie was most interested in a five-person firm that was at present operating out of the owner's home and would soon be moving. The president spent time on the phone with Julie and was very personable. In addition, this firm was close to where Julie lived. As you will see, Julie later changed her mind.

**Contact firms whether or not they have openings. If they agree to meet with you, *see them*. They'll hire the right person.**

## Do You Want a Job or Not?

When you do take a job, plan to work 12 weeks instead of 8 in the summer. You can still have a week or two off. A company will not be pleased if you're there a short time: It takes a while to learn how a company operates and to be truly productive. Make a good impression so you can get an offer from this firm after graduation or at least get good references. After graduation, you can take more time off before entering the big, bad work world.

*Living is a constant process of deciding what we are going to do.*

José Ortega y Gasset, Spanish philosopher

## How to Select a Good Place to Work

Julie was ambitious and eventually wanted to attend a top architectural graduate school. Therefore, she needed to select a good summer job now. It's okay for *high school kids* to work at camps all summer, but employers—and top graduate schools—expect more from college kids. Where Julie works this summer and next will matter when she tries to get into a good graduate school.

With this number of E-mails, Julie should be able to land something more appropriate to her long-term goals. When selecting a job, don't pick a job just because it pays a dollar or two more an hour. At The Five O'Clock Club, we say "Select the job that positions you best for the long term." Build your résumé because you will have to search again.

**Forget a buck an hour more. Select the job that positions you best for the long term.**

## How to Do What Is in Your Own Best Interests

Perhaps you will wind up with multiple offers. Great! Here's one way to decide which one to choose: If you were *graduating* from college and had to choose among these places to work, which one would you choose? That's the one you should work at right now.

Think in terms of **the people you will meet there**, the kinds of **projects they work on**, the work style you will pick up (**the professionalism of the place**), and—of course—the **assignments *you* will get**.

After her meetings, Julie should have plenty of offers to choose from. Maybe she will feel intimidated by a place that may be the best place for her. Some people—especially young people—may have low self-confidence. After all, they haven't worked at very many places.

Select the job that will position you best for the long term. If you know your approximate career direction and select a great company this time around, you may want to work at the same place next summer and then possibly after graduation.

## Preparing for the Interview

**Go to each company's website** before the interview so you know something about the company. Even managers at small companies will ask applicants, "So, how much do you know about us?" Because of the web, companies expect you to know something about them.

Julie had **visited each company's website to see the kind of work they did**, the number of employees they had, and other particulars so she would appear (and would actually be) very interested in each firm.

**Prepare a separate 3x5 card for each company**. Note the things you have seen on their website, such as the number of employees at each company and the kind of work they do. Right before going in for the meeting, pull out this card so the information will be fresh. For example, one of the firms Julie was interviewing with had done work at her college. They may be partial to students from her school. And she could ask them what they specifically did for the college.

Julie was fortunate in that she had so many interviews lined up. So the plan was that **if a company extended her an offer on the spot**—especially the early interviews—she would tell them how excited she was about the company, that she thought it was good chance that she would end up there (if she thought that), and that she would have to call them back on Wednesday. Julie could do this because of the way she conducted her search and because she was in demand.

When the situation is reversed and students are having a difficult time finding jobs, it's okay to accept an offer on the spot if you know it's a good one. Companies want employees who want them. They are turned off by job seekers who act as though they can take it or leave it.

**Be prepared to answer the question, "So tell me a little about yourself."** The answer to this question is in your cover letter and the top of your résumé. For example, Julie's answer was: "I am an architecture major with fairly strong administrative skills and some familiarity with AutoCAD. When I worked at the engineering firm, they could depend on me to handle just about anything. For example, I spoke with clients by phone, put together client proposals, organized hundreds of forms, and handled basic AutoCAD for the engineers. I'm excited about meeting with you today because of the kind of work you do and the size of your firm."

Julie memorized this, and you also should memorize your Two-Minute Pitch (covered in detail in an earlier chapter). You will feel more comfortable in the interview if you have it down pat. Put this information on a 3x5 card so you can pull it out right before you go in for the meeting.

**Ask each company what your duties will be**. You need to understand fairly clearly what you will be doing on the job. Will Julie learn anything about architecture or relating to the firm's clients? Or will she be doing work that could be done at any company, such as copying and mailing?

We keep saying, "**pick a job that positions you best for the long term.**" This means the place where you will gain the best experience. After all, we all have future job searches ahead of us.

**If they ask you to name an accomplishment** of which you are very proud or if they ask you if there is "anything else you would like to tell us about yourself," do not name anything having to do with your singing group or with your German class. Name something relevant to the job you are going after. In Julie's case, she could talk about how well she had done in her architecture class, citing the two times she had done better than the other students in projects. Julie was also prepared to talk about other specifics in her résumé, such as what she had done at other jobs and the courses she had taken in school.

One more thing: Do not forget to **bring an extra copy of your résumé with you on the interview**.

*An adventure is the deliberate, volitional movement out of the comfort zone.*

James W. Newman, *Release Your Brakes*

## The Interview Itself

When you go on the job interview, the hiring manager is likely to ask you how many other companies you are talking to. No company wants to hear that you are talking to seven companies and are considering all of them. Companies want people who really want to work for them. So, at the very least, tell hiring managers that you are talking to other companies but that you are especially interested in them because of. . . . And have an honest reason why this company appeals to you.

When you go on the interviews, **expect to be surprised**. Companies that sounded ideal before you went there may be a lot less interesting in person. Companies you considered a write-off may prove to give you the best experience. So go in excited and optimistic about each possibility.

**Notice the feel at each firm**. See if you like the way it looks. Notice how well people get along. Is your boss someone you trust to give you good assignments? Are there other young people there you can talk to to find out how they like it and *if they get good assignments*? Some firms, especially the larger ones, may look good on your résumé but give you very little in the way of real experience.

**Ask them how many other people they are considering** for the position. It is important for you to know how much competition you have.

As far as **salary negotiation** is concerned, it's best to **wait until you get an offer**. At the worst, you could say, "I was making $10 an hour in my last job, but I'm very interested in working here, so I'm open."

Then hear what they have to offer you. After you have a few offers, go back to the companies you are most interested in and say, "I've received a number of offers, but I'm most interested in working for you. Most of the companies have offered me $X. I was wondering what the chances were of increasing the pay by (for example) one dollar an hour. A dollar may not seem like much to you, but it means a lot to me. I'd really like to work for you."

Then wait to see what their final offer is. At that point, when you have heard everyone's best offer, you have to select the job you want.

But, again, the MOST important thing is to *select the job that positions you best for the long term* as opposed to the job that pays a buck an hour more.

**If you don't get an offer on the spot** from a firm that interests you, it may be that they are interviewing other people. This means that you have competition! Toward the end of the interview, especially if they ask if you are talking to other companies, ask them the following:

- "Where are you in the hiring process?" (Just getting started interviewing people; in the middle; you're the only one.)
- "How many other candidates are you talking to?"
- "Now that you've met a few people, how do you think the candidates stack up?" (You want to find out how they see you compared with the others.)
- "When do you think you'll make an offer to someone?"

*Here comes the future, rolling towards us like a meteorite, a satellite, a giant iron snowball, a two-ton truck in the wrong lane, careening downhill with broken brakes, and whose fault is it? No time to think about that. Blink and it's here.*

Margaret Atwood, *Good Bones and Simple Murders*

## After the Meeting

**Take notes after each meeting** (or during the meeting if you can) or you will get mixed up about who said what. What's more, if you have taken notes, you will feel more secure about what you are saying.

**To get offers from top firms**, you will most likely have to follow up. Lots of students contact those same firms. Even small companies have five or six applicants to choose from. You will need to make at least a phone call—and preferably send a fax or E-mail. If you write a letter to a firm you are especially interested in, do it immediately and use your notes from the meeting for your letter.

For example, if they mentioned special projects they would like you to work on, mention those projects specifically in the letter and say how good you would be at them. In your letter, tell them you have interviewed at a number of companies, have three offers (or whatever you have), but especially want to work there, and here's why. Tell them you will call later to see how things stand. And then call.

**You will need references later. So, pick a firm that is respected and where you will get good experience.**

*Hey, no matter what—it's better than working at the post office.*

Jerry Sterner, *Other People's Money*

## How to Select the Right Organization

To get a good job after graduation or go to graduate school, you will need references from your bosses. This may seem a little early to be thinking about references, but it's not.

Therefore, do your best to pick a firm that is respected and where you will get good experience. A reference from a great firm or one where you got great experience will have more weight than one from a lesser firm where you did menial work.

If you feel insecure about selecting the best firm for yourself, ask yourself what someone else who loves you (or God himself!) would want you to do—rather than asking yourself where you feel the most comfortable. I have had to do this myself many a time, although you may not feel the same insecurities I used to feel. When people feel insecure, they may gravitate toward the place where they feel the safest (i.e., the lowest level place) rather than the one that would be best for them in the long term. So ask someone who loves you or has some sense about these kinds of decisions which position would best use the terrific talents God gave you.

Don't bury your talents. Get into a place where you will learn the most (as opposed to the place where you might be the busiest). Select the job that will best fit into your future.

- Don't select a position just because it is closest to home.
- Don't select the one that pays a buck an hour more.
- Don't select the one that sounds like play.

Select the one that positions you best for the long term. Now's the time to make the right choice.

*The amount of money you receive will always be in direct proportion to the demand for what you do, your ability to do it, and the difficulty of replacing you.*

Napoleon Hill, paraphrased by Dennis Kimbro, *Think and Grow Rich: A Black Choice*

## Ah, the Offers Pour In

In the end, Julie went on **four interviews at top firms and got four offers**. As she got offers, she became pickier about the remaining firms on her list, ruling out those that would have required more than an hour and a half of travel. In her last job, Julie earned $10 an hour. Her first offer was at $11, two were at $12.50, and one offer had not yet come in.

**Julie seemed very desirable *because* she had so many possibilities in the works**. Companies were essentially in a bidding war for her. Remember that you need to **see 6 to 10 organizations concurrently to have a good search**.

When Julie interviewed at the last firm, she told them about her other offers, hoping for another offer at $12.50 per hour. They wooed her with the promise of being able to learn a lot about architecture on the job: She would visit some of the sites where the architects were building, go to client meetings, *shadow* an architect to see what was done all day. They said they would e-mail her an offer later that evening.

Julie would have been hard-pressed to turn down their offer, almost regardless of the salary they offered: The experience would have been so extraordinary compared with the others, and Julie was trying to keep her long-range future in mind.

However, Julie did not have to choose content over salary. The E-mail came that evening with an offer of $15.00 per hour!

The last firm knew what they were up against: three other offers. They also knew they had a difficult time recruiting architects in their neck of the woods. But for Julie, the location was perfect: only 45 minutes from her home.

**A TV journalist said kids show up for job interviews in tank tops with bellies showing! Of course, they don't get hired.**

*A very large amount of human suffering and frustration is caused by the fact that many men and women are not content to be the sort of beings that God had made them, but try to persuade themselves that they are really beings of some different kind.*

Eric Mascall, *The Importance of Being Human*

## Turning Down Offers

Congratulations on conducting a good job search. Now, you have to call those other very sweet companies that made you offers. **Call them the minute you accept an offer**. Tell them that you are so sorry. You would have loved to have worked there: You really liked the people, and you know the experience would have been worthwhile. But you have received an offer that you simply could not refuse.

**If they want to know anything about your offer, tell them!** They want to know what their competitors are doing to attract top talent like you. There is no reason to keep secret your salary offer, the training possibilities, and so on.

**Be very nice to the people you say "no" to**. They deserve it. And, you never know, but your new employer may have a huge cutback a month after you start. If you have handled things correctly with the other firms, you could simply call them and probably get an offer.

*Man is not made for society, but society is made for man. No institution can be good which does not tend to improve the individual.*

Margaret Fuller, American social reformer

## Dressing for Work

So you're going to start a big-time job on Monday. Here are some thoughts about dress code. Most students dress like students, and it's okay with some companies. It's almost as if the students are shouting, "I'm a kid." But this is the time to start dressing like an adult. You are at work, not at school. Work requires different clothes and a different mind-set, just as going to the beach requires a different set of clothes and a different mind-set!

At our small company, the young men wear a shirt and tie, no jacket. The young women have to wear a female equivalent of that. The men's dress code is easier to comply with.

The *female equivalent* of a shirt and tie means the ladies are not allowed to have their navels showing, their breasts showing (not even a little), or their thighs showing. You may not know this, but part of the reason men's suits evolved in business was so other workers would pay attention to a man's thoughts and not his body. The jacket is meant to cover up body lines. Women should use the same guidelines.

Some companies may tolerate *kid stuff* from students, especially when there is a labor shortage and workers are hard to find. But when there is a choice between two equally qualified students, the one who seems to understand the unwritten rules is more likely to get the good assignments, go on client meetings, and be retained in the long run.

Wearing the right clothes shows that you understand the system and want to participate in the adult world. There are students who say, "I want to be able to express myself and be proud of my pierced tongue and green hair. A company should accept me the way I am and judge me simply on my work." Okay. If you want to keep your pierced tongue, go work at a place where that's the norm. Business is a game, and it has its rules. Dress is one of them.

So, what is appropriate for women? Chances are, whatever you wear to school will not work on the job, unless you happen to dress up at school. Either dress pants or a skirt is fine. The skirts these days can be ankle length or perhaps two inches above the knee—no higher. Wear nice, work-type blouses. Regular shoes. Stockings. (No bare legs.) That's all it takes.

**Julie increased her pay 50 percent because she had so many offers and she contacted companies others ignored.**

Pay attention to your posture while at your desk. When we see a junior accountant in our office constantly slumped down in the chair, we know that he is doing a poor job. I know I'll have to check his work often, and chances are his work is sloppy.

The same is true in any office. If you enter data slouched over or simply sit in an unprofessional way, it sends a message. Companies will excuse a lot because, after all, "It's just a kid." **But you don't want to be thought of that way.** You are not at home or in your dorm. You are at work.

It may be that the company that hired Julie pays all interns $15 an hour, but probably not. It's more likely that **she got that amount because she had so many offers and because she contacted companies other students were ignoring**. In fact, it's likely that Julie was paid more than the typical intern at that company. So it's even more important that she look as professional as she can.

## A Changed Future

This job has the possibility of changing Julie's career path for the better. Instead of working as a camp counselor after her sophomore year and winding up with a weaker résumé, Julie is now on the right path. Theoretically, she could work at this same company the following summer and for one year after graduation before beginning graduate school.

So, make the most of your job searches while in school. As you go along in your job, be sure to keep in touch with your advisors.

Join Five O'Clock Club Junior and be in a small group with other students who are searching. It's your own Five O'Clock Club.

## The Denouement

A successful job search is just the beginning of anyone's story. How did the job work out for Julie? Was it the right place for her? Could she live up to their expectations?

Two weeks after she started, I got this E-mail from Julie, and I must say that I had tears in my eyes as I read it:

Dear Kate,

I got a few more E-mails asking me to come in for interviews. Well, too late for them! I'll hold on to them though. I know from you that I need to hedge my bets.

Work is going great. Got paid for the first time today. My check was the biggest I have ever seen made out to me, and it wasn't even for a full two weeks! But that is not the best part. I LOVE what I am doing! Yesterday I got to e-mail a contractor with some plans that I have been working on. I even got a call from him today! I was part of the staff meeting on Tuesday, which I was usually excluded from when I worked at the engineering firm. The meeting was very interesting, as I watched them assign people to teams, including me! I am assigned to definite projects and am drawing things that will definitely be built! I actually have to finish a set of foundation plans by tonight. . . . I have to rush rush! But it is so much fun! And I am getting GREAT experience.

Love,
Julie

*CYRUS (trying to be friendly):* I'll tell you what. You want to work, I'll give you a job. Nothing permanent, mind you, but that upstairs room over there—the one above the office—is a hell of a mess. It looks like they've been throwing junk in there for twenty years, and it's time it got cleaned up.

*RASHID (Playing it cool):* What's your offer?

*CYRUS:* Five bucks an hour. That's the going rate, isn't it? . . . If you can't finish today, you can do the rest tomorrow.

*RASHID (Getting to his feet):* Is there a benefits package, or are you hiring me on a freelance basis?

*CYRUS:* Benefits?

*RASHID:* You know, health insurance, dental plan, paid vacation. It's not fun being exploited. Workers have to stand up for their rights.

*CYRUS:* I'm afraid we'll be working on a strictly freelance basis.

*RASHID (Long pause. Pretending to think it over):* I'll take it.

Paul Auster, *Smoke*

# Are You Conducting a Good Campaign?

*The thing is to never deal yourself out . . . Opt for the best possible hand. Play with verve and sometimes with abandon, but at all times with calculation.*

L. Douglas Wilder, in "Virginia's Lieutenant Governor: L. Douglas Wilder Is First Black to Win Office," *Ebony,* April 1986

## The Quality of Your Campaign

Getting a job offer is not the way to test the quality of your campaign. A real test is when people say they'd want you—but not right now. When you are networking, do people say, "Boy, I wish I had an opening. I'd sure like to have someone like you here"? Then you know you are interviewing well with the right people. All you need now are luck and timing to help you contact or recontact the right people when they also have a need.

If people are not saying they want you, find out why. Are you inappropriate for this target? Or perhaps you seem like an outsider and outsiders are rarely given a break.

During the beginning of your search, you are gathering information to find out how things work.

Why should someone hire a person who does not already work in the field? Lots of competent people have the experience and can prove they will do a good job.

### How you know you are in a *campaign*:

You feel as though you know a critical mass of people within that industry. When you go on *interviews,* you contribute as much as you take away. You have gained a certain amount of information about the industry that puts you on par with the interviewer—and you are willing to share that information. You are a contributor. An insider.

You know what's going on. You feel some urgency and are more serious about this industry.

You are no longer simply *looking around*—playing it cool. You are more intense. You don't want anything to stand in your way because you know this is what you want. You become more aware of any little thing that can help you get in. Your judgment becomes more finely tuned. Things seem to fall into place.

You are working harder at this than you ever could have imagined. You read everything there is to read. You write proposals almost overnight and hand-deliver them.

Your campaign is taking on a life of its own.

At industry meetings, you seem to know everybody. They know you are one of them and are simply waiting for the right break.

When someone mentions a name, you have already met that person and are keeping in touch with him or her. The basic job-hunting *techniques* no longer apply.

You are in a different realm and you feel it.

This is a real campaign.

There is a test to see if you are perceived as an insider. If you think you are in the right target, talking to people at the right level, and are not early on in your search, you need feedback. Ask people, "If you had an opening, would you consider hiring someone like me?"

Become an insider—a competent person who can prove that he or she has somehow already done what the interviewer needs. Prove you can do the job and that the interviewer is not taking a chance by hiring you.

## The Quantity of Your Campaign

You need to find a lot of people who would hire you if they could. You know by now that you should **have 6 to 10 things in the works at all times**. This is the only true measure of the effectiveness of your campaign to get meetings in your target area. If you have fewer than this, get more. You will be more attractive to the manager, will interview better, and will lower the chances of losing momentum if your best lead falls apart.

Use the worksheet *Current List of Active Stage 1 Contacts*. At the beginning of your search, these will simply be networking contacts with whom you want to keep in touch. At this stage, your goal is to come up with 6 to 10 contacts you want to recontact later, perhaps every two months. In the middle of your search, the quality of your list will change. The names will be of the right people at the right level in the right organizations. Finally, the 6 to 10 names will represent prospective job possibilities you are trying to move along.

If you have 6 to 10 job possibilities in the works, a good number of them will fall away through no fault of your own (job freezes or hiring managers changing their minds about the kind of person they want). Then you'll need to get more possibilities in the works. With this critical mass of ongoing possible positions, you stand a chance of getting a number of offers and landing the kind of job you want.

*There is a tide in the affairs of men, Which, taken at the flood, leads on to fortune; . . . On such a sea we are now afloat; And we must take the current when it serves, Or lose our ventures.*

Shakespeare, *Julius Caesar*

## Developing Momentum in Your Search

A campaign builds to a pitch. The parts begin to help one another. You focus less on making a particular technique work and more on the situation you happen to be in. This chapter gives you a feel for a real campaign.

In your promotional campaign to get meetings, you see people who are in a position to hire you or recommend you. Keep in touch with them so they will . . .

- think of you when a job opens up
- invite you to create a job for yourself
- upgrade an opening to better suit you
- give you information to help you in your search

When you are in the heat of a real campaign, a critical mass of activity builds, so you start

- hearing the same names
- seeing the same people
- contributing as much as you are getting
- writing proposals
- getting back to people quickly
- feeling a sense of urgency about this industry
- writing follow-up letters and making follow-up phone calls

*. . . the secret is to have the courage to live. If you have that, everything will sooner or later change.*

James Salter, *Light Years*

*Eventually, and often after the survival of a long and profound crisis, often after the painful shedding of one skin and the gradual growth of another, comes the realization that the world is essentially neutral. The world doesn't care, and is responsible neither for one's spiritual failures nor for one's successes. This discovery can come as a profound relief, because it is no longer necessary to spend so much energy shoring up the self, and because the world emerges as a broader, more interesting, sweeter place through which to move. The fog lifts, as it were.*

Frank Conroy, *The New York Times Book Review,* January 1, 1989

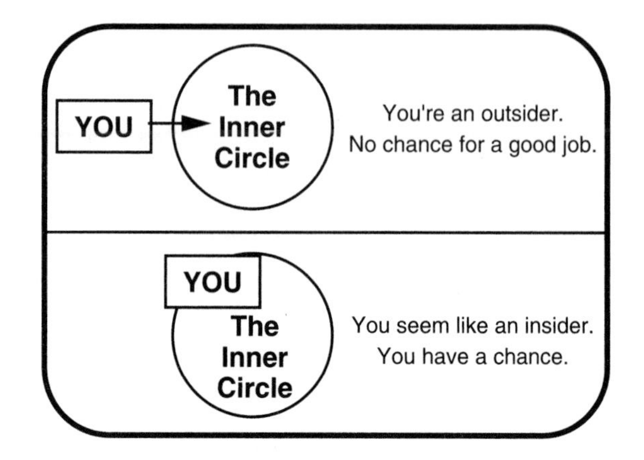

# How to Network Your Way In

*I use not only all the brains I have,*
*but all I can borrow.*
Woodrow Wilson

In the old days, networking was a great technique. We job hunters were appreciative of the help we got and treated those we met with respect and courtesy. We targeted a field and then used networking to meet people, form lifelong relationships with them, and gather information about the area. We called it *information gathering,* but it also often led to jobs.

Today, stressed-out, aggressive, demanding job hunters want a job quickly and expect their *contacts* to hire them, refer them to someone important (obviously not the person with whom they are speaking), or tell them where the jobs are. The old way worked; this new attitude does not. This chapter tells you how to network correctly.

**Network informally** by talking to acquaintances who may know something about your target area. **Network formally** by contacting people at their jobs to get information about their organization or industry. Networking is one way to find out what skills are needed where, what jobs may be opening up, and where you might be able to fit in. Talking to people because "they might know of something for me" rarely works. Use the networking—or information gathering—process **to gather information and to build new relationships**.

## Build Lifelong Relationships

You are also trying to build lifelong relationships. If a target area interests you, get to know the people in it and let them get to know you. It is unreasonable to expect them to have something for you just because you decided to contact them right now. Some of the most important people in your search may provide you with information and no contacts. Be sincerely grateful for the help you get, form a relationship that will last a lifetime, and plan to **recontact regularly the people you meet**.

Remember, you are not talking to people assuming they have heard of job openings. That approach rarely works. For example, if someone asked you if you happen to know of a position in the purchasing department in your old organization, your answer would be no. But if they said, "I'm really interested in your former organization. Do you happen to know **anyone** I could talk to there?" you could certainly give them the name of someone.

This is how people find jobs through networking. As time passes, the people you've met hear of things or develop needs themselves. If you keep in touch, they will tell you what's happening. It is a long-term process but an effective one.

As you talk to more and more people, you will gather more and more information about business situations and careers in which you think you are interested. And the more people you meet and tell about your career search, the more people are out there to consider you for a job or a referral to a job when they know of one. But, remember, they have to know you first. Networking allows you to meet people without asking them for a job and putting them on the spot. And the fact is, **if they like you and happen to have a job that's appropriate for you, they will *tell* you about it—you will not have to ask**.

People *like* to talk to sincere, bright people, and send on those who impress them. People will not send you on if you are not skilled at presenting yourself or asking good questions.

## CASE STUDY *Monica*

## Networking When You Don't Know Anyone

Monica moved to Manhattan from a rural area because she wanted to work in publishing. She found a temporary job and then thought of ways to network in a city where she knew no one. She told everyone she had always wanted to work in publishing and would like to meet with people who worked in that industry. She told people at bus stops, at church, and at restaurants. She read *Publishers Weekly*, the publishing trade magazine, to find out who was doing what in the industry, and she contacted some people directly. She also joined an association of people in the publishing industry. At meetings, she asked for people's business cards and said she would contact them later. She then wrote to them and met with them at their offices.

Monica found that one of the best contacts she made during her search was a man close to retirement who was on a special assignment with no staff. There was no possibility of her ever working for him, but he gave her great insights into the industry and told her the best people to work for. He saved her from wasting many hours of her time, and she felt free to call him to ask about specific people she was meeting.

Over time, lots of people got to know Monica, and Monica got to know the publishing industry. She eventually heard of a number of openings, and was able to tell which ones were better than others. Monica is off to a good start in her new profession because she made lifelong friends she can contact *after* she is in her new job.

Using the networking technique correctly takes:

- time (because setting up meetings, going on them, and following up takes time)
- a sincere desire for information and building long-term relationships
- preparation

# Questions You May Want to Ask

To repeat: People will be more willing to help you than you think *if* you are sincere about your interest in getting information from them *and* if you are asking them appropriate questions to which you could not get answers through library research or from lower level people.

If what you really want from them is a job, you will not do as well. At this point, you don't want a job, you want a meeting. You want to **develop a relationship with them**, ask them for information, tell them about yourself, see if they can recommend others for you to talk to, and build a basis for contacting them later.

Before each meeting, write down the questions you sincerely want to ask *this specific person.* (If you find you are asking each person exactly the same thing, you are not using this technique properly.) Some examples:

### The Industry

- How large is this industry?
- How is the industry changing now? What are the most important trends or problems? Which parts of the industry will probably grow (or decline) at what rates over the next few years?
- What are the industry's most important characteristics?
- What do you see as the future of this industry 5 or 10 years from now?
- What do you think of the organizations I have listed on this sheet? Which ones are you familiar with? Who are the major players in this industry? Which are the better organizations?

### The Company or Organization

- How old is the organization, and what are the most important events in its history? How large is the organization? What goods and services does it produce? How does it produce these goods and services?
- Does the organization have any particular clients, customers, or regulators? If so, what are they like and what is their relationship to the organization?
- Who are your major competitors?
- How is the company organized? What are the growing areas? The problem areas? Which areas do you think would be good for me, given my background?
- What important technologies does this organization use?
- What is the organizational culture like? Who tends to get ahead here?
- What important challenges is the organization facing right now or in the near future?

### The Job or Function

- What are the major tasks involved in this job? What skills are needed to perform these tasks?
- How is this department structured? Who reports to whom? Who interacts with whom?
- What is it like to work here? What is the organization's reputation?
- What kinds of people are normally hired for this kind of position?
- What kind of salary and other rewards would a new hire usually get for this kind of job?
- What are the advancement opportunities?
- What skills are absolutely essential for a person in this field?

### The Person with Whom You Are Meeting

- Could you tell me a little about what you do in your job?
- How does your position relate to the bottom line?
- What is the most challenging aspect of your job?
- What is the most frustrating aspect of your job?
- What advice would you give to someone in my position?
- What are some of the intermediate steps necessary for a person to reach your position?
- What do you like or dislike about your job?
- How did you get into this profession or industry?
- What major problems are you facing right now in this department or position?

*Our plans miscarry because they have no aim. When a man does not know what harbor he is making for, no wind is the right wind.*

Seneca the Younger, Roman statesman

## *You* Are the Interviewer

In an information-gathering meeting, *you* are conducting the meeting. The worst thing you can do is to sit, expecting to be interviewed. The manager, thinking you honestly wanted information, agreed to see you. Have your questions ready. After all, you called the meeting.

---

*If you have always done it that way, it is probably wrong.*

Charles Kettering

## The Information-Gathering or Networking Process

1. **Determine your purpose.** Decide what information you want or what contacts you want to build. Early on in your job search, networking with people at your own level helps you research the field you have targeted. At this point in your search, you are not trying to get hired. Later, meet with more senior people. *They* are in a position to hire you someday.

2. **Make a list of people you know.** In the research phase, you made a list of the organizations you thought you should contact in each of your target areas. You need lists of important people or organizations you want to contact. Then, when you meet someone who tends to know people, you can ask if that person knows anyone on your list.

Now make a list of all the people you already know (relatives, former bosses and coworkers, your dentist, people at your church or synagogue, former classmates, those with whom you play baseball). Don't say you do not know enough appropriate people. If you know one person, that's enough for a start.

Don't discard the names of potential contacts because they are not in a position to hire you. Remember, you are not going to meet people to ask for a job but to ask for information. These contacts can be helpful, may provide information, and most likely have other friends or contacts who will move you closer and closer to your targets.

**People to Contact in Each Target Area** In the chapter *Researching Your Job Targets,* you made a list of organizations you want to contact in each of your target areas. Then you used the *Sample Personal Marketing Plan* as a model for your own complete list. Now you want to get in to see the people at these and other organizations.

For each target, list on the following page the names of people you know, or know of, or even generic names (such as *lawyers who deal with emerging businesses*) who can help you in each target. Whether you contact them through networking or a targeted mailing, the meetings will all be networking meetings.

You will not be idly chatting with these people. Instead, you will have your pitch ready (see the chapter on the Two-Minute Pitch), and will tell them the target you have in mind. The target will include the industry or organization size, the kind of possible position you would like, and the geographic area. For example: "I'm interested in entrepreneurially driven, medium-sized private organizations in the Chicago area. I would do well in finance in that kind of organization. Can you suggest the names of people who might have contact with those kinds of organizations, or do you know anyone who works at that kind of organization or an organization on my list?"

Tell *everyone* the target you are going after—including people you meet on the train and at the barber shop or beauty salon. You never know who knows somebody.

3. **Contact the people you want to meet.** Chances are, you will simply call (rather than write to) people you already know—those on your *People to Contact* list. In the beginning of your search, practice on people who know you well. If you say a few things wrong, it won't matter. You can see them again later.

But as you progress in your search, most of the people you meet should not be people you know well. Extend your network beyond those people with whom you are comfortable. (See the graphic on the next page.)

As you build your network of contacts (people you know refer you to people you don't know, and they refer you to others), you will get further away from those people you originally began with. But as you go further out, you are generally getting closer to where the jobs are. Be willing to go to even further networking levels. Many people report that they got their jobs through someone six or seven levels removed from where they started.

You will probably want to contact by letter the people you do not know personally. Force yourself to write that letter and then follow up. People who are busy are more likely to spend time with you if you have put some effort into your attempt to see them. Busy people can read your note when they want rather than having to be dragged away from their jobs to receive your phone call. Often, people who receive your note will schedule an appointment for you through their secretary, and you will get in to see them without ever having spoken to them. (On the other hand, some job hunters are in fields where people are used to picking up the phone. *Cold calling* can work for them.)

- Identify the link between you and the person you wish to meet; state why you are interested in talking to that person.
- Give your summary and two short examples of achievements that would interest the reader.
- Indicate that you will call in a few days to see when you can meet briefly.

# People to Contact in Each Target Area

You made a list of organizations to contact in each of your target areas. Now you will show your list to those with whom you network because you want to get in to see those on your list and other organizations as well.

For each target, list below the names of people you know, or know of, or even generic names, such as *lawyers who deal with emerging businesses*. You will contact them through networking or a targeted mailing. The meetings you set up will be networking meetings. However, you will not be idly chatting with people. Instead, you will have your *pitch* ready (see Two-Minute Pitch), and will tell them the target you have in mind. The target will contain the industry or organization size, the kind of position you would like, and the geographic area. For example, "I'm interested in entrepreneurially driven, medium-sized private organizations in the Chicago area. I would do well in finance in that kind of organization. Can you suggest the names of people who might have contact with those kinds of organizations, or do you know anyone who works at that kind of organization?"

You will tell *everyone* the target you are going after—including people you meet on the train and at the barber shop or beauty salon. You never know who knows somebody.

| Target 1 | Target 2 | Target 3 | Target 4 | Other Names |
|---|---|---|---|---|
| | | | | such as: Dentist, Hairdresser, Neighbors |

## A Sample Note for Information-Gathering

Dear Mr. Brown:

Penny Webb suggested I contact you because she thought you could give me the information I need.

I'm interested in heading my career in a different direction. I have been with Acme Corporation for two years and I could stay here forever, but the growth possibilities in the areas that interest me are extremely limited. I want to make a move during the next year, but I want it to be the right move. Penny thought you could give me some ideas.

I'm interested in Human Resources Management. My two years' experience includes work on the development of an Executive Compensation System that measures human resources' complex variables. In addition, I have served as a liaison with other human resource departments in my organization regarding this system.

I'd like some solid information from you on the job possibilities for someone like me. I'd greatly appreciate a half hour of your time and insight. I'll call you in a few days to see when you can spare the time.

Sincerely,

Enclose your résumé if it supports your case. Do not enclose it if your letter is enough or if your résumé hurts your case.

4. **Call to set up the appointment** (first, build up your courage). When you call, you will probably have to start at the beginning. Do not expect a person to remember anything in your letter. Don't even expect anyone to remember that you wrote. Say, for example, "I sent you a letter recently. Did you receive it?"

Remind him of the reason you wrote. Have your letter in front of you—to serve as your script—because you may again have to summarize your background and state some of your accomplishments.

If the person says the organization has no openings at this time, that is okay with you—you were not necessarily looking for a job; you were looking for information or advice about the job possibilities for someone like yourself, or you wanted to know what is happening in the profession, organization, or industry.

If the person says he or she is busy, say, "I'd like to accommodate your schedule. If you like, I could meet you in the early morning or late evening." If he or she is still too busy, say, "Is it okay if we set something up for a month from now? I would call you to confirm so you could reschedule our meeting if it's still not a good time for you. And I assure you I won't take up more than 20 minutes of your time." Do your best to get on the calendar—even if the date is a month away. (Remember that you are trying to form lifelong relationships. Don't force yourself on people, but do get in to see them.)

**Don't let the manager interview you over the phone**. You want to meet in person. You need face-to-face contact to build the relationship and to be remembered by the manager.

*"I'll tell you why we need you on our team . . . you've got your finger on the pulse of today's youth."*

**Rather than leave a message, keep calling back to maintain control**. If no one returns your call, you will feel rejected. But be friendly with the secretary; apologize for calling so often. An example: "Hello, Joan. This is Louise DiSclafani again. I'm sorry to bother you, but is Mr. Johnson free now?"

"No, Ms. DiSclafani, he hasn't returned yet. May I have him call you?"

"Thanks, Joan, but that will be difficult. I'll be in and out a lot, so I'll have to call him back. When is a good time to call?"

**Expect to call seven or eight times**. Accept it as normal business. It is not personal. (See the article on our website, "How to Use the Telephone.")

5. **Prepare for the meeting.** Plan for a networking meeting as thoroughly as you would for any other business meeting. Follow the agenda listed in step 6. **Remember that it is *your* meeting. You are the one running it**. Beforehand,

- Set goals for yourself (information and contacts).
- Jot down the questions you want answered.
- Find out all you can about the person and the person's responsibilities and areas of operations.
- Rehearse your Two-Minute Pitch and accomplishments.

Develop good questions, tailoring them to get the information you need. Make sure what you ask is appropriate for the person with whom you are meeting. You wouldn't, for example, say to a senior vice president of marketing, "So, tell me how marketing works." That question is too general. Instead, do your research—both in the library and by talking with more junior people.

Decide what information you want or what contacts you want to build. Early on in your job search, networking with people at your own level helps you research the field you have targeted. At this point in your search, you are not trying to get hired. Later, meet with more senior people—the ones who are in a position to hire you someday. Then when you meet the senior vice president, ask questions that are more appropriate for someone of that level. You may want to ask about the rewards of that particular business, the frustrations, the type of people who succeed there, the group values, the long-range plans for the business. Prepare three to five open-ended questions about the business or organization that the person will be able to answer.

If you find you are asking each person the same questions, think harder about the information you need, or do more library research. The quality of your questions should change over time as you become more knowledgeable, more of an insider—and more desirable as a prospective employee. In addition, you should be giving information back. If you are truly an insider, you must have information to give.

6. **Conduct the meeting.** If this is important to you, you will continually do better. Sometimes people network forever. They talk to people, but there is no flame inside them. Then one day something happens: They get angry or just fed up with all of this talking to people. They interview better because they have grown more serious. Their time seems more important to them. They stop going through the motions and get the information they need. They interview harder. They feel as though their future is at stake. They don't want to chat with people. They are hungrier. They truly want to work in that industry or in that organization. And the manager they are talking to can sense their seriousness and react accordingly.

---

*. . . we know that suffering produces perseverance; perseverance character; and character hope.*

Romans 5:3–4

# Levels of Networking Contacts

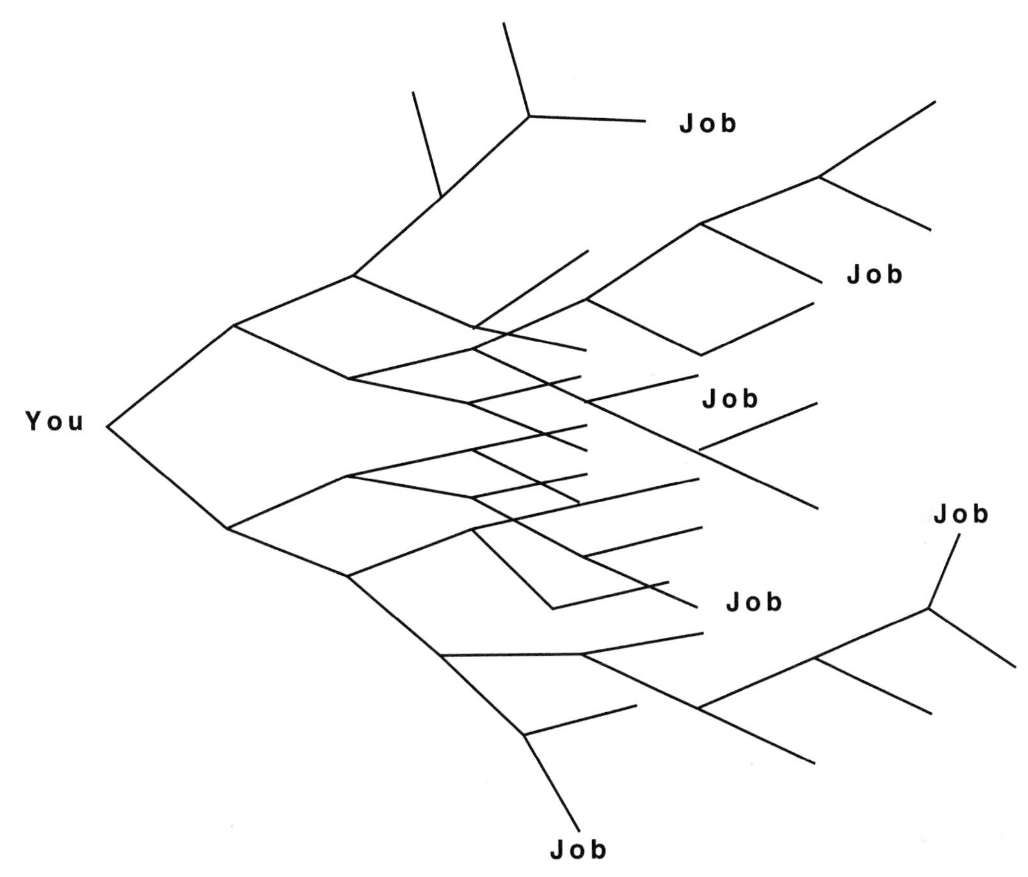


As you build your network of contacts (people you know refer you to people you don't know, and they refer you to others), you will get further away from those people you originally knew personally. But as you go further out, you are generally getting closer to where the jobs are.

Be willing to go to further networking levels. Many people report that they got their jobs six or seven levels removed from where they started.

*If there are obstacles, the shortest line between two points may be the crooked line.*

Bertolt Brecht, *Galileo*

## Format of an Information-Gathering Meeting

Prepare for each meeting. The questions you want to ask and the way you want to pitch, or position, yourself, will vary from one meeting to another. Think it all through. **Review *Format of a Networking Meeting* before *every* networking meeting. If you use it, you will have a good meeting.**

- Exchange Pleasantries—to settle down. This is a chance to size up the other person and allow the other person to size you up. It helps the person to make a transition from whatever he or she was doing before you came in. One or two sentences of small talk: "Your offices are very handsome" or "Your receptionist was very professional" or "You must be thrilled about your promotion."
- Why am I here? The nature of your networking should change over time. In the beginning, you don't know much and are asking basic questions. But you can't keep asking the same questions. Presumably, you have learned something in your earlier meetings. As you move along, you should be asking different, higher level questions—and you should also be in a position to give some information back to people with whom you are meeting. That's what makes you an insider—someone who knows a lot about the field.

This is a basic example of "Why I am here": "Thanks so much for agreeing to meet with me. David Madison thought you could give me the advice I need. I'm meeting with accounting managers in the Chicago area because I want to relocate here." If the meeting is *in response to a targeted mailing,* you may say something like: "I'm so glad you agreed to meet with me. I've been following your organization's growth in the international area and thought it would be great to meet with you." Remind the person of how you got his or her name and why you are there. He or she may have forgotten the contents of your letter or who referred you.

Here are additional suggestions on "Why I am here" (notice how there is a progression going from early on to later in the search process):

- I'm trying to decide what my career path should be. I have these qualifications and I'm trying to decide how to use them. For example, I'm good at ____ and ____. I think they add up to____. What do you think?
- I want to get into publishing, and I'm meeting people in the field. Dr. Cowitt, my dentist, knew you worked in this industry and thought you would be a good person for me to talk to.
- I've researched the publishing industry and think the operations area would be a good fit for me. I was especially interested in learning more about your organization's operations area, and I was thrilled when Charles Conlin at the Publishing Association suggested I contact you.
- I have met with a number of people in the publishing industry, and I think some meetings may turn into job offers. I'd like your insight about which organizations might be the best fit for me. I wrote to you because I will be in this industry soon and I know you are one of the most important players in it.
- I've worked in the publishing industry for five years and have also learned sophisticated computer programming at night. I am looking for a situation that would combine both areas because the growth opportunities are limited in my present firm. Vivian Belen thought I should speak with you, since your organization is so highly computerized.
- Establish credibility with your Two-Minute Pitch. (For more information about this important part of the meeting, see that chapter.) After you say why you are there, they are likely to say something like "How can I help you?" You

respond: "I wanted to ask you a few things, but first let me give you an idea of who I am." There are a number of reasons for doing this:

1. The person will be in a better position to help you if he or she knows something about you.
2. It's impolite to ask a lot of questions without telling the person who you are.
3. You are trying to form a relationship with this person—to get to know each other a bit.

- Ask questions that are appropriate for this person. Really think through what you want to ask. Perhaps have your list of questions in front of you: You will look serious and keep on track.
- As he or she answers your questions, talk more about yourself if appropriate. "That's interesting. The fact is that I've had a lot of pubic relations experience in the jobs I've held." By the time you leave the meeting, you should know something about each other.
- Ask for referrals if appropriate. This is an opportunity to extend your network. "I've made a list of organizations I'm interested in. What do you think of them?" "Are there other organizations you would suggest?" "Whom do you think I should contact at each of the good organizations on this list?" "Could you tell me something about the person you suggested at that organization?" "May I use your name?"

As you probe, they may respond that they do not know of any job openings. That's okay with you. You simply need to meet with more people in this industry, whether or not they have positions available: "I'm just trying to get as much information as possible."

Some job hunters get annoyed when they go away without contacts. They are thinking short-term and are not trying to build long-term relationships. But you were not *entitled* to a meeting with the manager. He or she was kind to meet with you at all.

If you get no contacts, be very grateful for what you do get. It may be that he or she has no names to give. On the other hand, so many people network incorrectly (aggressively and abrasively), and managers are often reluctant to give out names until the job hunter has kept in touch for a number of months and proved a sincere interest. Many managers feel used by job hunters who simply want names and are not interested in *them*.

- Gather more information about the referrals. (For instance, "What is Harvey Kaplan like?")
- Formal time of gratitude. Thank the person for the time spent.
- Offer to stay in touch. Constantly making new contacts is not as effective as keeping in touch with old ones. "May I keep in touch with you to let you know how I'm doing?" You might call later for future contacts, information, and the like.
- Write a follow-up note, and be sure to follow up again later. This is most important and a powerful tool. State how the meeting helped you or how you used the information. Be sincere. If appropriate, offer to keep the manager informed of your progress.
- Recontact your network every two to three months. Even after you get a job, these people will be your contacts to help you in your new job—and maybe you can even help them! After all, you are building lifelong relationships, aren't you? See the chapter *Following Up When There Is No Immediate Job*.

Remember:

- You are *not* there simply to get names. It may often happen that you will get excellent information but no names of others to contact. That's fine.
- Be grateful for whatever help people give you, and assume they are doing their best.

- Remember, too, that this is *your* meeting and you must try to get all you can out of it.
- This is not a job interview. In a job interview, you are being interviewed. In a networking meeting, you are *conducting* the meeting.

**Follow precisely the *Format of a Networking Meeting*.** If you use it, you will have a good meeting.

# Format of a Networking Meeting

Prepare for each meeting. The questions you want to ask, and the way you want to *pitch* or position yourself, will vary from one meeting to another. Think it all through.

Be sure to read this chapter in detail for more information on the networking, or information-gathering, process.

**The Format of the Meeting**

- **Pleasantries**—this is a chance to size up the other person and allow the other person to size you up. It's a chance to settle down. Just two or three sentences of small talk are enough.
- **Why am I here?** For example, "Thanks so much for agreeing to meet with me. Ruth Robbins thought you could give me the advice I need. I'm trying to talk to accounting managers in the Chicago area because I want to relocate here." Remind the person of how you got his or her name and why you are there.
- **Establish credibility with your Two-Minute Pitch.** After you tell the person why you are there, they are likely to say something like: "Well, how can I help you?" Then you respond, for example: "I wanted to ask you a few things, but first let me give you an idea of who I am." There are a number of reasons for doing this:
    1. The person will be in a better position to help you if he or she knows something about you.
    2. It's impolite to ask a lot of questions without telling the person who you are.
    3. You are trying to form a relationship with this person—to get to know each other a bit.
- **Ask questions** that are appropriate for this person. Really think through what you want to ask. For example, you wouldn't say to the marketing manager: "So what's it like to be in marketing?" You would ask that of a more junior person. Consider having your list of questions in front of you so you will look serious and keep on track.
- As the person is answering your questions, **tell him or her more about yourself if appropriate.** For example, you might say: "That's interesting. When I was at XYZ Company, we handled that problem in an unusual way. In fact, I worked on the project. . . ."
- **Ask for referrals if appropriate.** For example, "I'm trying to get in to see people at the organizations on this list. Do you happen to know anyone at these organizations? . . . May I use your name?"
- **Gather more information about the referrals.** (Such as: "What is Ellis Chase like?")
- **Formal time of gratitude.** Thank the person for the time spent.
- **Offer to stay in touch.** Remember that making a lot of new contacts is not as effective as making not quite so many contacts and then *recontacting* those people later.
- **Write a follow-up note, and be sure to follow up again later.**

**Remember**

- You are *not* there simply to get names. It may often happen that you will get excellent information but no names of others to contact. That's fine.
- Be grateful for whatever help people give you and assume they are doing their best.
- Remember, too, that this is *your* meeting and you must try to get all you can out of it.
- This is not a job interview. In a job interview, you are being interviewed. In a networking meeting, *you* are conducting the meeting.

---

*Business is a game, the greatest game in the world if you know how to play it.*

Thomas J. Watson, Jr., former CEO of IBM

## Other Meeting Pointers

- The heart of the meeting is relating your good points in the best way possible. Be concise and to the point. Don't be embarrassed about appearing competent. Be able to recite your Two-Minute Pitch and key accomplishments without hesitation.
- Keep control of the meeting. Don't let the person with whom you're meeting talk too much or too little. If he goes on about something inappropriate, jump in when you can and relate it to something you want to say. Remember, this is *your* meeting.
- Find out which of your achievements he's really impressed with. That's his hot button, so keep referring to the achievements he likes.
- Be self-critical as you go along with this process. Don't become so enamored with the process that you become inflexible. Don't become a professional information gatherer or job hunter.
- Interview hard. *Probe.* Be prepared to answer hard questions in return.
- Take notes when you are getting what you want. This lets the manager know that the meeting is going well and encourages more of the same. The person to whom you are talking is just like everyone else who is being interviewed—everyone wants to do well.
- Show enthusiasm and interest. Lean forward in your chair when appropriate. Ask questions that sincerely interest you, and sincerely try to get the answers.
- Don't be soppy and agree with everything. It's better to disagree mildly and then come to some agreement than to agree with everything 100 percent.
- Remember your goals. Don't go away from any meeting empty-handed. Get information or the names of other contacts.
- Don't overstay your welcome. Fifteen minutes or half an hour may be all a busy person can give you. Never take more than one and a half to two hours.
- If you are meeting over lunch, go someplace simple so you are not constantly interrupted by waiters.
- If you are looking for a job, don't conceal that fact.
- **If the person you are meeting with suggests passing on your résumé to someone else, that is usually not helpful**—unless you know who the person is and can follow up yourself. Say, "I hate to put you to that trouble. Would you mind if I called her myself and used your name?" If the manager does not agree to this, then you must accept his or her wishes.
- **If the person you are meeting tells you of a job opening**, say, "I'd like to know more about that job possibility, but I also had a few questions I'd like to ask you." Continue to get your questions answered. If you follow up only on the job lead, you will probably wind up with no job and no information.
- It is important to remember that these are only suggestions. You must adopt your own style, your own techniques. You'll find that the more you meet with people, the better you'll get at it. Start out with friends or in low-risk situations. You do not want to meet with your most promising prospects until you are highly skilled at networking meetings. The more you practice, the better you will become.

---

*Nothing great was ever achieved without enthusiasm.*

Ralph Waldo Emerson, *Circles*

## Who Is a Good Contact?

A contact is any connection between you and the person with whom you are hoping to meet. Most often the contact is someone you've met in another information-gathering meeting, but think a little, and you will find other, creative ways to establish links with people. (Also see the chapter *Targeted Mailings: Just Like Networking.*) Here are a few real-life examples:

**Example one**: A man's mother used to clean the office of the president of a good-sized corporation. One day the son wrote to the president, "My mother cleaned your office for 12 years." He was granted a meeting with the president and shown a good deal of courtesy. This may seem far-fetched, but it happened.

**Example two**: Clara wanted to leave an organization where she had worked for three years. She thought about the person who had taught her data processing years earlier. Her teacher had left the organization to form his own business. She had never kept track of him, but he had impressed her as worldly, and she thought he would be a good person to give her advice.

She wrote to him on personal stationery:

> Dear Mr. Jones:
>
> You taught me data processing in 1999. I remember it well, since it was the start of my career, and I thought you would be a good person to give me the advice I need.
>
> I'm interested in making a move during the next year or so, but I want it to be the right move.
>
> I now have three years of computer experience, specializing in financial and personnel systems. I have used state-of-the-art languages and have worked on complicated systems. You may be interested in some of the specific things I've done:
>
> - Worked on a three-person team in developing a human resources system that linked salary administration, performance reviews, and employee benefits packages.
> - Worked on a sophisticated accounting system that allowed all of the PCs in the organization to access certain information on the mainframe.
>
> I'll call you in a few days to set up a mutually convenient time to get together.

Of course, the man did not know Clara from Adam. She had been one of 28 students in the class he taught at a large organization and was probably the shyest of the group. In fact, after she wrote to him, she became afraid and did not call for two weeks.

When she finally did call, she was told the business had been acquired by another firm and her former teacher had moved from Philadelphia to Chicago. She felt like a fool calling Chicago, but she finally got up the nerve.

When she identified herself to the secretary, she heard, "Clara Horvath! We've been trying to reach you everywhere. Your note didn't contain a phone number!" The secretary said Clara's former teacher was now a senior vice president in Chicago—and had sent the note to the head of the Philadelphia office.

When she called the Philadelphia office, the secretary said, "Clara Horvath! We were hoping you would call. Your note didn't have your phone number."

The secretary arranged for Clara to see the head of the Philadelphia office, who developed a job description for her. According to organizational policy, the job would have to be posted internally and the head of the Philadelphia office would have to interview qualified in-house candidates. After developing a job description to suit Clara, however, the chances were good that he would not find someone internally with her same qualifications.

Clara went to work at the company, and it was many months before she finally met the man who was her former teacher. Neither one of them recognized each other, but that was fine!

---

*Many things are lost for want of asking.*

George Herbert, *Jacula Prudentum*

## Other Sources of Contacts

Be sure to read the chapters on research for lots of ideas about associations, alumni groups, and so on. In addition, you can consider

- Contacting acquaintances—even more than friends. Friends may be reluctant to act as contacts for you. You are more of a reflection on them than you would be for an acquaintance. And if things don't work out, they could lose your friendship—but acquaintances don't have as much to lose.

- Network every chance you get—on the bus, at parties. Don't be like those job hunters who don't tell anyone they are looking for a job. You never know who knows someone who can help you. Everyone you meet knows lots of people.
- Don't contact someone on the strength of *Dun and Bradstreet, Poor's,* or other directories. There is no true link between you and that person. Use your imagination to think of a better link.

## Out-of-Town Search

The principles are the same wherever you are. If you have targeted another city, sometimes it is difficult to get face-to-face meetings with some of the people you would like to talk to. But plan ahead. If you are making business trips to, attending seminars or taking a vacation in that city, think about with whom you would like to make contact there for your network. Telephone or write to him or her well in advance for an appointment. Keep your ears open about who might be coming through your area, and try to get time with him or her if you can.

## Summary

Networking is a powerful job-hunting tool—if it is used properly, which most often it is not. It is also a life skill that you can and should use throughout your career. Become expert at it, and do not abuse people. Give them something back.

*Keep away from people who belittle your ambitions. Small people always do that, but the really great make you feel that you, too, can become great.*

Mark Twain

*Our dignity is not in what we do but what we understand. The whole world is doing things.*

George Santayana, *Winds of Doctrine*

*No matter what accomplishments you make, somebody helps you.*

Althea Gibson, in *Time,* August 26, 1957

*It is better to die on one's feet than to live on one's knees, but some individuals appear actually to believe that it is better to crawl around on one's bare belly.*

Nathan Hare, in *The Black Scholar,* November 1969

*God does not die on the day when we cease to believe in a personal deity, but we die on the day when our lives cease to be illuminated by the steady radiance, renewed daily, of a wonder, the source of which is beyond all reason.*

Dag Hammarskjold

*Life is a series of collisions with the future; it is not a sum of what we have been but what we yearn to be.*

José Ortega y Gasset

# Networking Cover Letters

**Asking for advice is appropriate early on in your search.**

Jared Kreiner

20 Trinity Place
New York, New York 10000
(222) 555-2231
JKreiner@earthlink.net

March 10, 20XX

Mr. David Madison
Executive Vice President
Young & Rubicam
285 Madison Avenue
New York, New York 10017

Dear Mr. Madison:

I am following up the suggestion of Michael Saunders, who refers to himself as a fan of yours, and am writing to ask for your counsel on my current career plans.

I have recently decided to leave my present company, McGraw-Hill Publishing, and continue my career elsewhere. Michael thought you could give me the advice I need.

I have targeted the advertising industry as part of my search strategy because I believe that with my skills in financial planning, combined with my degree in international business, I could make an important contribution to good business management. In addition, I believe I would enjoy working in the dynamic and creative environment of most agencies.

Thus, Michael suggested that I particularly ask for your response to my thoughts on how my experience in finance in the publishing industry can be productively employed in advertising.

I look forward to speaking with you, and will call in a few days to see when we can meet.

Sincerely,

Jared Kreiner

**This note was handwritten on informal off-white stationery.**

May 19, 20xx

Dear Mr. Sims,

Angie Cayo suggested I contact you because she thought you could give me the information I need.

I'm interested in heading my career in a different direction. I've been with Rohm and Haas for two years and I could stay here forever, but the growth possibilities in the areas that interest me are extremely limited. I want to make a move during the next year, but I want it to be the right move. Angie thought you could give me some ideas.

I'm interested in human resources. My two years' experience in data processing included work on Rohm and Haas' Salary Administration system. What I'd like from you is some solid information on the job possibilities for someone like me.

I'd greatly appreciate half an hour of your time and insight. I'll call you in a few days to see when you can spare the time.

Sincerely,

Mariya Katsnelson

# How to Contact Organizations Directly

*I don't know anything about luck. I've never banked on it and I'm afraid of people who do. Luck to me is something else: hard work and realizing what is opportunity and what is not.*

Lucille Ball

Julie got all of her job leads through a direct-mail campaign. She developed the list for her campaign through Internet research. Direct-mail campaigns can also be done using snail mail, and they can be even more effective. So be sure to consider snail mail as well.

Beth also used direct mail but delivered her message through snail mail. To develop her interviewing skills and investigate each target area, Beth first had meetings at firms she did not care about. She treated these meetings as networking meetings. Beth probed, for example, to find out what the manager thought of other organizations on her list. If the comments were generally negative, she dropped those organizations. If the comments were positive, she asked if the manager might know someone in that organization she could contact. She got a lot of mileage out of her campaign because she combined direct mail with networking and worked the system with great energy.

The entire process took only one and a half months. Beth had clear targets, followed the process, and prepared thoroughly for her meetings. She explored career possibilities in which she had been somewhat interested and refined her career direction. She turned down a number of job offers before she accepted a high-level position that allowed her to combine her strongest skill area with something that was new to her and satisfied her long-range motivated skills. Beth took a two-week vacation before she started that job. She deserved it.

Jack's campaign strategy was very different. Jack is intelligent, articulate, research-oriented—and also very shy. He targeted an industry that would result in a career change for him. He had read a lot on this industry, and wanted to find out the job possibilities within it.

Jack meticulously researched organizations and selected 20 in which he was seriously interested. They were huge corporations, and that made it relatively easy to get the names of people to contact. If he had simply mailed to that list, however, he might have gotten no response. As you will see later, 20 names is generally not enough for a direct-mail campaign. The effort would have been even more futile in Jack's case because he had, essentially, no hands-on experience in that field.

Jack did a targeted mailing—that is, he wrote to the 20 people and *followed up with phone calls* to all of them. His well-written and convincing letter proved his sincere interest in and knowledge of the field. He sent it—without a résumé, because he was making a major career change—and told each of the 20 he would call him or her. He sent all the letters at once, and called every person. It was quite an effort. Jack got in to see just about every person on his list, and—as usually happens—some of them took a personal interest in his case. They gave him the names of others and told him how to break into the field. Two of his contacts volunteered to sponsor him in their organization's training program.

## How It Works

Approximately 20 percent of all jobs are found through direct-mail campaigns. This technique is even more effective when you combine it with networking—as both Beth and Jack did.

You will do better in your direct-mail campaign when you:

- have clearly identified your target market
- are familiar with the problems faced by organizations in that market
- know what you have to offer to solve its problems

Know enough about your target market to compose an appropriate cover letter and to hold your own in a meeting. If you don't know enough, learn more through library research or networking. If you feel that you may be caught off-guard in a meeting because of a lack of knowledge of your target market, do not use this technique until you have gained at least some knowledge. These are not job interviews, but exploratory meetings that may lead to:

- more information
- names of other people to contact
- a job interview

*Conduct the meeting using the same format as that of a networking meeting.*

Don't let the interviewer know you blanketed the market. If an organization wants to see you, quickly do a little research on it. Tell the manager you wrote to him as a result of your research, and name something specific about the organization that interested you.

It doesn't matter if your meetings come from a direct contact or from networking. What matters is that you get in to see people who are in a position to hire you.

## Benefits of This Technique

Direct mail blankets the market. In one fell swoop, you can find out what the chances are for someone like you in that market. You *market test* what you have to offer and also get your name out quickly to prospective employers. This technique is fast and as complete as you want it to be, as opposed to networking, which is slower and hits your target in a spotty manner.

## What Is a Targeted Mailing?

A targeted mailing is direct mail followed by a phone call. Use it when you would like to see every person on your small list. Research so you can write customized letters (you may want to call for annual reports, for example, or talk to people to get information about an organization). Follow the process for networking, paying special attention to the follow-up call, which requires a great deal of persistence. As with networking, you want to meet with people whether or not they have a job to offer.

## An Easy Way to Contact Lots of People

Typically, job hunters do not contact many people. Either the job hunter is unemployed and has the time to contact lots of people but may be suffering from low self-esteem or is employed and simply does not have the time to contact people during the day. The direct-mail campaign allows a person to contact lots of potential employers despite reluctance or a lack of time.

Sometimes job hunters hit a slump and find networking overly stressful. Direct mail can help you get unstuck. You can hide away for a short while and grind out a mailing. You can sound more self-confident on paper than you actually feel and get your act together before you go out and talk to people. A direct-mail campaign can be a way out of a bind. But eventually you must talk to people. You cannot get a job through the mail.

Don't use this technique to avoid people forever. Remember, you are writing so you can get in to see them.

## The Numbers You'll Need

In a small industry, your list will be smaller. In a larger industry, your list may be so large that you'll want to hit only a portion of it, as a test, and then hit another portion later.

The *response rate* is measured by the number of meetings you get divided by the number of pieces you mailed. Meetings count as responses; rejection letters do not. Meetings count because there is the possibility of continuing your job search in that direction. Rejection letters, no matter how flattering, have ended your search in that particular direction.

In direct mailing, a 4 percent response rate is considered very good. The basic rule of thumb is this: A mailing of 200 good names results in 7 or 8 meetings, which result in 1 job offer.

If your list is smaller, you may still do okay if you are well suited to that target and if there is a need for your services. If, however, your list has only 10 names, you must network in or use a targeted mailing with a follow-up phone call.

Another factor that affects your response rate is the industry to which you are writing. Certain industries are very people-oriented and are more likely to talk to you. Targeting industries that have a great demand for your service should result in a lot of responses.

Assuming that the job you are seeking is reasonable (that is, you have the appropriate qualifications and there are positions of that type available in the geographic area you are targeting), persistent inquiries will eventually turn up some openings.

## Should You Enclose Your Résumé?

If your résumé helps your case, enclose it. Beth enclosed her résumé; Jack did not. Direct-mail experts have proved that the more enclosures, the greater the response rate. You never know what may *grab* the reader, and the reader is likely to glance at each enclosure. Your résumé, if it supports your case and is enticing, is another piece to capture the reader's attention. I have been called for meetings because of what was on page three of my résumé.

If, however, your résumé hurts your case, change it—or leave it out altogether. A résumé may hurt your case when you are attempting a dramatic career change, as Jack was. (Read the chapter *How to Change Careers* to get more ideas on how you can support your case.)

---

*Passion costs me too much to bestow it on every trifle.*

Thomas Adams

# Format for a Cover Letter

*What makes men happy is liking what they have to do. This is a principle on which society is not founded.*

Claude Adrien Helvetius

The format you follow for your cover letter essentially can be the same whether you enclose your résumé or not. Your cover letter focuses your pitch more precisely than your résumé does and makes the reader see your résumé in that light. You can pitch to a very precise segment of the market by making only minor changes in the letter. The format for your cover letter follows.

**Paragraph 1—The grabber.** Start with the point of greatest interest to your target market. This is the equivalent of a headline in an ad.

If your background is enough of a grabber for the target market to which you are writing, use it. For example, if you want a job in sales and have an excellent track record in that area, then open with a terrific sales accomplishment. The following *verbal* pitch was used by a student who worked part-time at the same company for three years while he was in school.

> I've been in sales for three years. Although I was hired by my employer to do public relations, I ended up also selling. First, I sold our company's services to individuals who called to ask about our company. I just happened to be the one answering the phone. I did so well, that my boss asked me to do follow-up calls to corporations encouraging *them* to purchase our services. I was assigned 150 companies, spoke with them only over the phone, and had landed three major accounts within the first four months.

When he wrote it in a cover letter, here is how it read:

> I've been in sales for three years and have been responsible for 150 corporate accounts. I landed three major corporate sales within the first four months strictly through cold calling.

On the other hand, you can open your letter with a statement that shows you understand the problems faced by the industry to which you are selling your services. A successful letter to accounting firms started like this:

> Many accounting firms are being deluged with résumés from young hopefuls with an MBA or even an accounting degree. While the educational background of the applicants may give firms some comfort, many companies find the new hires don't last long. You may need more than good credentials. You may need someone who has a track record of loyalty, hands-on experience in accounting as well as five accounting courses.

Here's a variation on the same theme—but aimed at organizations that are probably doing well financially:

> I know this is a time of rapid growth and high activity for biotech firms. I believe this is also a time when biotech firms must be as effective as possible to maintain their competitive edge. If you are looking for new sci-

entists—either on an ad hoc or a permanent basis—consider a person like me.

If you have done an internship or part-time work for a well-known organization in an area that would be of interest to your target market, you could start your letter like this:

I am at present with SONY Music Company in a position where I. . . .

If you are targeting a small number of organizations, mention your specific interest in each one:

I have been interested in [your organization] for a while because of. . . .

**Paragraph 2—A summary of your background** aimed at a target—perhaps taken from the summary statement on your résumé.

**Paragraph 3—Your key accomplishments** that would be of interest to this target market. These can be written in a bulleted or paragraph format. Make them lively and interesting.

**Paragraph 4** (optional)—**Additional information**. This could include references to your education or personality or other relevant information.

I am high in energy and integrity—persuasive, thorough, and self-confident—a highly motivated self-starter accustomed to working independently within the framework of an organization's policies and goals. I thrive on long hours of work, and enjoy an atmosphere where I am measured by my results, where compensation is directly related to my ability to produce, and where the job is what I make it.

**Final paragraph—The close** (if a targeted mailing, you make a follow-up phone call).

I would appreciate a brief meeting where I can find out more about your organization and I can tell you more about myself. I will call you in a few days to set up a mutually convenient time for us to meet.

Or use this statement for a direct-mail campaign, when you will *not* be making follow-up phone calls, especially to a list to which you have some relationship, such as that of an organization of which you are a member:

I can understand how busy you must be, and therefore do not want to bother you with a follow-up phone call. However, I trust that you will give me a call if you come across information that would be helpful to me in my search. (Or: I trust you will give me a call if you are half as interested in meeting as I am.)

**Be sure to look once more at the cover letter Julie used for her E-mail. You could use the same format for snail mail as well.**

(See the chapter *Case Study: Julie—Getting and Doing Well in Interviews*)

*You gain strength, courage and confidence by every experience in which you really stop to look fear in the face. You are able to say to yourself: "I lived through this horror. I can take the next thing that comes along." . . . You must do the thing you think you cannot do.*

Eleanor Roosevelt

*Happiness is not a matter of events; it depends upon the tides of the mind.*

Alice Meynell

*Pain: an uncomfortable frame of mind that may have a physical basis in something that is being done to the body, or may be purely mental, caused by the good fortune of others.*

Ambrose Bierce

*The man without purpose is like a ship without a rudder—a waif, a nothing, a no man. Have a purpose in life, and, having it, throw such strength of mind and muscle into your work as God has given you.*

Thomas Carlyle

# Targeted Mailings: Just Like Networking

*Life is like playing a violin solo in public and learning the instrument as one goes on.*

Samuel Butler

Networking is not the only way to job hunt. Consider targeted mailings when

- You want to see a particular person but have no formal contact. You must think of how you can create some tie-in to that person and contact him or her directly.
- You have selected 20 to 30 organizations in your target market that you really want to get in to see, and there are only a few jobs that would be appropriate for you in each company.

For the 20 or 30 organizations you have chosen, research the appropriate person to contact in each one. Ask each for a meeting—whether or not they have a job for you. You want to get in to see them *all* because your target is very small.

---

*There's nothing to writing. All you do is sit down at a typewriter and open a vein.*

Walter ("Red") Smith,
in *Reader's Digest,* July 1982

## The Letter

- **Paragraph 1:** The opening paragraph for a targeted mailing would follow the format for a networking letter: State the reason you are writing and **establish the contact** you have with the reader.

> Congratulations on your new position! I know you are extremely busy (I've heard about it from others). After you are settled in, I would be interested in meeting with you. I think it would be mutually beneficial for us to meet, although I have no fixed idea of what could come of it.

After you have found out something about the person or the organization, pretend you are sitting with that person right now. What would you *say* to him or her? Your opening should reflect whatever you know about the organization or the person

> Whenever people talk about organizations with excellent internal temporary services departments, Schaeffer's name always comes up. In fact, the people who run the Amalgamated Center, where I am now assigned, speak often of the quality of your work. I am interested in becoming a consultant in this field, and I hope to meet with you.

- **Paragraph 2:** Give a **summary about yourself.**
- **Paragraph 3:** Note a few **key accomplishments that would be of interest to this target.**
- **Paragraph 4:** Ask for **half an hour** of their time, and say you will **call them in a few days.** For example,

I hope you will allow me half an hour of your time and insight to explore this area. I will call you in a few days to set up a mutually agreeable time.

If you plan to follow up with a phone call, say so. (But if you say so, do it—or you may get no response while they wait for your call.)

*There is no way of writing well and also of writing easily.*

Anthony Trollope, *Barchester Towers*

## Out-of-Town Search

For an *out-of-town search* (perhaps placed next to the last paragraph):

As a result of many years' residence in Seattle, I would prefer to live and work in that area. In fact, I am in Seattle frequently visiting family and can arrange to meet with you at your office.

## Scannable Letters

As we have seen, other variations include the use of **underlining key points,** which can increase your response rate. This helps the busy reader scan the letter, be drawn in, and want to read the rest. Underlining makes certain key points pop out at the reader—anywhere in your text. Underline parts of sentences in no more than five places. Read the underlined parts to make sure they sound sensible when read together, have a flow, and make your point.

Even when I look at my own letters, I sometimes don't want to read them before I make them scannable. I rephrase my letters, underlining in a way that will make sense to the reader. People will read the salutation, then the first few words of your letter, and then the parts you have underlined. If they find these things compelling, they'll go back and read the rest of your letter.

Underlining should make sense. Don't underline the word *developed,* for instance, because that doesn't make sense. Underline the word *after,* which is *what* you developed, because that's probably the compelling part.

*Who has begun has half done.*
*Have the courage to be wise. Begin!*

Horace, Epistles

## Do What Is Appropriate

Strange as it may seem, **sometimes it can be very effective to ignore all of this.** Do what works in your target market. It is sometimes better to follow your instincts rather than listen to the experts. You're smart. Think it through. Then make up your own mind.

## The Follow-Up Call (after a Targeted Mailing)

When you call, you will probably have to **start again from the beginning.** Do not expect them to remember anything in your letter. Do not even expect them to remember that you wrote to them. For example, when you phone:

- Say, "I sent you a letter recently. Did you receive it?"
- Remind them of the reason you wrote. You may again have to summarize your background and state some of your accomplishments.
- If they say they have no job openings at this time, that is okay with you—you were not necessarily looking for a job *with them;* you were looking for information or advice about the job possibilities for someone like you, or perhaps you wanted to know what is happening in the profession, organization, or industry.

**Leave messages that you called, but do not ask to have them call you back.** Chances are, they won't, and you will feel rejected. However, be friendly with the secretary, and apologize for calling so often. If she would like to have her boss call you back, tell her thanks, but you will be in and out and her boss will be unable to reach you: You will have to call again. After the first call, try not to leave your name again. **Expect to call seven or eight times.** Do not become discouraged. It is not personal.

*Take calculated risks. That is quite different from being rash.*

Gen. George S. Patton, letter to his son, June 6, 1944

## The Meeting

When you go in for your meeting, **handle it as you would a networking meeting** (unless the manager turns it into a job interview):

- Exchange pleasantries.
- State the reason you are there and why you wanted to see this particular person.
- Give your Two-Minute Pitch.
- Tell the manager how he or she can help you. Get the information you want, as well as a few names of other people you should be talking to.

As we have said, **be grateful for whatever help people give you.** They are helping you the best they can. If they do not give you the names of others to contact, perhaps they cannot because of a feeling of insecurity in their own jobs. Appreciate whatever they do give you.

## Form a Relationship

Take notes during your meeting. Your follow-up notes will be more appropriate, and then you will feel free to contact this person later. Keep in touch with people on a regular basis. Those who know you well will be more likely to help you.

A targeted mailing is a very powerful technique for hitting *every* organization in a small target area. A direct-mail campaign hits every organization in a larger target. Both can dramatically move your job hunt along. Try them!

## Follow Up

**Follow up with a customized note specifically acknowledging the help you received.** These notes follow the same concept as follow-ups to networking meetings.

## Final Thoughts

You will strike sparks with certain people you meet. They will develop a true interest in you and will surprise you with their help. I have had people invite me to luncheons to introduce me to important people or call me when they heard news that would interest me. I have even made new friends this way.

Of course, I have done my part, too, by keeping in touch to let them know how my campaign was going. If you are sincere about your search, you will find that the people you meet will also be sincere and will help. It can also be a very heartwarming experience.

*The way to get good ideas is to get lots of ideas and throw the bad ones away.*

Linus Pauling, American chemist

## CASE STUDY *Ahmed*

## Research and Focus

Ahmed, 26, had just moved to the United States from Turkey, so he had no contacts here. He had a background in international sales and trading.

He targeted nine major employers and did extensive research on each one. Then he wrote to the head of international sales at each of the nine companies. In his introductory paragraph, he said things like "I notice that your international sales have declined from 6 percent to 3 percent over the last year. I find that very disturbing. I was wondering why that is happening, given the state of the market now. . . ."

Paragraph two was his summary. Paragraph three was his bulleted accomplishments. Paragraph four was the close: "I would really appreciate meeting you. . . ."

He called only two of them—because the other seven called him before he had a chance. This targeted mailing resulted in nine meetings and three job offers.

## Direct Contact Requires Research and Excellent Writing Skills

Targeted mail works only if you've done your research and if you're a good writer. Furthermore, you must target the right person and have something interesting to say to each person you are contacting. That's why direct contact works best for job hunters who clearly understand their target markets and the issues that are important in them. And that's also why most people do not attempt direct contact until after they have done their research—through preliminary networking or the library.

## Are You Sincere?

It's not enough to write to people and expect to get in to see them. They are probably busy with their own jobs, and may be contacted by quite a few people.

Unless you sincerely want to see a person, you won't develop strategies to figure out how to get in to see him or her. You won't do your research. You won't do the follow-up phone calls that are required to prove your sincerity. You won't prevail when someone doesn't return your phone calls.

If you really want to see this person, you'll persevere. And you won't mind asking for an appointment one month from now if he or she is too busy to see you now. You may even say, "I know you're busy now. How about if we schedule something for a month from now, and I'll call you in advance to confirm?"

## To Enclose Your Résumé or Not?

A cover story in *Time* magazine was titled "Junk Mail." People said, "Why do junk-mail companies enclose so many things in these envelopes that we get? They're wasting paper." In the Letters to the Editor, the junk-mail companies said they had no choice because the response rate increased so dramatically with the number of additional enclosures that have the same message. If they have fewer enclosures, their response rate decreases dramatically.

The same is true for the mailings you are sending. Some people say, "If they see my résumé, they'll know I'm job hunting." But they'll probably know it anyway from your letter. People are very sophisticated today.

My rule of thumb is this: If it supports your case and it has a message that complements your cover letter, then enclose your résumé. You can say, "I've enclosed my résumé to let you know something more about me." If you have a brilliant résumé, why not enclose it?

On the other hand, if you want to make a career change, you may not want to enclose your résumé because you can probably make a stronger case without it.

Do what is appropriate for you. Try it both ways and see which works better for you and your situation.

## Stating Your Accomplishments in Your Cover Letter

Think of which of your accomplishments are of interest to your target market. You may want to list different accomplishments for the different industries to which you are writing.

Rank your bulleted accomplishments generally in order of importance to the reader, as opposed to chronologically or alphabetically. It may be that some other logic would be more appropriate in your case. Then do that.

## CASE STUDY *Rick*
## Out-of-Town Search

A Five O'Clock Club job hunter was looking for a job in Denver. He conducted research by getting a listing of companies from the Denver Chamber of Commerce. He called each company and asked for the name of the department head for the area in which he was interested. He wrote to each one, and followed up with a phone call.

He was employed at the time. Yet most of his effort did not take time away from his job. He did his research and wrote his letters on the evenings and weekends. Net-working would have been an impossible way for him to start his search, especially in another part of the country. But after he had made these initial contacts and had traveled to Denver, then he could network around.

He wound up with something like 80 companies to contact—too many for follow-up phone calls. Even 20 is a lot. He followed up with 20 companies and scheduled a three-day trip to Denver. Before he went, he had set up eight meetings—for the first two days of his trip. When he met with those first eight, he networked into four additional companies and held those meetings on the third day of his trip.

He didn't have a lot of money, so he couldn't stay long in Denver. But this is also the best way to conduct an out-of-town search—a few days at a time.

When job hunters visit a city for two weeks and hope that something will happen, they usually come home empty-handed. It's better to do your research, contact all of the organizations ahead of time, and go there with meetings already set up. The meetings could be with search firms, in answer to ads, or through networking or direct contact.

Go for three days. Tell the people you meet that you are planning to be in town again in a few weeks and would like to meet with other people in their organization or in other organizations. Go back home, do more work, return in another three or four weeks, and stay for another three days. Then you develop momentum in your out-of-town campaign. A one-time visit rarely works.

Rick went back again six weeks later. It took a few more visits to land the job he wanted, but he did it all with direct and targeted mail as the basis for his campaign, supplemented by networking.

The following pages contain case studies of people who have been successful with targeted mailings. Rather than simply copying their letters, **think of *one* actual individual on your list to whom you are writing, and think of the compelling things you should say to make that person want to meet with you.** Even if you write exactly that same kind of letter to 20 people, it will sound more sincere and have more life if you write that first letter with a particular person in mind.

---

*Without effort we cannot attain any of our goals in life, no matter what the advertisements may claim to the contrary. Anyone who fears effort, anyone who backs off from frustration and possibly even pain will never get anywhere. . . .*

Erich Fromm, *For the Love of Life*

**Here's the cover letter that Julie had written earlier to land an internship. We've modified it to make it a targeted mailing (requires a follow-up phone call).**

Julie Angelo

---

julieangelo@umich.edu

University of Michigan
Box #3124; 76 North Churchill Rd.
Ann Arbor, MI 99999
555-666-4693

angelo555@hotmail.com

863 Erie Avenue
Brewster, MI 99945

**Most Five O'Clock Club letters use exactly the same format:**
Paragraph 1: The opening.
Paragraph 2: A summary about yourself.
Paragraph 3: A few key accomplishments of interest to this target.
Paragraph 4: Ask for a meeting; state who will call whom.

Notice that she used a moderate amount of underlining and bolding to make it easier for the reader to scan the letter to see what she had done.

May 11, 20xx

Mr. James Spiegler
President
Green Tree Architects, Inc.
888 Sixth Avenue
New York, New York 10000

Subject: **Administrator/CAD Drafter—Architecture-related—top student.**

Dear Mr. Spiegler:

I am writing to you because yours is a prestigious firm in the architecture industry, and I am an architectural student interested in summer work at a firm such as yours. I'd like to meet with you or someone else in your firm to find out more about your company and to tell you about myself. Even if you have no openings right now, you never know when you may need someone like me.

I have 10 months' experience with a civil engineering firm. You may be interested in some of the specific things I have done:

- Served as an **assistant office manager,** organizing client proposals and setting up manuals. I also answered an 8-line phone.
- My **basic AutoCAD experience** includes becoming the person engineers turned to when they wanted routine things done.

As an Architectural Studies major, I tend to **be among the best in my class,** winning contests and doing excellent work. I would be excellent at client contact, helping architects get ready for meetings, putting proposals together, and assisting with AutoCAD work. I would appreciate a meeting and will call your secretary in a few days to find out who you would like me to meet with and when.

With thanks,

Julie Angelo

**Attachment:** résumé

**This letter was sent after a cold call to Ms. Rosenberg about the possibility of a stockbrokering position.**

James J. Borland, III

140 West 81st Street
New York, New York 10000
JBorland678@landmine.net

July 17, 20xx

Ms. Renée Rosenberg
Merrill Lynch
Liberty Place
165 Broadway
New York, New York 10000

Dear Renée:

I appreciate your offer to review and forward on my résumé. I think you'll see how I've used my skills of persuasion throughout the years. For example, while working on the "Friends of Bill Thomas" Mayoral Campaign, I was on the phone all day long convincing politicians across a broad spectrum to either publicly commit to my candidate or, as was the case at the outset when resistance was strong and reactions negative, to cooperate behind the scenes. The continual give and take involved a lot of listening as people wanted to state their case, vent frustrations with personalities, and so on. One had to cajole and "massage" the local political types in an effort to have them deliver us an audience at events that we staged in their communities. These same techniques—reasoning with people, getting my message across, listening, possessing a desire to please—all these would be assets in a job where rejection is the norm.

On the other hand, I find I enjoy analyzing business. For example, in my current job I monitor revenue and other statistics daily to determine trends and affect policy. I co-ordinate 22 city marshals who participate in the street impoundment program and also deal directly with 3 garage towing operations under contract to us.

I enjoy working in an atmosphere where there is a lot of activity, where I'm measured by my results, where compensation is directly related to my ability to produce, and where the job is what I make it. I want to be with interesting people, people that matter, people that can have an impact. I feel that the securities business and the opportunity to train and grow the best at Merrill would be a challenge and an education. In this situation, I feel the most severe limitations and constraints would be my own and I like that.

I would be pleased to meet with someone in your organization to further discuss how my qualifications may lead to a career with Merrill.

Sincerely,

# Direct-Mail Campaigns

*Perfection of means and confusion of goals seem, in my opinion, to characterize our age.*

Albert Einstein

## Does Direct Mail Work?

A technique *works* if it helps you to get meetings in your target market. When you are mounting a full campaign, your goal is to have the organizations in your target market know about you as quickly as possible. You can supplement your networking by using search firms and answering ads, but you will still not have hit most of the organizations in your market. Regardless of how you get in, if you find you are being well received by some organizations in your target market, consider direct mail and/or targeted mail for the rest.

If you use direct mail, consider mounting campaigns to a number of targets. Out of four campaigns, for example, maybe two will be effective and result in meetings, and two won't work at all. Part of it is selecting a target that is likely to be interested in you. Another part is being able to express yourself clearly and compellingly in writing. And a third part is a numbers game. If you get no response when you mail to a very small number, that mailing was not a good test.

Most job hunters expect every letter they write to result in a meeting. That's unreasonable. They don't expect every search-firm contact or every ad to result in a meeting. The same is true for direct contact.

CASE STUDY ***Diane***

## Getting More Job Possibilities in the Works

Last week, Diane accepted a job offer. She had uncovered two job possibilities through networking, but she wanted to have the requisite *6 to 10 things in the works*. So she did a mailing of 250 letters, which resulted in 4 more job leads. Admittedly, that's a very small response rate from a mailing, but she wound up with 4 more job interviews than she would have had exclusively through networking.

## Act as If This Company Is Important to You

One time I wrote a direct-mail letter to 200 companies. A manager at one company said to me, "How did you hear of us? No one ever writes to us." I said, "Oh, a number of people have mentioned your company." "Really. Who?" I said, "Pierre Charbonneau and Lillian Bisset-Farrell, to name two [making up the first two names that came to my mind]." The manager said, "I don't know them." "Well," I replied, "they've heard of you!"

If they take your letter personally, you cannot tell them that you sent that same letter to 200 people.

# Bruce: Before and After Direct-Mail Letters

Bruce Faulk (his real name) is a young actor who was working as a receptionist while waiting for his big break. Like most actors, he kept in touch with those who might advance his career. But like most job hunters, he left out the substance in his letters.

Because of The Five O'Clock Club approach, he became more methodical about everything he did in his search for his next acting job. Bruce's "after" letter is on the next page.

By the way, after appearing on Broadway as the youngest actor in *Hamlet,* Bruce toured the United States, and then toured Europe with *Hair*.

Bruce's letter proves that the approach works for anyone—regardless of their profession. At The Five O'Clock Club, we have worked with everyone from orchestra conductors to fine artists.

This just in from Bruce:

**The "before" version of Bruce's direct-mail letter**

Dear Martin Reed:

I am sending you my picture and résumé on the advice of Casey Childs, who has directed a number of *A Different World* episodes. I hope you will keep me in mind for any upcoming project for which I might be right. I will keep you apprised of my situation. Thank you.

Sincerely,

Bruce Faulk

Kate—

Europe is all I expected and more—so much so that I've extended my tour here a few more months. So far, most of the tour has been all over—and I do mean *all* over Germany; but there's still a lot of time for Zurich (where I am now), for the rest of Switzerland, for Austria, and a month and a half right outside Amsterdam. Next month, I'm off to Cannes, France, and a week in Sweden.

Not too shabby for a former receptionist?

Hope all is well with you. Please give everyone my love.

Always,
Bruce

**The "after" version of Bruce's direct-mail letter**

**BRUCE J. FAULK**
286 North 50th Street—Apt. HL
New York, NY 10099
212-555-9809

March 18, 20XX

Dear Mr. Reed:

Casey Childs, who has directed *A Different World,* suggested I contact you. He thought you and I might be able to work together.

I am a graduate of the High School of Performing Arts and Carnegie-Mellon University. I have performed repeatedly off-Broadway in New York. You may be interested in some of my specific experiences. For example:

- I am particularly proud of my work in *The Island,* a South African one-act by Athol Fugard. Many people said it was the best thing done that year at Carnegie. In fact, we were asked to repeat the show for Black History Month at the Pittsburgh Civic Center. (In addition, I was interviewed on TV as part of the show's promotion.) It was extremely well received and many people came up to me on the streets of Pittsburgh and said how much it meant to them; I have a video of the performance if you are interested in seeing it.
- Another example of my work is *Broadway Cabaret.* I played the part of the emcee, warming up the audience for about 10 minutes before opening the show and then singing and dancing throughout. We played to a packed house and a standing ovation every night of the run; it was the most popular show of the season and was extended. I was glad to develop a serious working relationship with the director/choreographer Billy Wilson.

I am a professional, I know how to put a part together and get a job done and I work very hard on whatever I take on. In addition, I am easy to work with and have a good sense of humor.

I will keep you apprised of my situation so you may have a chance to see me in a piece. Casey thought you and I could work together. I hope we can.

Sincerely,

Bruce J. Faulk

# Following Up after a Networking/ Direct-Contact Meeting

*Opportunities are usually disguised as hard work, so most people don't recognize them.*

Ann Landers, Syndicated advice columnist, in Rowes, *The Book of Quotes*

The follow-up after a networking meeting—or a meeting resulting from having directly contacted an organization (through a direct-mail campaign or a targeted mailing)—is very different from the way you follow up after a job interview.

Analyze the meeting. In your letter, thank the interviewer. State the *specific* advice and leads you were given. Be personable. Say you will keep in touch. *Do* keep in touch.

**Follow up every few months with a *status report* on how your search is going, an article, or news of interest to the manager.**

**Make sure people are thinking about you.** You may contact the manager just as he or she has heard of something of importance to you.

**Recontact those you met earlier in your search.** Otherwise, you're like a salesman who works to get new leads while ignoring his old relationships. Get new leads but also keep in touch with people you've already met.

**It's never too late to follow up.** For example: "I met you three years ago and am still impressed by____. Since then I have______and would be interested in getting together with you again to discuss these new developments." Make new contacts. Recontact old ones. It's never too late.

**Trouble getting started? What would you say to the person if he or she were sitting across from you right now? Consider that as the opening of your follow-up letter.**

**Job hunters make a mistake when they fail to *recontact* people with whom they have formed relationships earlier in their search. Keep in touch on a regular basis so you increase your chances of contacting them just at a time when they have heard of something that may interest you—or may have a new need themselves.**

*If you know anything that will make a brother's heart glad, run quick and tell it; and if it is something that will only cause a sigh, bottle it up, bottle it up.*

*Old Farmer's Almanac,* 1854

*If (a man) is brusque in his manner, others will not cooperate. If he is agitated in his words, they will awaken no echo in others. If he asks for something without having first established a (proper) relationship, it will not be given to him.*

I Ching: *Book of Changes*
China, c. 600 B.C.

**Follow up with a customized note specifically acknowledging the help you received.**

**JOHN WEITING**

163 York Avenue—12B
New York, New York 10000
(212) 555-2231 (day)
(212) 555-1674 (message)
jweiting@attnet.net

June 25, 20xx

Ms. Rachel Tepfer
Director of Outplacement
Time-Warner Communications
8 Pine Street
New York, NY 10001

Dear Ms. Tepfer:

Thanks so much for seeing me. Your center is very impressive and seems very well run. But of course, that's what I had heard before I met you.

As you suggested, I sent for information on ASTD, and was pleasantly surprised to see your name in there! It sounds like a great organization, and I can't wait until they start to have meetings again in the fall.

I will definitely follow up with both Ann Brody and Jack Kaufman, and appreciate your giving me their names. I've called them each a few times, but they are very busy people.

After I left your place, I wished I had asked you more about your own career. It was only at the very end that you brought up the interesting way you got your job. I had wrongly assumed that you came up through the ranks at Time-Warner Communications. Perhaps some other time I can hear the rest of the story.

I will keep you posted regarding my activities, and perhaps I'll even run into you at ASTD meetings.

Thanks again for your time and insight. Till we meet again.

Cordially,

John Weiting

*In differentiation, not in uniformity, lies the path of progress.*

Louis Brandeis, U.S. Supreme Court Justice,
*Business—A Profession*

**Follow-up letters don't have to be long, but they do have to be personal. Make sure the letters you write could not be sent to anyone else on your list.**

**SYLVAN VON BURG**

To: Judy Acord

I enjoyed our conversation, which I found most helpful.

I will meet with Betsy Austin when she returns from overseas, and will talk to Jim about seeing Susan Geisenheimer. I'll also contact Bob Potvin and Clive Murray, per your suggestion.

Again, thanks for your help. I'll let you know how things develop.

*Sylvan*

**CARL ARMBRUSTER**

To: Nancy Abramson

Thanks again for contacting Brendan for me and for providing all those excellent contact names.

There's such a wealth of good ideas in the list it will take me a while to follow up with all of them, but I'm working hard at it and will let you know what develops.

Again, thanks for your extraordinary effort.

Cordially,
*Carl*

Mr. Miguel Villarin
President
Commerce and Industry Association
Street Address
City, State

Dear Miguel:

Thank you for the time from your busy schedule. I enjoyed our discussion and appreciated your suggestions about marketing myself in the northern part of the state. Your idea on using the Big 8 firms as pivot points in networking is an excellent one. As you requested, I have enclosed copies of my résumé. I plan to call you next week, so that I can obtain the names of the firms to which you sent my résumé.

I have been thinking about using Robert Dobbs (Dobbs & Firth) in my networking efforts. Since he is a past president of Commerce and Industry, I would be foolish not to tap such a source. Thanks again, Miguel.

Sincerely,
Janet Vitalis

Enclosures

# How to Work with Search Firms

*Once-in-a-lifetime opportunities come along all the time—just about every week or so.*

Garrison Keillor
*A Prairie Home Companion*

If you understand how search firms work, your expectations will be more reasonable, and you will better understand how to approach them.

Contrary to what some people think, a recruiter in a search firm does not place hundreds of managerial and professional people per year. Their search assignments are very specific and require extensive research, networking, and screening prior to presenting qualified individuals to their client organizations. Therefore, the average recruiter places one or two people a month.

The work recruiters do is in some respects similar to the work done by realtors. Recruiters *represent* positions that need to be filled (the equivalent of houses for sale), and they recruit qualified people to fill those positions (house hunters). They match up qualified candidates with their job opportunities, just as realtors match up house hunters with the houses on their lists. In both fields, possibilities are sometimes presented as *once-in-a-lifetime* opportunities.

There are reputable, professional search firms, just as there are reputable, professional realtors. But recruiting is basically a sales profession, and recruiters are interested in working with individuals who are marketable—just as realtors prefer houses that are marketable. Therefore, the more marketable you are, the more likely a search firm will be interested in handling you. If you are too difficult to categorize, want to make a major career change, require unreasonable compensation, or have other drawbacks, search firms are unlikely to work with you.

Make it easy for search firms to market you. Here are a few suggestions:

- Summarize your marketable characteristics in your cover letter. Recruiters need to categorize you anyway, so make it easy for them.
- Clearly state your target market (geographic area, industry, and position) and your salary range. For example: "I'm interested in a financial position in the direct-marketing industry in the New York or Chicago areas. I'm looking for a salary in the $65,000 to $70,000 range."
- Next, state your key selling points—your summary and accomplishments. Recruiters present your *accomplishments* to client organizations—not your job description. Tell them what to say to sell you. It will make their jobs easier and thus make them more likely to want to handle you.
- Be honest. According to Barbara Bruno, president of H&R Consulting in Chicago, "Search firms will check references and verify whatever information you give to them. Their reputations are based on the caliber of individuals they represent. If you misrepresent information, it could cost you the perfect career opportunity."

## Sample Search Firm Cover Letter

Search firms need to know your target: the kind of job you want and where. They also need to know your salary requirements. The letter on the following page uses our formula for cover letters presented earlier.

## A Typical Search Firm Marketing Call

Here is what may happen if you have made it easy for them. They place a few phone calls. "Joe," they say, "I've got someone you may be interested in. He's a highly skilled individual who has the exact profile you have hired through me before." And then they may read from your cover letter. "He's got two years of financial experience in the direct-marketing industry. [Then they will stress your accomplishments, especially those that saved a past employer time or money.] He's an energetic, ambitious person—a real self-starter. When would it be convenient for us to set up a meeting? He's available next Tuesday or Wednesday morning. . . . Oh, I know you don't have any positions currently available. After I met him, I just thought of you. I really think he'd be worth your time to interview."

## Should I Follow Up with a Phone Call?

The short answer is no. Recruiters are very aware of the positions they are trying to fill at the moment, and all of their energies are going into finding good matches for their client organizations. If they have a position in-house that is appropriate for you and if they are not already too far along with the search, they may call you in. A follow-up phone call from you will do no good and just cuts into their busy day. We advise job hunters to send their résumés to search firms and then get on with other aspects of their searches.

It is better to form long-term relationships with reputable search firms. You can do this by helping them when they have an assignment they are trying to fill—even though it is not right for you. Perhaps you could suggest the names of other people they should call. Then when you are ready to make a move, they are already aware of you and your character and are more likely to consider you when they have an opening that *is* right for you.

---

*Life will give you what you ask of her if only you ask long enough and plainly enough.*

E. Nesbitt

# Search-Firm Cover Letter

**Search firms need to know your target: the kind of job you want and where.**

**They also need to know your salary requirements. This letter follows our formula format:**

**Paragraph 2—Summary.**

**Paragraph 3—Bulleted accomplishments.**

Dear Ms. Bruno:

In the course of your search assignments, you may have a requirement for a technically knowledgeable IBM AS400–System 38 professional.

I have experience with the phases of the System Development Life Cycle having worked at General Motors for the past two years. My accomplishments include the following:

- Conversion of RPG and COBOL programs;
- Development and programming;
- Quality Assurance and Testing;
- Optimization of performance for Applications and Systems.

At this juncture, after years of commuting to Detroit, I'm interested in seeking permanent employment in Ann Arbor, where I live.

The enclosed résumé briefly outlines my experience. My base is now in the $50,000 range plus the usual fringes.

If it appears that my qualifications meet the needs of one of your clients, I would be happy to further discuss my background in a meeting with you.

Yours truly,

**Do not send your résumé to search firms unless you know their reputation. A disreputable agency could *blanket* the market with your résumé, and cheapen your value. Make sure the search firm tells you before they send your résumé to anyone.**

## Which Organizations Use Search Firms?

Search firms are used by small to mid sized organizations that have limited personnel departments. The search firm acts as an extension of their human resources staff. In addition, smaller organizations often must use search firms because applicants don't contact them as often as they do larger organizations.

Search firms are also used by major organizations that have specific needs. Major organizations expect the search firm to identify the best individual in their industry nationwide—and usually in a very short period of time. Search firms are expected to know—or be able to find out quickly—the important players in a specialty.

Search firms are also used to fill jobs where there is a labor shortage. This could be for a specialty that is much in demand at the moment, an executive-level position, a field that is so unusual that the search firm may have to look outside the organization's normal geographic area, or even for common positions that the organization is having difficulty filling.

To find the names of search firms, use the *Directory of Executive Recruiters.* Despite its title, it lists firms for most job levels and job categories, and also by geographic area. It is carried by many libraries, or you can get your own copy from Kennedy Publications, Phoenix Mill Lane, Peterborough, NH 03458.

## Retainer versus Contingency Search Firms

The *search firm* field has become more complex in recent years. It now includes new services, such as temporary service firms.

Whether retainer or contingency, search firms are hired by organizations to fill positions. Organizations pay search firms about a third of the new person's salary. Retainer firms receive an exclusive assignment to fill a position and get paid whether or not they find the person for it. Contingency firms are paid only if they fill the position, and a number of contingency firms could be working on filling the same position. The one that fills it gets the fee.

Do not send your résumé to search firms unless you know their reputation. There may be a disreputable agency that could blanket the market with your résumé, and cheapen your value. Make sure the search firm tells you before it sends your résumé to anyone. If a search firm has sent your résumé to lots of places, it will have gotten to organizations before you have had a chance to get in on your own. If an organization has a policy of not paying a fee to search firms, it will not consider you for a position because you were *introduced* by a search firm. If it *is* willing to pay a fee, but two search firms have sent in your résumé, the organization will not hire you because it does not want to get into an argument about which search firm to pay. Simply have a search firm tell you ahead of time which organizations it wants to contact on your behalf. You can find good search firms by asking your networking contacts for the names of the firms they use.

## Can I Get the Search Firm to Increase the Salary Being Offered?

The answer is: In most cases, you can't. A search firm is hired by a client organization to fill a certain position at a certain salary. A search firm needs to know your salary requirements. The salary cap can sometimes be negotiated based on the level or experience of the candidate. However, if the search firm does not put you in for the job because your salary requirements are too high, you should contact the firm directly.

Let's remember the purpose of search firms: They cannot get you a job. Search firms can help you get *meetings* in your target market. You can also get meetings through ads, networking, and direct contact. When a search firm tells you about a specific job at a specific salary, decide if you want the *meeting.* Once they get you a meeting; you have to do the rest yourself.

Also remember our basic principle regarding salary negotiation: Do not negotiate the salary until you have received an offer. After you have gotten the interview, turn it into an offer by following up with the organization itself. Once you have the offer, get involved in the negotiating process yourself. There are some search firms that are excellent at negotiating on your behalf if the organization really wants you. In general, however, you will want to do the deal yourself.

## Develop Long-Term Relationships: Become a Referral Source

As you go through your career, establish a rapport with headhunters who contact you. Their current job opening may not be appropriate for you, but if they know what you will accept, they will contact you when the right thing crosses their desk. Become a referral source—someone who recommends candidates—and you will receive calls on a regular basis.

In addition, keep the good firms regularly apprised of your situation—over the long term. For your current search, contact those with whom you already have a relationship and write, "It has been a while since we last spoke, and I wanted to send you an updated résumé for your files." Then be sure to include the other paragraphs of our search firm letter.

When you accept a new position, send each organization with whom you have a relationship the same kind of note and an updated résumé.

## A Final Word about Search Firms

Some search firms give the industry a bad name. If you are belittled or badgered by a search firm, do not take it personally, but do move on. The possible damage to your ego isn't worth it. A recruiter may, for example, hurt your ego so that you will accept a position that is rather low in salary.

Search firms work for the organizations that hired them, not for you. A firm may want the best fee and not care about a good placement for you. That firm may want to place you quickly at a low salary level and move on.

If you refuse a job offer, a search firm will still present you to their other client organizations. Getting an offer proves you are marketable. If you've gotten one offer, most will conclude you can get another. They will drop you, however, if they feel you are just shopping the market and are not interested in making a move. After all, they are running a business. So don't be frivolous in refusing offers.

But don't be afraid to turn down an offer if it is not appropriate for you. It is important that you not be talked into accepting an offer you don't want by a recruiter who is trying to satisfy the needs of the client organization. Recruiters are just trying to do their job: selling the benefits of the client organization's position. Contact a number of search firms in your specialty. Depending on your target market, they may be a very important tool for getting meetings.

---

*For God sake hold your tongue.*

John Donne, *The Canonization*

# How to Answer Ads

*Of all sad words*
*Of tongue and pen*
*The saddest are these:*
*"It Might Have Been."*

*Let's add this thought*
*unto this verse:*
*"It Might Have Been*
*A Good Deal Worse."*

Anonymous

Some people get excited after they have answered an ad in the paper or on the Internet. They know this is the job for them.

Do not be surprised if you answer 30 or 50 ads and get no meetings. Your résumé is with perhaps thousands of other responses. What's more, your résumé is not being screened by the hiring manager.

Chances are, your cover letter and résumé will be screened by someone like a 20-year-old I met. She reviewed résumés on behalf of blue-chip companies, screening thousands of professionals and managers in the $40,000 to $100,000 range. *She* decided who would get interviewed!

This young woman was good at her job and often took a personal interest in the people whose résumés she saw—but she was only 20 years old. Writing a cover letter to "intrigue" or strike a responsive chord in her wouldn't have worked.

While intrigue, subtlety, and personality may work in direct-mail campaigns and networking, stick to the basics in answering ads. If the ad asks for specific qualifications and experience, highlight those areas from your background. Respond point by point to each item mentioned. Show how you have everything they want. Keep your cover letter crystal clear. Remember, the reader of your letter may be 20 years old. If you don't fit exactly, you will probably be screened out.

If an average ad in *The Wall Street Journal* or *The New York Times* gets a thousand responses, you have 999 competitors. Ads on the Internet may get tens of thousands of responses. Answer ads—I believe in doing everything to help your job hunt.

If you qualify for the job, make that apparent by following the format of the letter on the following page. If you do *not* qualify, use the paragraph format used in networking cover letters. If you don't get in by responding to the ad, *network* into the company or contact someone there directly (not the person mentioned in the ad).

**If you meet all the requirements of the job, then make it very clear to the screener that you should not be screened out. And also try to get in through direct contact or networking.**

ROBERT HENRY
38 Cicily Place
West Hamstart, MO 59684
RobHenry@worldwidenet.com

March 23, 20XX

Nancy Friedberg
Employment Manager
National Data Labs
22 Parns Avenue
East Hamstart, MO 59684

Dear Ms. Friedberg:

I believe I am a good fit for the Assistant Accountant position that was advertised in the *Hamstart Times* on March 20, 20XX.

I have been continually challenged at Toronto Local Bank, and I have a proven track record in accounting functions. I've worked on the general ledger, accounts receivables and payables, the year-end closing and bank reconciliations. Toronto Local has a cost accounting process, similar to National Data Labs, and this has contributed to the success of the organization.

Here is a breakdown of my experience vs. your requirements:

| Your Requirements | My Experience |
| --- | --- |
| • 2 years experience in accounting | • 4 years' accounting experience in a financial services firm |
| • A BBA, MBA a plus | • BBA in Finance MBA in Financial Management |
| • Financial Analysis/ Cost Accounting Skills | • Strong Financial Analysis skills—worked directly with Controller |
| | • Strong Cost Accounting skills—Implemented Cost Accounting/ Unit Cost Methodologies |

I consider myself a dedicated and exacting professional with a significant number of business accomplishments, coupled with an excellent ability to communicate both orally and in writing.

I would welcome an interview with you to review my experience in accounting and related areas.

Sincerely,

Bob Henry

# How to Handle Rejection Letters

*In nature, there are neither rewards nor punishments—there are consequences.*

Robert Green Ingersoll

Organizations generally send the same rejection letter to everyone complementing the applicant on his or her credentials and offering regret that there are no appropriate openings at that time. A rejection letter is truly a rejection only when it follows a job interview.

## Rejection Letters in Response to a Direct-Mail Campaign

If you received a respectable number of responses (meetings) from your campaign, try another campaign of the remaining organizations in a few months. Direct marketers say you should then expect approximately half the response you got with your first mailing. As an alternative, network into the organizations that interest you, contact someone else in the same firm, or use a targeted mailing approach.

If the response rate from your mailing was poor, you picked the wrong market for what you have to offer, or the package you sent was lacking. Chances are, you were not as knowledgeable about this market as you thought. Research or network to learn more, or network to find out what was wrong with your package.

## Rejection Letter in Response to an Ad

This is par for the course. The organization probably received a thousand résumés. Or perhaps the ad was not for a legitimate opening.

If an organization's name was listed, network in, do a targeted mailing to someone who could be close to the hiring manager, or contact a search firm that handles the type of position mentioned. Your résumé was probably rejected by someone other than the hiring manager, so it's worth further effort if you're interested in the position. Some organizations have a policy of immediately sending out rejection letters to everyone. Then they call those people they're interested in—even though the applicants have already been *rejected*. For organizations that always send rejection letters, this approach saves time.

## Rejection Letter in Response to a Networking Contact You Tried to Make

The person did not understand that what you wanted was information. If many people respond to you this way, reassess your approach to networking.

## Rejection Letter Following a Job Interview

This is a true rejection letter. It used to be that it took seven job interviews to get one offer. That figure may now be higher. If you are still interested in the organization, don't give up. (Read what Michael did in the chapter *Following Up When There Is No Immediate Job*.)

## Lessons to Learn

When you get a rejection note in response to a job interview, think about it. How interested are you in that firm? Did you hit it off with the interviewer? If you think there was some mutual interest, see if there might be other jobs with the organization later—perhaps in another department. Or perhaps the person hired instead of you might not work out. Keep in touch. People rarely do, but we all like to hire people who truly want to work for us.

CASE STUDY ***Stan***

## Turning a Rejection into an Offer

Stan was told an offer was being made to another candidate. He was crushed, but he immediately dashed off a letter to the hiring manager and hand-delivered it. A brief letter, it said, in part:

> I was disappointed to hear that you have offered the position to someone else. I truly believe I am right for the position, and wish you would keep me in mind anyway. You never know—something could happen to the new person, and you may need a replacement. Please consider me no matter when this may occur, because I believe I belong at your institution.

The next day, Stan received a call with an offer. Some people may think the offer to the other candidate fell through. However, I believe Stan's letter influenced the hiring manager. When he saw the letter, he thought to himself, We're offering the position to the wrong person! and he allowed the negotiation with the other candidate to lapse.

# Following Up When There Is No Immediate Job

*Contrary to the cliché, genuinely nice guys most often finish first, or very near it.*

Malcolm Forbes

During each meeting, you have taken up the time of someone who sincerely tried to help you. Writing a note is the only polite thing to do. Since the person has gone to some effort for you, go to some effort in return. A phone call to thank a person can be an intrusion and shows little effort on your part.

In addition to being polite, there are good business reasons for writing notes and otherwise keeping in touch with people who have helped you. For one thing, few people keep in touch, so you will stand out. Second, it gives you a chance to sell yourself again and to overcome any misunderstandings that may have occurred. Third, this is a promotional campaign, and any good promoter knows that a message reinforced soon after a first message results in added recall.

If you meet someone through a networking meeting, for example, he or she will almost certainly forget about you the minute you leave and just go back to business. Sorry, but you were an interruption.

If you write to people almost immediately after your meeting, this will dramatically increase the chance that they will remember you. If you wait two weeks before writing, they may remember meeting someone but not remember you specifically. If you wait longer than two weeks, they probably won't remember meeting anyone—let alone that it was you.

So promptly follow the meeting with a note. It is important to remind those to whom you write who you are and when they talked to you. Give some highlight of the meeting. Contact them again within a month or two. It is just like an advertising campaign. Advertisers will often place their ads at least every four weeks in the same publication. If they advertised less often than that, few people would remember the ad.

---

*As a splendid palace deserted by its inmates looks like a ruin, so does a man without character, all his material belongings notwithstanding.*

Mohandas Gandhi

## What Michael Did

This is a classic—and it worked on me. I wanted to hire one junior accountant for a very important project and had the search narrowed down to two people. I asked my boss for his input. We made up a list of what we were looking for and we each rated the candidates on 20 criteria. The final scores came in very close, but I hired Judy instead of Michael.

In response to my rejection, Michael wrote me a note telling me how much he still wanted to work for our organization and how he hoped I would keep him in mind if something else should come up. He turned the rejection into a positive contact. Notes are so unusual, and this one was so personable, that I showed it to my boss.

A few months later, Michael wrote again saying that he had taken a position with another firm. He was still very much interested in us, and he hoped to work for us someday. He promised to keep in touch, which he did. Each time he wrote, I showed the note to my boss. Each time, we were sorry we couldn't hire him.

After about seven months, I needed another helping hand. Whom do you think I called? Do you think I interviewed other people? Do you think I had to sell Michael to my boss? Michael came to work for us, and we never regretted it. Persistence pays off.

### Sample Follow-Up to a Networking Meeting

PETER SCHAEFER

To: Alexandra Duran

Thanks again for contacting Brendan for me, and for providing all those excellent contact names.

There's such a wealth of good ideas in that list that it will take me a while to follow up on all of them, but I'm getting hard at it and will let you know what develops.

Again, thanks for your extraordinary effort.

Cordially,

Peter

## What to Say in Your Follow-Up Note

Depending on the content of your note, you may type or write it. Generally use standard business-size stationery, but sometimes Monarch or other note-size stationery, ivory or white, will do. A *job* interview follow-up should almost always be typed on standard business-size ivory or white stationery. However, if the organization seems to do a lot by E-mail, you can write follow-up notes via E-mail.

After an information-gathering meeting, play back some of the advice you received, any you intend to follow, and so on. Simply be sincere. What did you appreciate about the time the person spent with you? Did you get good advice that you intend to follow? Say so. Were you inspired? Encouraged? Awakened? Say so.

If you think there were sparks between you and the person with whom you met, be sure to say that you will keep in touch. Then do it. Follow-up letters don't have to be long, but they do have to be personal. Make sure the letters you write could not be sent to someone else on your list.

To keep in touch, simply let interviewers/network contacts know how you are doing. Tell them whom you are seeing and what your plans are. Some people, seeing your sincerity, will keep sending you leads or other information.

It's never too late to follow up. For example: "I met you a year ago and am still impressed by. . . . Since then I have . . . and would be interested in getting together with you again to discuss these new developments." Make new contacts. Recontact old ones by writing a *status report* every two months telling how well you are doing in your search. **Keeping up with old networking contacts is as important as making new ones.**

Some job hunters use this as an opportunity to write a proposal. During the meeting, you may have learned something about the organization's problems. Writing a proposal to solve them may create a job for you.

Alan had met with the head of a senior citizens' center, where he learned that they needed new programs to keep the residents active. He visited a number of senior centers to see what their programs were, selected the ones he knew he could lead, and gathered the newsletters that each center had. He then developed a *proposal* of programs he could run, such as bingo games and ballroom dance lessons.

In his follow-up note, he said that he had visited a number of centers, had some ideas including the following, and also gathered sample newsletters so he could put together a newsletter for the center. Equally important, he said that he would like to visit with her again to discuss his proposal.

She went over the proposal with Alan, and they created a position for him.

However, you are not trying to turn every networking meeting into a job possibility. You *are* trying to form lifelong relationships with people. Experts say that most successful employees form solid relationships with lots of people and keep in touch regularly throughout their careers. These people will keep you up-to-date in a changing economy, tell you about changes or openings in your field, and generally be your long-term ally. And you will do the same for them.

---

*Has a man gained anything who has received a hundred favors and rendered none? He is great who confers the most benefits.*

Ralph Waldo Emerson, "Essay on Compensation"

# PART SIX

# Getting What You Want

## THE FIVE O'CLOCK CLUB APPROACH TO INTERVIEWING AND NEGOTIATING

# Basic Interview Techniques

*Just know your lines and don't bump into the furniture.*

Spencer Tracy's advice on acting

An interview is not simply a conversation; it's showtime, folks. You will be competing against people who are well rehearsed and know their lines.

## Develop Your Lines

In an interview, an inability to express yourself clearly is worse than a lack of experience. Refine your sales pitch by listing on a 3x5 card:

- the main reason the employer would want to hire you
- what you have to offer in the way of experience, credentials, and personality
- two key accomplishments to support your interest in this position
- an answer to what you think might be the employer's main objection to you, if any
- a statement of why you would want to work for this company

Keep this card in your pocket or purse and review it just before going in for the interview so that you will know your lines.

---

*Make yourself necessary to someone.*

Ralph Waldo Emerson

## Look and Act the Part

Remember, this is show biz. Even if you don't feel self-confident, act as if you do. If you come in looking defeated, like a loser, why would anyone want to hire you? *Act* as if you are successful and feel good about yourself, and you will increase your chances of actually *feeling* that way. Enthusiasm counts. Every manager is receptive to someone who is sincerely interested in the company and the position.

---

*I have always tried to be true to myself, to pick those battles I felt were important.*

Arthur Ashe

**First, read the chapter:**
***Case Study: Julie—Getting and Doing Well in Interviews***

## During the Interview—Play the Part of a Consultant

Pretend for a minute that you own a small consulting company. When you first meet a prospective client, you want to probe to better understand the problems this person is facing. If the client has no problems or if you cannot solve them, there is no place for you.

You are also there to sell your company. Therefore, as the manager talks about company problems, you reveal your own company's experience and credentials by asking questions or by telling how you have handled similar situations. You want to see how your company fits in with this company.

If the conversation goes astray, lead it back to the topics on your 3x5 card—the work you would do for them and your abilities. That way, you can make your points in context.

It is your responsibility to reassure the hiring manager that everything will work out. The manager does not want to be embarrassed later by discovering he's made a hiring mistake. It is almost as if you are patting the manager on the arm and saying, "There, there. Everything will be just fine. You can count on me."

**If the interviewer has no problems, or if you cannot solve them, there is no place for you.**

You must display self-confidence in your ability to handle the position. If you are not confident, why should the hiring manager take a chance on you? If you want the job, take a stand and say that you believe it will work.

If you are asked how you would handle a situation, reassure the manager that even though you do not know specifically what you would do (because, after all, you are not on the job yet), you know you can figure it out because:

- It won't be a problem. I'm good at these things.
- I'm very resourceful. Here's what I did as company controller. . . .
- I've been in that situation before. I can handle your situation even though I don't know the specifics.

Let the manager air his or her doubts about you. If you are told what these reservations are, you can reassure the manager right then, or you can mull it over later and reassure the manager in writing.

Do not appear to be *shopping around.* Be sincerely interested in this particular company—at least during the interview.

Follow up on your meetings. Address the important issues, stress your interest and enthusiasm for the job, and state your major selling points—especially since you now know what is of interest to the interviewer.

**Follow-up will dramatically increase the number of job offers you get. It is one of the most powerful tools you have to influence the situation.**

*We're a society that's not about perfection, but about rectifying mistakes. We're about second chances.*

Harry Edwards, in "Hardline,"
*Detroit Free Press,* May 1988

## Questions You Might Ask in an Interview

You are there not only to answer the interviewer's questions but also to make sure you get the information you need. Ask questions that are appropriate. What do you really want to know? Here are a few to get you thinking in the right direction:

**Questions to Ask Personnel**

- Can you tell me more about the responsibilities of the job?
- What skills do you think would be most critical for this job?
- Is there a current organization chart available for this area?
- What happened to the person who held this job before?
- What kinds of people are most successful in this area?
- What do you see as the department's strengths and weaknesses?

**Questions to ask Managers (and Perhaps Peers)**

- What are the key responsibilities of the job?
- What is the most important part of the job?
- What is the first problem that would need the attention of the person you hire?
- What other problems need attention now? Over the next six months?
- How has this job been performed in the past?
- Are there other things you would like someone to do that are not a formal part of the job?
- What would you like to be able to say about the new hire one year from now?
- What significant changes do you see in the future?
- May I ask what your background is?
- What do you find most satisfying about working here? Most frustrating?
- How would you describe your management style?
- How is the department organized?
- May I meet the other people who work in the area?
- How is one's performance evaluated? By whom? How often?
- What skills are in short supply here?

## Do Your Homework

Before the interview, research the company and the industry. If you're asked why you are interested in them, you will have your answer. Do library research. Call the company's public relations department and ask for literature or an annual report. Ask others about the company. Show up early and read company literature in the reception area, talk to the receptionist, and observe the people. Get a feel for the place.

*It may sound like a contradiction, but you achieve spontaneity on the set through preparation of the dialogue at home. As you prepare, find ways of making your responses seem newly minted, not preprogrammed.*

Michael Caine, *Acting in Film*

## The Rehearsal

Even experienced job hunters need practice. Each interview smooths out your presentation and responses. As you get better, your self-confidence grows.

By now, you've had networking or information-gathering interviews. You will have practiced talking about yourself and will have information about your area of interest and the possibilities for someone like you.

When I was unemployed, I had lots of interviews, but I was not doing well in them. I was under so much stress that I kept talking about what *I* wanted to do rather than what I could do *for the company*. I knew better, but I could not think straight. An old friend, who belongs to The Five O'Clock Club, helped me develop my *lines* for my 3x5 card. Then we practiced. After that, my interviews went well.

**Be sure to record every networking and job interview on the interview record.**

*To take what there is and use it, without waiting forever in vain for the preconceived—to dig deep into the actual and get something out of that—this doubtless is the right way to live.*

Henry James

## Get a Job Offer

Sincerely intend to turn each interview into a solid job offer. Do your best to make the position and the pay into something acceptable. Make the most of each interview. Negotiate changes in the job itself. Suggest additional things you can do for the company—jobs often can be upgraded a level or two. Or perhaps the manager could refer you to another area of the company. You should make every effort to turn an interview into a reasonable job offer.

- This is an opportunity to practice your negotiation skills and increase the number of interviews you turn into offers. You can always turn the job down later.
- Getting job offers helps your self-esteem. You can say you received a number of offers, but they didn't seem right for you. This puts you in a stronger negotiating position.
- Even if you turn down an offer, stay friendly with the hiring manager. This may lead to another offer later that is more appropriate.
- When you get an offer you are not sure about, say that you have a few other things you must attend to, but will get back to them in a week. Then contact other companies that were of real interest to you. Tell them you have received an offer but were hoping to work something out with them. They may tell you to take the other offer—or they may consider you more seriously because the other offer makes you more valuable. Sometimes knowing you got another offer is the only thing that will make a company act.
- You may be surprised: Perhaps what you originally found objectionable can be changed to your liking. If you end the process too early, you lose the possibility of changing the situation to suit you. Having a job created especially for you is the best outcome.

---

*The world is moving so fast these days that the man who says it can't be done is generally interrupted by someone doing it.*

Harry Emerson Fosdick

## Coming in as a Freelancer or Consultant

Some job hunters are willing to work for a company as a freelancer or consultant and hope the company will later put them on the payroll. This may happen, but don't count on it. If you are doing a great job for little money, the company has no incentive to change that arrangement. If you want to be *on salary,* consult only if you are sure you have the self-discipline to continue job hunting after you start consulting.

You can parlay a consulting assignment into a full-time job at a decent salary if you do outstanding work on the assignment and get a decent offer somewhere else. Then tell your manager that you enjoy what you are doing and would like to be a salaried employee—but have received another job offer. You would prefer working for his company, but this temporary arrangement is not what you want.

## Aiming for the Second Job Out

Sometimes the job you really want is too big a step for you right now. Instead of trying to get it in one move, go for it in two moves. Make your next job one that will qualify you for the job you really want.

---

*I am proud of the fact that I never invented weapons to kill.*

Thomas A. Edison

*If I had known, I should have become a watchmaker.*

Albert Einstein, on his role in making the atomic bomb possible

## What Do You Really Want?

To get ahead, many people compromise what they want. A lot of compromising can result in material success but also feelings of self-betrayal and not knowing who you really are.

It can be difficult to hold on to your values and live the kind of life that is right for you. You may feel there is no hope for change. If you are really honest, you may discover that you have tried very little to make changes. Ask yourself what you have done to improve your situation.

Deciding where you want to work is a complex problem. Many unhappy professionals, managers, and executives admit they made a mistake in deciding to work for their present companies. They think they should have done more research and more thinking before they took the job.

The stress of job hunting can impair your judgment. You may make a decision without enough information simply because you want to *get a job*. Ego can also be involved: You want to get an offer quickly so you can tell others and yourself that you are worth something. Or you may deceive yourself into thinking you have enough information. Even if you are normally a good decision maker, you can short-circuit the decision-making process when it comes to your own career.

You will make better decisions when you are not deciding under pressure. Start now to see what your options are. Then you already will have thought them through in case you have to make a move quickly later.

Objectively evaluate the information you come up with, and develop contingency plans. Decide whether to leave your present position, and evaluate new opportunities. List the pros and cons of each possibility for you and those close to you.

You may decide, for example, that a certain position is higher level, higher paying, and more prestigious, but you will have less time for your personal life, and the job will make demands on your income because you will have to take on a more expensive lifestyle. You may even decide that you don't like the kind of work, the conditions, or the people, or that your lack of leisure time will push you further away from the way you want to live.

Depending on your values, the job may be worth it or not. If you list the pros and cons, you are more likely to adhere to your decision and have fewer regrets. You are more likely to weigh the trade-offs and perhaps think of other alternatives. You will decide what is important to you. You will have fewer negative surprises later and will be warned of areas where you may need more information. You will make better decisions and have more realistic expectations about the future.

*If one man says to thee, "Thou art a donkey," pay no heed. If two speak thus, purchase a saddle.*

The Talmud

## What If Your Interviews Are Not Turning into Job Offers?

*Listen to gather better information.* You may find that your target market is declining, or that you don't have the required background, or whatever. One of my clients kept saying that managers insulted her. If you have the same experiences again and again, find out what you are doing wrong.

*Perhaps you are unconsciously turning people down.* A job hunter may make unreasonable demands because, deep inside, he or she knows there are things dramatically wrong with a situation. The requests for more money or a better title are really to make up for the unacceptable working conditions. Then the company rejects the applicant. One job hunter thought he was turned down for the job. In reality, *he* turned down the job. He did not let an offer happen because he knew the job was not right, and he made it fall through. There is nothing wrong with this—so long as he knows he could have had a job offer if he had wanted one.

Job hunters are under tremendous pressure to answer to a lot of people who want to know *how your job hunt is going*. If you say you are still looking and have not gotten any offers, you may feel bad. That's another reason why you may want to get a few offers—even though you are

*"Dude, touring with a punk rock band was fun, but what I'd really like to do is be CEO of a Fortune 500 company."*

not interested in those particular jobs. On the other hand, if your job hunt seems to be going very quickly, you may not want to waste your time on practice offers.

*Make sure you are addressing the company's problems—not your own.* A major mistake that I have made myself is focusing on what I wanted rather than on what the company or the manager needed.

*Perhaps you are not talking to the right people.* Are you interviewing with people two levels higher than you are—those in a position to hire you? If you are spending a lot of time talking to people at your own level, you can learn about the field, but this is unlikely to result in job offers.

*If you don't know why, ask them.* If appropriate, you may want to call a few of the people with whom you interviewed to find out why you did not get the job. If you are really stuck and feel you are not interviewing well, this can be very valuable feedback for you. You may even be able to turn a negative situation around.

---

*. . . you ought to say, "If it is the Lord's will."*

James 4:15

## Do Your Best, Then Let It Go

You are trying to find a match between yourself and a company. You are not going to click with everyone, any more than everyone is going to click with you. Don't expect every interview to turn into a job offer. The more interviews you have, the better you will do at each one.

And don't punish yourself later. Do your best, and then do your best again.

Hang in there. Get a lot of interviews. Know your lines. And don't bump into the furniture. You will find the right job. As M. H. Anderson said: "If at first you don't succeed, you are running about average."

---

*So to avoid all that horror, prepare. Apart from anything else, preparation uses up a lot of the nervous energy that otherwise might rise up to betray you. Channel that energy; focus it into areas that you control. The first step in preparation is to learn your lines until saying them becomes a predictable reflex. And don't mouth them silently; say them aloud until they become totally your property. Hear yourself say them, because the last thing you want is the sound of your own voice taking you by surprise or not striking you as completely convincing.*

Michael Caine, *Acting in Film*

*A man should always consider how much he has more than he wants, and how much more unhappy he might be than he really is.*

Joseph Addison

# Difficult Interview Questions and Possible Answers

**Do not allow the interview to get off track. When the interviewer brings up something that takes you in a direction in which you don't want to go, briefly give a response that satisfies the interviewer, and then *get back on track*.**
**Give your answer, and then say, for example, "But I really wanted to tell you about a special project I worked on."**
**It is *your* responsibility to get the conversation back on track.**

*A sudden, bold, and unexpected question doth many times surprise a man and lay him open.*

Francis Bacon, "Of Cunning"

Business is a game, and interviewing is part of the game. You are asked a question to see how well you handle it—and to see how well you play the game. This is not like a discussion with a friend. Don't take questions literally.

For example, if the interviewer asks you why you didn't finish college, should you tell the truth? Should you say, for example:

- I couldn't decide on a major

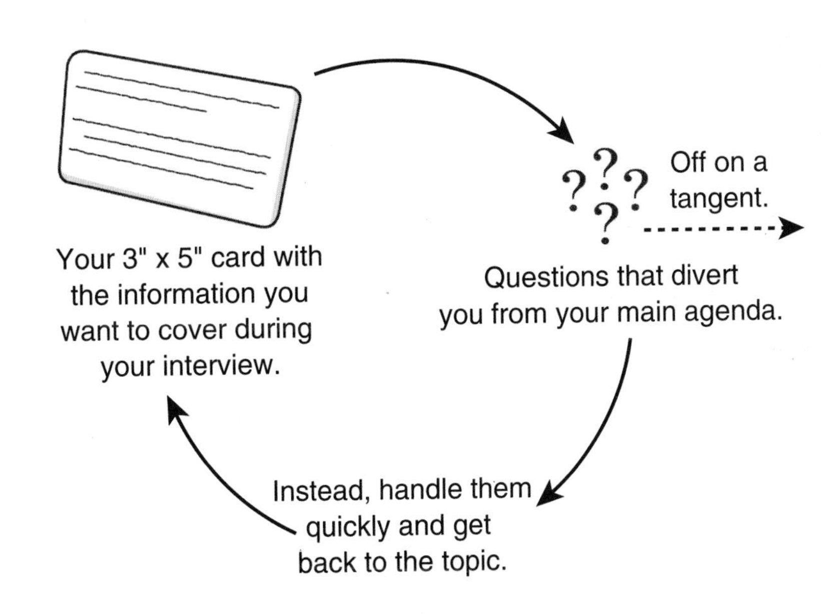

- My mother died and I had to help out
- I ran out of money

These answers are not wise because they're negative and they also take you both away from what should be the main discussion: the company's needs and how you can help.

The interviewer is not interested in you and your mother. There is a job to fill. Talking about certain subjects weakens your position—regardless of who brought them up. Keep the interview positive, and try not to discuss subjects that detract from your case. Many times hiring managers say to me, "Why did Joe (the applicant) have to tell me that? I was ready to hire him, but now I'm not so sure. When my boss confronts me about Joe's lack of college, I don't have a good answer."

Some job hunters insist on being "honest." They think, "I'll just tell them the way it is, and if they don't hire me, then so be it." These job hunters are putting their responsibility on the interviewer. We've all had problems. The interviewer doesn't have to hear about them.

A businesslike answer, however, moves the interview along. Let's try the question again—keeping the goal of the interview in mind.

**Do not go into long discussions. *Briefly and politely* handle those questions that might take you off course, then smoothly move the conversation back to the company's needs or your abilities—the things on your 3x5 card that you had planned to cover. Give your answer, and then say, for example, "but I really wanted to tell you about a special project I worked on." It is your responsibility to get the conversation back on track.**

Lettice: *Let me play the interviewer for once: you be the victim.*

Peter Schaeffer, *Lettice & Lovage*

---

*Midway in our life's journey, I went astray from the straight road and woke to find myself alone in a dark wood.*

Dante, *The Inferno*

## Why Didn't You Finish College?

"I like to be out there doing things. I finished several semesters, but I wanted to get more done. And that's what my bosses have always said about me: I'm someone who gets things done. They've all been happy with me."

Let's try a few others, but remember that you must find your own answers depending on your situation.

## What Would You Like to Be Doing Five Years from Now?

"Actually, I'd like to do the best job I can possibly do in the position we're talking about right now. I know that if I do a great job, good things will happen to me later. They always have."

## Tell Me about Yourself

See Your Two-Minute Pitch.

## Tell Me About the Worst Boss You've Ever Had

If you say that the worst boss you've ever had simply did not have enough time for his subordinates, they'll wonder why you needed so much of your boss's time. If you say your worst boss yelled and screamed at people, they'll wonder what you did to make your boss so angry.

No matter what your bosses have been like: "I've been really lucky. I've been blessed with good bosses. They've all been different, but I've learned from each of them."

## Why Are You Looking? Why Are You Leaving?

You can count on being asked this because it's their job to ask it. Have your answer ready and then move back to the topics on your 3x5 card. They're just checking off items on a list to make sure there are no problems. Keep it brief. You are the only one who cares about the gory details.

Some job hunters have very solid reasons for being out of a job. One Five O'Clock Clubber lost the best job of his life when his boss died and the new boss brought in a friend. He was out through no fault of his own, and there was no better answer than what really happened to him.

Other than a story like that one, the best strategy is to describe your job loss as something you were proactive about—as if you had some say in the matter—and are also glad about. At the very least, do not describe your job loss as having to do with your own performance. Here are a few examples of positive responses:

"My company is going through a reorganization. I had the option of taking another job internally, but I decided to look elsewhere."

*Or*

"X company has been great for me, but the career possibilities in the areas that interest me are extremely limited."

*Or*

"Perhaps you heard that the _______ industry has been going through a major restructuring. I was caught along with three thousand others."

- If you're still employed, or if you're in outplacement and are allowed to look for a job back in your old firm:

  "I don't know that I *am* leaving. I'm talking to people around the company. They sure would like me to take another job there, but I feel like I want to look outside as well."

- If you lost your job and received even a little severance, you can say:

  "I had the opportunity to grab a package and I took it. I'm so lucky. I was not growing as much as I would have liked and now I can move my career along. That's why I'm glad to be talking to you today. I understand that your department is very involved in the new technologies."

They'll rarely ask how long you will be getting paid, and it's none of their business anyway.

Do what's appropriate for you and for your comfort level. Talk it over with your counselor or with those in your small group. Maybe there's a variation of these answers that's right for you.

- If you had been working long hours: "I decided I couldn't work 75 hours a week and also look for a job. I couldn't do justice to my former employer. I left the company so I could conduct a proper search."
- If you didn't get along with your boss: Generally speaking, it's not a good idea to say that you left because of personality conflict. People may suspect that *you* are a difficult person. When you're tempted to talk about conflict with a boss, it's best to say instead: " I want to move my career in a different direction. My expertise is not the most important thing at my present company, and I want to move to a company where my skills will be put to better use."

## What Are You Looking For?

It takes a lot of thinking to be ready for this question. Nothing turns off interviewers more than candidates who don't know what they want. So don't speak in generalities, "I'm looking for a job that excites me" or, even worse, "I'm not sure." This amounts to asking the interviewer to come up with ideas for you! You shouldn't be going on job interviews if you're not hungry and *focused.*

Be prepared to name the kinds of positions you think would be appropriate for you. If your Two-Minute Pitch is polished, you will be able to talk persuasively about the kind of things you can do for the company.

*That is the essence of science: ask an impertinent question, and you are on the way to a pertinent answer.*

Jacob Bronowski

## How Would You Handle This?

The interviewer describes a problem situation and asks how you would handle it. You can't think that quickly.

"I'd have to give it some thought. I'm the type who likes to think things through. I've been up against problems like this before, such as when we were behind schedule at X company. I thought about the problem, and quickly decided we should do a, b, c. This reduced our processing time and everyone was happy.

"Everywhere I've worked, I've been able to assess situations and resolve them, and I'd do the same for you. I don't know how to answer your question at the moment, but I know I would handle the problem the way I have handled things in the past. I have a good track record."

## What Are Your Greatest Weaknesses?

After taking time to mull it over: "Actually, I can't think of any work-related weakness. My bosses have always thought I was great. I'm the kind not only to do my own job but also to notice what else needed to be done in other areas and pitch in to help."

Or, name a weakness and show how you have dealt with it, such as: "Sometimes I get impatient with people because I want the job to get done, but I make sure I find out what's going on and help them with whatever may be stopping them."

## What Are Your Strengths?

Don't simply say, "I'm organized, dependable and honest." They won't remember your strengths unless you also give an example to illustrate each one. For example: "I'm very organized. I was asked to straighten out a library of 3,000 boxes of files. Within just three months, everyone in the department could find anything they wanted."

## What Is Your Current Salary? See Salary Negotiation

The most important strategy is to postpone the discussion of salary until you get an offer. And remember, the person who names a number first is in a weak position.

## They Ask You to Fill Out Your Salary on a Form

If you find you are always filling out forms before you get into the interview, it may mean that you are getting most of your interviews through search firms, ads or human resources. Instead, try to get in through networking or through contacting someone directly. Then you won't find yourself filling out so many forms.

## How Long Have You Been Unemployed?

If you've been unemployed for a long time, and you answer, "26 months," how likely are you to be hired? I have run job-hunt groups of people who have been unemployed two years or more. The first thing we work on is an answer to this question.

From a moral point of view, I must help these people develop a good story so they can get back to work. It would be cruel for me to insist that they tell the truth. Who will hire an applicant who says, "When I was fired, I got depressed for 6 months and couldn't move, and then my mother got sick and I had to help. By then, I had been unemployed 11 months, and no one would hire me. I'm hoping you will give me a chance."

Very few people are willing to give this person a chance, and you can't fault them for that. After all, the *truthful* job hunter is saying, "I've had all these problems, but I'm better now. Will you risk your organization for me?" It's not fair to burden the interviewer. All the interviewer wants to do is fill a job—not save lives.

The solution is to develop a good answer you can live with. Think of what you have actually been doing. Have you been working on your computer? Helping at your church or synagogue? Helping friends with their businesses? Most people can think of something they've been doing—even something little—that they can build a story around.

If you really haven't been doing anything at all, then *go do something.* You are unlikely to interview well if you haven't been out there at all. Get your adrenaline going. Walk dogs, pick strawberries, usher at church. Get active.

Better yet: Learn a new skill. Master new software. Take refresher courses. Volunteer your skills, or get paid something nominally. You might even consider saying you were paid for volunteer work, if you think they would back you up. Then think up a good story:

1. "I've actually been *looking* only a month or so. After I left X company, I spent some time working on a special project for a small company."

   *Or*

2. "I've been looking only a few weeks now. After working since I was 16, this was my first time off, and I took advantage of the time to (take care of a sick family member, learn tax accounting, etc.). I was glad to have the opportunity to (help out, learn something new, etc.). But now I'm ready to get back to work and put in 20 years."

   *Or*

3. Take the work you've done: "I've been doing public relations work for a small firm. I thought it would be fun to try after working for a big corporation, but now I know I like corporate life and I want to get back."

If your answers aren't working—if you're not getting second interviews or job offers—change your answers. Be creative, brainstorm with family and friends, and try new approaches. Positioning is everything; things won't go well until you've positioned yourself correctly.

## How Many Other Companies Are You Talking To?

"I've been very pleased with the response to my résumé. I'm looking at several opportunities." Don't tell them the names of the other companies unless you think it's in your best interest.

If you are *not* talking with other companies, you can say that you are just getting started and expect to be talking to a good number shortly. It is *not* a good strategy to pretend that you are on the verge of another offer if you are not. The hiring manager may tell you to *take* the other offer. Instead, get out there and talk to other companies.

## We Have Two Different Positions. Which Would You Prefer?

Hedge your bets. "I could see myself doing [this] and I could also see myself doing [that]."

## What Is Your Working Style?

This is a common question, so don't be blindsided by it. Be prepared to give examples. Think of stories that demonstrate your work style. Some may be fresh in your mind after having done the Seven Stories. "When sales dropped in my old company, staff was cut while workload was increasing. . . ."

## How Good Are You at . . . ?

If they ask, "How good are you at computer programming?" it's not good enough to say, "Very good." Instead, elaborate on how good you are: "I'm excellent at what I do, I have always been selected for the toughest assignments, the ones that no one else could do. For example. . . ."

## What Questions Do You Have for Us?

I go into the interview with an $8\frac{1}{2} \times 11$ pad. At the top of the pad, I put the four or five questions that I want to ask, and I integrate those questions into the conversation. I also take notes during the interview because I want to remember the details for the follow-up letters. If I meet with five people in one day, I cannot possibly remember what each person said. The notes are crucial even if you talk with only one person.

At the end of the meeting, when the interviewer asks, "Do you have any questions for us?" I make a point of looking at my questions (even though I know that I've already asked them all) and say, "No thanks, we've covered them all." But because the questions were written on the pad, I look prepared.

That's what consultants do. They go into a meeting with pen and paper in hand and try to figure out how things work so they can create an assignment for themselves.

What do you need to know? **If they were going to offer you a job that started a week from Monday, what is the gap between what you know now and what you need to know to get started there on Monday**? Ask those questions. For example:

- "I'd like to talk to someone else who is doing accounting here so I can get an idea of what they do."
- "I'd like to talk to some of my prospective peers so I can figure out exactly how I would interface with them."
- "I need to give this some thought and then I'd like to meet with you again. I'll have some ideas to discuss with you then." (Then do some research and find out more about this industry.)
- "What are the most important things that need attention right now?"

And then a consultant will ask:

- "Where are you in the decision-making process?"
- "What other consultants are you talking to?"
- "How do you see me stacking up against them?"

If you ask questions like these—as if you were going to start working there a week from Monday, you will be much more proactive in the interview process. You will be thinking like a consultant.

*The secret of science is to ask the right question, and it is the choice of problem more than anything that marks the man of genius in the scientific world.*

Henry Tizard

## Level the Playing Field

Job hunters feel as though they are at a disadvantage. After all, the organization is meeting with lots of candidates and will pick only one. It seems as though the hiring team has all the power. But you can have power, too.

You can *put yourself* in a position of power. Get 6 to 10 things in the works. They're talking to other people. Why shouldn't you? Then you can walk away from an abusive company just as easily as a company gets rids of candidates that are not up to the job.

Having 6 to 10 things in the works is also the reason why Five O'Clock Clubbers who have been unemployed a long time still get jobs at market rates. Employers are likely to focus on what you have been doing for the last 18 months or on what you were making in your last job. Instead, the emphasis shifts to the fact that you're talking to a host of other companies about jobs in the $35,000 to $40,000 range, or whatever.

*Any job that has defeated two or three men in succession, even though each performed well in his previous assignments, should be deemed unfit for human beings and must be redesigned.*

Peter Drucker

## Get 6 to 10 Things Going—Not All Good Ones

When you have your 6 to 10 things in the works, they're not all going to be brilliant possibilities. A good number will be with organizations you don't ever want to work for.

But getting the offers serves a purpose: It boosts your ego, helps you to better compare one situation with another, and increases your chances of getting offers from the companies that are of most interest to you. You will be able to say, "I've got four offers right now but I don't want to work for the others. I want to work for you." Prospective employers will see you as more marketable. So get some offers—even ones that are not right for you.

## Don't Stand in Your Own Way

I was doing a workshop for lower level workers at a major retailer. Richard, the head of the mailroom, had supervised about 30 people—a responsible job. For some reason, he was sensitive to the fact that he had been head of the mailroom for "only" two years.

When we practiced the Two-Minute Pitch, he himself brought up what he considered a weakness. He shot himself in the foot at the outset, "Well, I'm head of the mailroom at Bloomingdale's, where I have 30 to 50 people reporting to me and it's going very well *despite the fact that I've been on the job for only two years."*

When Richard positions himself that way, the hiring manager is going to think there's something wrong with his having been in the job two years.

If you feel that something is a handicap for you, think twice about mentioning it—don't bring it up! If you think your age is a problem, you may inadvertently say, "Despite the fact that I'm young" or "Despite the fact I'm still in school." Remember, positioning is everything. Be careful what you say.

Your attitude should be, "Problem? What problem?" Be sensitive to your own sensitivities and get over them.

## The Good Interviewer

It probably won't happen to you during your entire job search, but be prepared for the person who conducts a good interview. In a good interview, the hiring manager may start with the beginning of your career, asking, "What did you do in this job?" "Why did you leave that job and go on to the next one?" "What did you like best about that job?" "What about your boss?"

Then he or she asks you about the next job in a methodical, organized way. "What did you enjoy?" "What did you do best in that job?" "Why did you leave it?" "Tell me about the next one."

You're not going to get very many interviewers like that.

## How to Handle Discrimination

If the interviewer asks you questions that are illegal (such as questions about pregnancy or your plans to have children), assume they are not being asked maliciously. Instead of answering the question itself, answer the *concern* that may have prompted the question. For example, if someone asks, "Are you married?" You cannot say, "It's illegal to ask that." They'll apologize, but you won't get the job. Who needs a troublemaker?

Instead, try to figure out why they're asking you that question and answer their concern. You could say, for example, "Are you concerned that I might not show up at work? I've never missed a day in three years."

## Remember the Following:

- Be prepared.
- Have your 6 to 10 things in the works so that you're not at a disadvantage.

- The purpose of the first interview is not to get a job offer. The purpose of the first interview is to get the second interview.
- You're trying to give and get information so that you can get that next meeting.
- Half of the interview process is being prepared, but the other half is having that right attitude. They'll sense your self-confidence and you are less likely to buckle under when they ask you idiotic questions—often they don't care about the answers anyway.

**Do not drop your search activities when an offer seems almost certain. If it doesn't materialize, the lost momentum is difficult to recover.**

—Advice from a successful job hunter at The Five O'Clock Club

*Shy persons often act like they were captured and are being interrogated.*

Garrison Keillor

*My formula for success?*
*Rise early, work late, strike oil.*

J. Paul Getty

*Maybe they call it take-home pay because there is no other place you can afford to go with it.*

Franklin P. Jones

# How to Use the Interview Record

*Until you value yourself, you will not value your time. Until you value your time, you will not do anything with it.*

Dr. M. Scott Peck

On the next page is a very important worksheet: the interview record. Make a lot of copies of this page for your own personal search. Every time you have a meeting—**whether a networking meeting or a job interview**—fill it out. Make note of with whom you met, to whom they referred you, and what happened in the meeting. Attach to the interview record a copy of your notes from the meeting, the follow-up letter that you sent, perhaps the letter that led to the meeting.

Two weeks after the meeting, you may not remember what you discussed. If you are having a productive search and you are meeting with 10 to 15 people each week, you will not be able to remember what each person said, let alone how you met that person. To keep track of your meetings, maintain a record of each one.

Some job hunters use a three-ring binder and arrange all of the interview records alphabetically or by industry or in some other logical order, with their letters attached. Some job hunters methodically cross-reference the names by noting who referred whom.

At the beginning of your search, you may think you will be searching for a short time. But part of a good search is to follow up with your contacts at least every two months. You can have a more intelligent follow-up if you have an interview record to refer to.

---

*Obviously the way you move will be affected by the character you are playing; but natural movement comes from your "center," from the same place as a natural voice. When you walk from your center, you will project a solid perspective of yourself. Walk with that certainty and ease, and your path becomes a center of gravity. Your force pulls all eyes to you. Slouch or poke your head forward, or pull your shoulders back uncomfortably, and that power seeps away. Only a relaxed, centered walk creates a sense of strength. A centered walk can be very menacing, too. Even if you don't get film work on the basis of this advice, follow it and you'll never get mugged, either. Mind you, if you look like I do you'll never get mugged anyway because people generally think I have just been mugged.*

Michael Caine, *Acting in Film*

*What convinces is conviction. Believe in the argument you're advancing. If you don't, you're as good as dead. The other person will sense that something isn't there, and no chain of reasoning, no matter how logical or brilliant, will win your case for you.*

Lyndon Baines Johnson

# Interview Record

Name: ______________________

Position: ______________________

Company: ______________________

Address: ______________________

______________________

______________________

Phone: Bus: ______________________

Home: ______________________

E-mail: ______________________

Referred by: ______________________

______________________

Link to referral: ______________________

______________________

People spoken to (May require separate sheets.):

______________________

______________________

Issues (advice, problems, plans, etc.): ______________________

______________________

______________________

______________________

Key points to remember: ______________________

______________________

______________________

______________________

Referrals (Write additional names on back.):

Name: ______________________

Position: ______________________

Company: ______________________

Address: ______________________

______________________

______________________

Phone: Bus: ______________________

Home: ______________________

Date of initial contact: ______________________

Method used: ______________________

(If letter, copy and attach to this sheet.)

Planned date of follow-up call to set up appointment: ______________________

(Also record date on job-hunting calendar.)

Actual dates of calls to set up appointment:

______________________

______________________

______________________

______________________

Appointment:

Follow-up note mailed: ______________________

(Copy attached.)

Follow-up 2: ______________________

Follow-up 3: ______________________

Follow-up 4: ______________________

Follow-up 5: ______________________

Follow-up 6: ______________________

(Copy attached.)

Other comments:

- tone of the meeting
- objections to you
- logical next steps
- your feelings about the job
- positives about you
- key issues to address
- influencers

# How to Handle Your References

*Great minds have purposes, others have wishes.*

Washington Irving

Oops. You went through the entire interview process, and then they asked for references. The dot-com you worked for has gone out of business. They loved you there. Too bad you don't know where to find your old boss. The Gap manager you worked for didn't like you all that much, and you didn't like him either. And you forgot to ask any of your professors to serve as a reference for you, and now it's summer. Don't wait until you get a job offer to think about your references. Take care of them now.

1. **Make a list of people you want to use as references.** Former bosses, teachers, even former coworkers could be used as references. If you are in an internship or a part-time job, be sure to add your current boss to the list.
2. **Ask them if they would serve as a reference for you.** Get the agreement of three or four people, at least one of whom should be a boss or former boss. Call your references to ask their permission, tell them about the kinds of jobs you are looking at, and remind them of the good things you did for them—things you would like them to tell others about you.

   Say to the prospective reference: "I was hoping to use your name as a reference in my job search. Do you think you would feel comfortable providing a strong reference for me?" If a person is not willing to give you a great reference, you don't want to use that person. If the person promises to be *very fair* and *provide a balanced picture*, get someone else. Hiring managers expect you to give them the names of people who will glow about you. If a reference starts naming an equal number of good and bad points, you may not stack up well against the other applicants.

   If there is no way you can risk giving your boss's name as a reference, be prepared with names of peers, subordinates, or your boss's boss as stand-in references.

   Position your references so that the hiring company talks to your best ones first. Tell your prospective employer that Judy is tied up in meetings for a few days, and that Helen is available immediately.

3. **Help your references to help you.** Some time ago, I received a call from a prospective employer checking on Bessie, a woman who worked for me and used to head up the accounting department. The caller asked, "Is Bessie the type who was happiest heading up the accounting department?" I raved about Bessie's managerial and organizational skills. The caller said, "That's just what I was afraid of. We were considering her for an analytical position." So I had to backtrack and praise Bessie's analytical skills and ability to work alone. Call your references and tell them the kind of job you are applying for and what you would like them to say about you. Help them to help you.

   You can even put some points in writing so the references can refer to your sheet when they get a call about you. This leaves nothing to chance.

4. **Keep in touch with your references over time.** People change jobs a lot. By the time you need the great reference, that person may have moved on. E-mail your references every six months to a year. Send them a holiday card. Don't lose track of them. Eliminate the problem of not being able to locate someone who could provide the perfect reference when you need it.
5. **Protect your references from too many phone calls.** If lots of prospective employers call the same person, you will look like a loser. "I wonder why Joe is having such a hard time finding a job." Therefore, do not give out your references too soon. If the employer asks for references before you've even had a meeting, that is too soon—except in academia where it is more standard to give references up front. Instead, tell the prospective employer that your references are very important to you and the employer is relatively serious about hiring you.
6. **Ask your references to follow up with you.** You need to know whether someone was called. Ask your references to let you know when they are contacted. If you have given out three names and none of them has been called within a week or two, you are probably not as close to an offer as you think. Call the hiring company and try to uncover any possible hidden objections.
7. **Thank your references.** After you get a job, let them know what happened and thank them for their help.

## How Employers Can Get Information about You

Companies need to protect themselves against lawsuits, so many are cautious and have a policy of giving out only your title and dates of employment.

In some cases, this could work to your advantage, but actually it would not be good if your prospective employer called your references and everybody *pleaded the fifth*. Your future boss would worry that something was wrong. It's best if prospective employers are able to get good information about you. So you need to be prepared to provide the names of good references and be thorough in preparing for this part of the search process.

Often, after you receive an offer, you will be asked to sign a statement releasing your former employer from liability about anything they may say about you. This means that your former employer can feel free to tell you the truth as she sees it.

## If You Left under Bad Circumstances

In the case of an unhappy departure, it's best if you and your former manager could settle on a mutually agreeable story. If this is impossible, think of a substitute reference, such as someone who used to be your boss, even if it was a while back. Then say, "I worked for Jane for two years, so she knows me better than my most recent boss."

If they *still* insist on speaking with your former boss, it's time for a preemptive strike to warn them that they might not hear good things. You might want to say something like this: "I'll be happy to give you Jonathan's phone number. I'm sure he'll be able to tell you details about the work I did. But I wanted to become part of a productive and organized team, which was not the case in my last position. Jonathan's style is more flamboyant and seat-of-the-pants, so please keep that in mind when you speak with him. And definitely do give him a call.

"But I really wanted to tell you about a special project I worked on when Jane was my boss. . . ."

## If a Former Boss Is Sabotaging You

If you're getting interviews everywhere, and second interviews, and then no job offers, then your references may be suspect.

You could approach your former boss and say that you are having a problem getting a job and think that it's because of your references. Ask him or her directly what they are saying about you. Tell them what you'd like them to say. Focus on whatever you did well in that organization, not on your most recent failure.

Think of it this way: *Many* of the people we meet at The Five O'Clock Club have had a recent problem despite an otherwise fine career. Yet they wind up getting jobs. They have to focus on their successes and downplay their recent situation.

---

*Being entirely honest with oneself is a good exercise.*

Dr. Sigmund Freud

## Asking for a Written Reference

It's not a bad idea to ask an employer for a written reference. But don't be like Jeff. Jeff was about two years out of college, working for a company where the president had great influence in the industry. Jeff thought a letter of reference would help him tremendously as he applied for positions in the future.

Jeff sent an E-mail to the company president asking for a written letter of recommendation.

The president said he would help Jeff in any way he could, but Jeff was aghast that "he wanted ME to write the letter, and then pass it along to him for editing."

Jeff should count his blessings. You can only imagine how many requests for a reference the president of a company gets. He cannot spend his time writing references—he has to manage the company. Yet, what a nice guy he is for offering to *help in any way he could.*

But Jeff has to make the president's job easier. He has to put in a little effort if he wants a reference. I often ask employees to give me a draft when they want a reference from me. Then I know what aspects of their personalities and their jobs they want to have emphasized. They are also reminding me of what they have done. If I'm trying to help them, the last thing I need is someone complaining that I left out an important project he or she worked on!

So, if you want a written reference, ask your boss and volunteer to write a draft. You'll see how difficult it is to do.

---

*Writing is easy. All you have to do is stare at a blank sheet of paper till drops of blood form on your forehead.*

Gene Fowler (writer)

## How to Write a Reference Letter (Also Called a "Letter of Commendation")

As for guidelines, put "To Whom It May Concern" at the top, then use the first sentence to place you in context: "Jeff worked with us for two years in the capacity of. . . ." Next, give a general appraisal ("Throughout his time with the company he was a top-notch employee and . . ."), followed by some details of what you've accomplished. Don't be afraid to brag a little. Finally, you could conclude with something like, "I would highly recommend Jeff for whatever position he believes is appropriate."

Then your manager will modify your letter to suit his or her style and perhaps include things she knows about you.

## Then, Keep Up the Good Work

I once wrote a terrific letter of reference for Stan, an employee. (Of course, he first wrote a draft.) Once Stan had that letter in his hot little hands, he stopped coming to work. He figured he had what he needed.

Au contraire! A few weeks later, I received a phone call from a prospective employer who asked about Stan. This would be an absolutely plum job for a recent graduate. Stan would be the assistant to the president of a prestigious venture capital organization. He would travel with the president and help him get ready for meetings. All of the other students who worked there did copying and stuffing envelopes but were glad just to be in that firm.

I urged them to hire Stan but mentioned that he sometimes had to take off from work for personal reasons, although I thought those reasons were behind him (this was true). I was trying to give them a hint that he may have problems, although I didn't want to ruin his chances of getting this plum job.

A few months later, the venture capital firm called me again to say that they *had* hired Stan—but they had just *fired* him too! He routinely missed work and gave very lame excuses. The vice president said to me, "He must have thought we were stupid!"

The problem with trying to pull a fast one is that you take your character with you. The person you've tricked most is yourself. Your character will develop in that direction and your character flaw will become more pronounced as you get older. So, take care now to develop good habits. It becomes more difficult to change habits the more entrenched they become. And people around you probably see *much* more than they let on.

*"I would've dressed better, but my tie was dirty."*

## Developing Your Character

When you are younger, you can get away with some character flaws: arrogance, pettiness, impatience, recklessness, impulsiveness, distractedness (to name a few suggested by the students in our office!). Managers excuse you because of your youth, and they expect that you'll grow out of it. But, as employees get older, managers are less tolerant—they figure you ought to know better. Bad habits catch up with you. When you were young, you got ahead in *spite* of your arrogance (and so on) not because of it. When you are older, you are likely to *lose* your job because of your arrogance.

There are LOTS of bright people around. Study after study shows that managers pick those who get along well with others over those who are simply competent. So, work on those character traits now.

## If You've Made a Big Mistake

Here's a sticky one, and I'm sure some readers (especially older ones) will not agree with me. One mother wrote to me about Julian, her 16-year-old son (and three others) who were fired from their jobs at a local grocery store because they stole soda, candy, and/or money. Julian made restitution, wrote a letter of apology, and asked the owner for forgiveness. The owner said he'd forgive him but could not give him a job reference.

People of all ages make mistakes, but especially young people. Julian seems to have learned his lesson. I hope he's now hanging around a different group of kids, for his own sake. Although shoplifting is common, most managers won't hire someone they know was caught stealing. What if it happens again? Who gets blamed for hiring them?

Here's the sticky part—and remember that the topic right now is protecting your references: If Julian were my son, I would advise him *not* to put the grocery job on his record. Just pretend this part of his life never happened, resolve to do better in the future, and get a fresh start at age 16½.

## Developing Character on the Job

Your early jobs are important in your development. Don't quit just because you think your coworkers are not doing their fair share or your bosses don't dote on you the way your parents do. You would also be likely to leave the *next* job when it is not exactly right. However, if you stay a while, you will not only pick up new skills that you can market to other places, you can learn about yourself and other people.

People tend to develop traits early on that they take with them throughout their work lives. One of our clients, the chief financial officer for a midsized company, did factory work when he was young. There, he learned persistence and determination, traits that have served him well throughout his impressive career.

When you are young, you can train yourself to be a slacker, trying to get away with doing as little as possible. Then you will probably behave like that on your next job, staying at the bottom rung. Or you can train yourself to pitch in, help out wherever the boss needs help, and do it cheerfully. Then you are more likely to rise through the ranks.

Richard Bayer, an ethicist and author on employment economics, notes specific character traits that are essential in today's information age. These include cooperation, hard work, persistence, creativity, optimism, planning, regard for the welfare of others, flexibility, trust in the future, and patience for long-run results.

**Character traits essential today: cooperation, hard work, persistence, creativity, optimism, planning, regard for the welfare of others, flexibility, trust in the future, and patience for long run results.**

You will learn a lot in your early jobs. If your coworkers are slackers, while you are not, you may learn that life isn't fair—at least in the short run and sometimes in the long run. But maybe management will notice that you are working harder than the others and give you more responsibility. Or maybe you'll learn to speak up to get additional assignments and move up that way. Maybe you'll learn to do an honest day's work for an honest day's pay regardless of what others are doing, and maintain a pleasant attitude rather than feeling too resentful.

Studies have shown that cheery workers tend to get ahead at all levels more than those who are unhappy complainers. Even at your junior level, learning to work hard with a pleasant disposition will groom you for future success. As I mentioned earlier, managers select enthusiastic workers over those who are simply competent when deciding who should stay or be fired.

Your first job may not seem so important now, but you are laying the foundation for the rest of your work life.

---

*The heights by great men reached and kept*
*Were not attained by sudden flight,*
*But they, while their companions slept,*
*Were toiling upward in the night.*

Henry Wadsworth Longfellow

*Courage is doing what you are afraid to do. There can be no courage unless you're scared.*

Eddie Rickenbacker

# Follow-Up after a Job Interview: Consider Your Competition

*Bullock shrugged. He'd been thinking about Bill that afternoon, trying to decide how to fit him into Deadwood Brickworks, Inc. It wasn't a question he could be useful. Anybody could be useful when you decided where they fit. That was what business was.*

Pete Dexter, *Deadwood*

So far in the interview process, we have considered you and the hiring manager. By acting like a consultant, you can negotiate a job that's right for both you and him or her. But there are other players and other complexities in this drama. First, there are all the other people you meet during the hiring process. They are influencers and, in fact, may influence the hiring decision more than the hiring manager does. These are people the hiring manager trusts and on whose opinions she or he relies. In addition, there are complexities such as outside influencers, the timing of the hiring decision, and salary considerations. Finally, you have competitors. They may be other people the interviewer is seeing, or your competition can be an ideal candidate in the interviewer's mind.

This chapter contains case studies of how some people considered and dealt with their competition. In the next chapter, we'll give you the guidelines they followed, which helped them decide what they could do to win the job. Remember, the job hunt really starts after the interview. What can you do to turn the interview into an offer? This is the part of the process that requires the most analysis and strategic thinking. Think *objectively* about the needs of the organization and of everyone you met, and think about what you can do to influence *each* person.

*If you're in a seller's market,* however, you may not need to follow up: You'll be brought back for more meetings before you have a chance to breathe. *If you're in a buyer's market,* you will probably have to do some thoughtful follow-up to get the job.

Because effective follow-up is a lot of work, your first decision should be: Do I want to get an offer for this job? Do I want to *go for it*? If you are ambivalent, and are in a competitive market, you will probably *not* get the job. Someone else will do what he or she needs to do to get it.

Follow-ups will not guarantee you a specific job, but extensive follow-ups on a number of possibilities increase the number and quality of your offers. If you focus too much on one specific situation and how you can *make* them hire you, that won't work. You need both breadth and depth in your job hunt: You have both when you are in contact on a regular basis with 6 to 10 people who are in a position to hire you or recommend that you be hired. You must have 6 to 10 of these contacts in the works, *each* of which you are trying to move along.

Ideally, you will get to a point where you are moving them along together, slowing certain ones down and speeding others up, so you wind up with three concurrent job offers. Then you can select the one that is best for you. This will usually be the job that positions you best for the long run—the one that fits best into your Forty-Year Vision. It will rarely be sensible to make a decision based on money alone.

Therefore, if one situation is taking all of your energy, stop right now for 10 minutes and think of how you can quickly contact other people in your target area (through networking, direct contact, search firms, or ads). It will take the pressure off, and prevent you from trying to close too soon on this one possibility.

## CASE STUDY *The Artist*

## Status Checks Rarely Work

Most people think follow-up means calling for the status of the search. This is not the case.

At Citibank, a project I managed needed an artist. I interviewed 20 and came up with two piles: one of 17 rejects, and another of the 3 I would present to my boss and my boss's boss. A few people called to *follow up*. Here's one:

Artist: "I'm calling to find out the procedure and the status. Do you mind?"
Me: "Not at all. I interviewed 20 people. I'll select 3 and present them to my boss and my boss's boss."
Artist: "Thanks a lot. Do you mind if I call back later?"
Me: "No, I don't mind."

The artist called every couple of weeks for three months, asked the same thing, and stayed in the reject pile. To move out, he could have said things like:

- Is there more information I can give you?
- I've been giving a lot of thought to your project and have some new ideas. I'd like to show them to you.
- Where do I stand? How does my work compare with the work others presented?

If all you're doing is finding out where you are in the process, that's rarely enough. *The ball is always in your court.* It is your responsibility to figure out what the next step should be. Job hunters view the whole process as if it were a tennis game where—*thwack*—the ball is in the hiring manager's court. Wrong.

Me to job hunter: "How's it going?"
Job hunter to Kate: *(Thwack!)* "The ball's in their court now. They're going to call me."

When they call, it will probably be to say, "You are not included." If you wait, not many of your interviews will turn into offers.

---

*Mediocrity obtains more with application than superiority without it.*

Baltasar Gracian, *Oraculo Manual*

## CASE STUDY *Rachel*

## Trust Me

*A man is not finished when he's defeated; he's finished when he quits.*

Richard Milhous Nixon

Rachel had been unemployed for nine months. This was her first Five O'Clock Club meeting. She was disgusted. "I had an interview," she said. "I know what will happen: I'll be a finalist and they'll hire the other person."

Rachel was nice, enthusiastic, and smart: She was always a finalist. Yet the more experienced person was always hired.

Here's the story. Rachel, a lobbyist, was interviewing at a law firm. The firm liked her background but it needed some public relations help and perhaps an internal newsletter. Rachel did not have experience in either of those areas, though she knew she could do those things. She wrote a typical thank you note playing up her strengths, playing down her weaknesses, but essentially ignoring the firm's objections. She highlighted the lobbying, and said that PR and a newsletter would not be a problem. She could do it. She was asking the firm to "trust her."

## Lots of Job Hunters Take the *Trust Me* Approach

The following occurred during a group meeting at The Five O'Clock Club:

Me: "Do you want this job? Are you willing to go through a brick wall to get it?"
Rachel: "Yes. I am. I really want this job."
Me: "Let's think about overcoming their objections. If you can write a PR plan after you get hired, why not do it now? Why ask them to trust you?"

Two people in the group had old PR plans, which they lent her. Remember: The proposals or ideas you write will probably be wrong. That's okay. You're showing the company you can think the problem through and actually come up with solutions.

Rachel's lack of experience with newsletters was also an objection. We suggested Rachel call law firms in other cities and get their newsletters.

After doing research, Rachel sent a very different note. In this one she said she had been giving it more thought and was very excited about working for the firm. She had put together a PR plan, *which she would like to review with them,* and had gotten copies of newsletters from other law firms, which gave her ideas of what she could do in a newsletter for them. Of course, she got the job.

## Uncovering Their Objections

Rachel got the job because she overcame the objections of the hiring committee. Start thinking about how you can overcome objections. This will change the way you interview, and you will become more attuned to picking up valid objections rather than quashing them. Then you can even solicit negatives. For example, you can ask:

- Who else is being considered?
- What do they have to offer?
- How do I stand in comparison with them?
- What kind of person would be considered an ideal candidate?
- What would you like to say about a new hire one year from now?

Get good at interviewing so you can solicit valid objections to hiring you.

---

*Without competitors there would be no need for strategy.*

Kenichi Ohmae, *The Mind of the Strategist*

## Act Like a Consultant

Since most jobs are created for people, find out what the manager needs. Hiring managers often decide to structure the job differently, depending on who they hire. Why not influence the hiring manager to structure the job for you?

Probe—and don't expect anything to happen in the first meeting. If you were a consultant trying to sell a $30,000 or $70,000 project (your salary), you wouldn't expect someone to immediately say, "Fine. Start working." Yet job hunters often expect to get an offer during the first meeting.

Forget about job hunting. This is regular business. You're selling an expensive package. Do what a consultant or a salesperson does: Ask about the company's problems and its situation; think how you could get back to the interviewer later. Get enough information so you can follow up and give the interviewer enough information so he'll want to see you again. Move the process along: Suggest you meet with more people there. Do research. Have someone influence the interviewer on your behalf. Then get back to him again. That's what a consultant does. Remember to move the process along; outshine and outlast your competition.

CASE STUDY ***Leon***

## How Did He Get the Job?

Leon came to The Five O'Clock Club after 15 months of interviews. After three Club meetings, he got two job offers simply because he followed the group's advice and wrote proposals. When he told the group his good news, someone asked him how he got the two jobs. He said that one offer was from an ad and one was from networking. Leon had been pursuing jobs through networking and search firms for 15 months, but it wasn't until he decided to do real follow-up on these that he was offered a job.

*He said, however, that the real secret of his fortune was that none of his mules worked as hard and with so much determination as he did himself.*

Gabriel Garcia Marquez, *Love in the Time of Cholera*

## The Other Decision Makers/ Influencers

*The people you want to reach . . . should be viewed as distinct target audiences that require different approaches and strategies.*

Jeffrey P. Davidson, marketing consultant
*Management World*, September/October 1987

Many job hunters assume the hiring manager is the only person who matters. Big mistake. Others are not only influencers; in some cases, they may actually be the decision makers.

I'm a good example. I make terrible hiring decisions: Everyone I interview seems fine to me. So I have others meet with the candidates. Their opinions weigh more than mine. Any applicant who ignores them is ignoring the decision makers—or at least the serious influencers.

Take seriously every person you meet. Don't be rude to the receptionist. She may say to the boss, "If you hire him, I'm quitting." That receptionist is definitely an influencer.

## What Happens as Time Passes

*He had made a fortune in business and owed it to being able to see the truth in any situation.*

Ethan Canin, *Emperor of the Air*

Most jobs are *created* for people: Most interviewers don't know clearly what they will want the new person to do. Yet job hunters expect the hiring manager to tell them exactly what the job will be like and get annoyed when the manager can't tell them.

Generally the job description depends on who will be in the job. Therefore, help the hiring manager figure out what the new person should do. If you don't help him, another job hunter will. This is called *negotiating the job*. You are trying to remove all of the company's objections to hiring you, as well as all of *your* objections to working for them. Try to make it work for both of you. But time is your enemy. Imagine what happens in the hiring process as time passes:

You have an interview. When I, your counselor, ask how it went, you tell me how great it was: The two of you hit it off, and you are sure you will be called back. You see this interview as something frozen in time, and you wait for the magical phone call.

But after you left, the manager met with someone else, who brought up new issues. Now his criteria for what he wants have changed somewhat, and consequently, his impression of you has also changed. He was honest when he said he liked you, but things look different to him now. Perhaps you have what he needs to meet his new criteria, or perhaps you could convince him that his new direction is wrong, but you don't know what is now on his mind.

You call to find out *how things are going*. He says he is still interviewing and will call you later when he has decided. Actually, then it will probably be too late for you. His thinking is constantly evolving as he meets with people. You were already out of the running. *Your call did nothing to influence his thinking*: You did not address his new concerns. You asked for a status report of where he was in the hiring process, and that's what you got. You did nothing to get back into the loop of people he might consider or find out the new issues that are now on his mind.

*Oh I could show my prowess,*
*be a lion not a mou-esse,*
*if I only had the nerve.*

The Cowardly Lion in the movie *The Wizard of Oz* (from the book by L. Frank Baum) by E. Y. Harburg and Harold Arlen

The manager meets more people and further defines the position. Interviewing helps him decide what he wants. You are getting further and further away from his new requirements.

You are not aware of this. You remember the great meeting you two had. You remind me that he said he really liked you. You insist on freezing that moment in time. You don't want to do anything to rock the boat or appear desperate. You hope it works out. "The ball is in his court," you say. "I gave it my best. There's nothing I can do but wait." So you decide to give it more time . . . time to go wrong.

---

*Annie:*. . . you want to give it time—
*Henry:* Yes—
*Annie:*. . . time to go wrong, change, spoil.
Then you'll know it wasn't the real thing.

Tom Stoppard, *The Real Thing*

You have to imagine what is going on as time passes. Perhaps the hiring manager is simply very busy and is not working on this at all. Or perhaps things are moving along without you. Statistics prove that the person who is interviewed last has the best chance of being hired. That's because the last person benefits from all the thinking the manager has done. The manager is able to discuss all of the issues of concern with this final applicant.

## What You Can Do during the Interview

If you go into an interview with the goal of getting a job, you are putting too much pressure on yourself to come to closure. When you walk away without an offer, you feel discouraged. When you walk away without even knowing what the job is, you feel confused and lost.

Instead of criticizing managers who do not know what they want, try to understand them: "I can understand that there are a number of ways you can structure this position. Let's talk about your problems and your needs. Perhaps I can help."

Your goal in the interview is not to get an offer but to build a relationship with the manager. This means you are on the manager's side—assessing the situation and figuring out how to move the process along so you can continue to help define the job.

---

*Boone smiled and nodded. The muscles in his jaw hurt. "What I meant was did you ever shoot anybody but your own self. Not that that don't count."*

Pete Dexter, *Deadwood*

## Pay Attention to Your Competition

Most job hunters think only about themselves and the hiring manager. They don't think about the others being considered for the position. But you are different. You are acutely aware at all times that you have competition. Your goal is to get rid of them.

As you move the process along, you can see your competitors dropping away because you are doing a better job of addressing the hiring manager's needs, coming up with solutions to her or his problems, and showing more interest and more competence than they are.

You are in a problem-solving mode. Here's the way you think: "My goal isn't to get a job immediately, but to build a relationship. How can I build a relationship so that someday when this person decides what he or she wants, it'll be me?" You have hung in there. You have eliminated your competition. You have helped define the job in a way that suits both you and the hiring manager. You have the option of saying, "Do I want this job or don't I?"

# Four-Step Salary Negotiation Strategy

*I've got all the money I'll ever need*
*if I die by four o'clock.*

Henny Youngman

**First, read the chapter: *Case Study: Julie—Getting and Doing Well in Interviews***

Now you know you not only have to impress the hiring manager but also other influencers so they will want to have you on board. In addition, you have to think about your likely competitors, and how you can convince everyone you meet that you are the best choice. During the interview, a job hunter may also think about salary.

When job hunters ask about salary negotiation, they usually want to know how to answer the questions, What are you making now? and What are you looking for? We'll cover these issues in detail a little later, but it is more important to first look at salary negotiation from a strategic point of view. From the very first meeting, you can set the stage for compensation discussions later.

Most job hunters think about salary—unconsciously and anxiously—during their first meeting. They think, I'm making $40,000 now, but I know this person won't pay more than $30,000. Most job hunters try to get rid of the anxiety. They don't want to waste their time if this person isn't going to pay them fairly. So when the hiring manager mentions money, the job hunter is relieved to talk about it.

Hiring manager: How much are you making now?
Job hunter: I'm making $40,000.

**Dear Five O'Clock Clubber,**

**Think strategically. From the very first meeting, set the stage for compensation discussions later. If a job pays $5,000 less than you want, that's okay for now. Postpone salary discussions, and remember that you are there *not* for this specific job, but for a position that has not yet been completely defined—and in which you have some say.**

**A skilled negotiator has a completely different approach—and much more power—than someone who does not know these techniques. A skilled negotiator knows that he or she is not *chasing jobs, but chasing companies.* This position may not be right, but you want to make a good impression anyway because there may be other places in the organization that are better.**

**The important salary negotiation issues are strategic, not tactical. Those are the issues we will cover here. Good luck.**

**Cordially, Kate**

Hiring manager: That's a little rich for us. We were thinking about $30,000.
Job hunter: I couldn't possibly take $30,000.

End of discussion. Another wasted interview. But there is a better way. Intend to turn every job interview into an appropriate offer. Overcome the company's objections to hiring you, and overcome your own objections to working there. If the salary or something else bothers you about the job, think about how you can change it.

Think more consciously and more strategically. Intend to negotiate. Most job hunters don't negotiate at all.

- They don't negotiate the job. They listen passively to what the job is, and try to fit themselves into it—or reject it.
- They certainly don't negotiate the salary. They listen to the offer, and then decide whether they want to take it.

**Don't accept or reject a job until it is offered to you.**

Job hunters decide whether or not they want the job without negotiating to make it more appropriate—and without even getting an offer! Career counselors have a maxim: Don't accept or reject a job until it is offered to you.

We'll see how you can be more proactive rather than passive. The following guidelines will allow you to take more control and more responsibility for what happens to you. Following these steps will not guarantee you the compensation you want, but you will certainly do much better than if you do not follow them.

*There arises from the hearts of busy [people] a love of variety, a yearning for relaxation of thought as well as of body, and a craving for a generous and spontaneous fraternity.*

J. Hampton Moore, *History of The Five O'Clock Club,* written in the 1890s

Remember the four steps you will learn here—and pay attention to where you are in those steps.

**If you can remember these four steps with regard to a particular company, you will do better in your salary negotiation *—and in your entire search as well.***

## Step 1: Negotiate the Job

By now, you have already negotiated the job. You have created a job that suits both you and the hiring manager. Make sure it is at an appropriate level for you. If the job is too low-level, don't ask about the salary—*upgrade the job.* Add responsibilities until the job is worth your while. Make sure the hiring manager agrees that this new job is what he or she wants. Don't negotiate the salary yet.

## Step 2: Outshine and Outlast Your Competition

By now, you have already killed off your competition. You have kept in the running by offering to do more than your competitors. You have paid more attention to the progress made in your meetings, and you have moved the process along. You have satisfied every need and responded to every objection. For some jobs, it can take five interviews before the subject of salary is discussed. All the while, your competitors have been dropping out. It is best to postpone the discussion of salary until they are all gone.

## Step 3: Get the Offer

Once a manager has decided that you are the right person, you are in a better position to negotiate a package that is appropriate for you. Until you actually get the offer, postpone the discussion of salary.

## Step 4: Negotiate Your Compensation Package

Most job hunters hear the offer and then either accept or reject it. This is not negotiating. If you have never negotiated a package for yourself, you need to practice. Why not try to get some offers that don't even interest you, just so you can practice negotiating the salary? Here are some hints to get you started.

- Know the company's and the industry's pay scales.
- Know what you want in a negotiation session, and know what you are willing to do without. Negotiate one point at a time. Negotiate base pay first and then the points the employer would easily agree to. Save for last the issues of conflict. Be prepared to back off, or not even bring up, issues that are not important to you.
- You are both on the same side. Each of you should want a deal that works now and works later—not one that will make either of you resentful.
- Care—but not too much. If you desperately want the job—at any cost—you will not do a good job of negotiating. You must convince yourself, at least for the time you are interviewing, that you have alternatives.
- Try to get them to state the first bid. If they say: "How much do you want?" You say: "How much are you offering?" If pressed about your prior salary, either say instead what you are looking for, or be sure to include bonus and perks. Some include an expected bonus or increase in salary.
- If the manager makes you an unacceptable offer, *talk about the job.* Look disappointed and say how enthusiastic you are about the position, the company, and the possibility of doing great things for this manager. Say everything is great and you can't wait to start—but your only reservation is the compensation. Ask what can be done about this.

Be reasonable. As the saying goes: Bulls win, and bears win, but pigs never win.

---

*If your ship doesn't come in, swim out to it.*

Jonathan Winters

## It Works at All Levels

Once I did a salary negotiation seminar for low-level corporate people. One person had been a paper-burster for 25 years: He tore the sheets of paper as they came off the computer. But because he had been at the company for 25 years, his salary was at the top of the range of paper-bursters. He had the same kind of salary problem a lot of us have.

The four steps worked for him, too. He told the hiring managers, "Not only can I burst the paper, but I can fix the machines. This will save you on machine downtime and machine repair costs. And I can train people, which will also save you money."

He was:

1. **Negotiating the job.**

And:

2. **Outshining and outlasting his competition.**

And after he:

3. **Gets the offer.**

He'll have no trouble:

4. **Negotiating the salary.**

Know where you are in the four steps. If you have not yet done steps one, two and three, try to postpone step four.

## CASE STUDY *Bessie*

### It Can Even Work against *Me*

Once when I was a chief financial officer for a small firm, I wanted to hire an accounting manager who would supervise a staff of four.

I told an excellent search firm exactly what I wanted and the salary range I was looking for: "someone in the $45,000 range."

I received lots of résumés—all of which the search firm had marked at the top: "Asking for $45,000." I interviewed a lot of people, but Bessie stood out from the crowd. I had Bessie meet with a peer of mine and also with the company president. Everyone loved her.

Finally, I told Bessie that we were pleased to offer her the $45,000 she wanted. Bessie said, " I would love to work here, but I would not be happy with $45,000. I didn't put that there."

I was stunned, but I was also stuck. We had made an investment in Bessie. Everyone had met her and loved her, and she wisely stayed mum about the money until she received the offer. A more anxious job hunter might have said early on, "I see that it says $45,000 at the top of my résumé, but I just want you to know that I am already making more than that." That would have been admirable honesty but the person would have been out of the running.

Bessie wound up with $50,000, which is what she was worth—and we wound up with an excellent employee. Bessie had followed the four steps exactly.

1. **Negotiate the job.**
2. **Outshine and outlast your competition.**
3. **Get the offer.**
4. **Negotiate your package.**

Remember, too, that *salary negotiation* involves more than salary. It can involve negotiating for anything you need to do the job well, in addition to your compensation package. For example, you may need to have company-paid attendance at a trade association meetings.

**Be sure the person with whom you are negotiating is at the right level. If you find yourself constantly bumping up against the salary level of the people with whom you are negotiating, the problem is not your salary negotiation technique. The problem is that you are talking to people who are at the wrong level.**

**Have you already received an offer? If they are *thinking* about making you an offer, that's not the same as actually *making* you an offer. Don't negotiate your compensation until you *receive* an offer.**

**Where is your competition? You cannot assess your negotiating leverage until you know how the hiring team sees you compared with your competition. You may have already received the offer, but could the company easily consider someone else? If the hiring team wants nobody but you, you are in a stronger negotiating position.**

*No modest man ever did make a fortune.*

Lady Mary Worthy Montagu

By now, you know where you are in the four steps. In fact, for each company with whom you are meeting, you know exactly where you are in the process. If you are conscious of where you are, you will do much better than if you simply do what seems reasonable without regard to where you are in the process.

In addition, the more experienced you become in negotiating your compensation, the more you can assess what is appropriate for a given situation and deviate from the rules. However, until you are an experienced negotiator, it is best to play by the rules.

## What Are You Making Now? What Are You Looking For?

Now we'll look at the questions you've been waiting for. But we'll look at them strategically—so you can *plan* an appropriate answer depending on your situation. First, you need to develop some background information before you can plan your strategy for answering the questions. The strategy will also give you hints for postponing the discussion of salary until you have an offer.

### Background Information: Figure Out What You Really Make

If you are being paid hourly as a student, that rate does not translate to a full-time salary after gradation. There is no connection. When you are a student, you are considered *in training*. Once you are in the regular workforce (degree or not), it's a whole other ballgame.

Those who are in the regular workforce, however, do need to look at what they are currently making. Start with your base salary, but also include your bonus and any perks, such as a company car, a savings plan, deferred compensation, company lunches, and company contribution to insurance plans. That's what you really make—but that may not be what you will tell the prospective employer.

### Background Information: Figure Out What You Are Worth in the Market

Talk to search firms, ask people at association meetings, look at ads in the paper, and—most of all—network. At networking meetings, ask, "What kind of salary could someone like me expect at your company?" A few networking meetings will give you a good idea of the market rates for someone like you.

However, you must remember that you are worth different amount in different markets. You may be worth a certain amount in one industry, field, or geographic area and a different amount in other industries, fields, or geographic areas.

What's more, you may be worth more to one company than you would be to another.

Research what you are worth in each of your target markets. And when you are interviewing at a specific company, find out as much as you can about the way they pay.

### Background Information: Compare What You Are Making (Total Compensation) with What the Market Is Paying

You need to know if you are presently at market rates, below market, or above market. *This is the key* to how you will answer a hiring manager or search firm that asks you, "What are you making?" or "What are you looking for?"

### How to Answer: If You Are within the Market Range

Most companies want to know what you are making and, if you are within the market range, they will pay you 10 to 15 percent above what you are currently making. Therefore, if you are making $40,000 and you know the market is paying $43,000 to $45,000, then you could say, "Right now I'm at $40,000, but I'm looking to move a little away from that." The only time you can safely state your current compensation is when you are at market rates.

### How to Answer: If You Are above Market Rates

A counselor asked me to have a meeting with his client Sam, who was having problems finding a job because of his high salary. I did an interview role play with Sam. At one point I said, "So, Sam, what are you making now?" Sam replied, "Eighty thousand dollars plus-plus-plus." I said, "I know you're a very competent person, but we simply cannot afford someone at your high level." Sam's salary was not hurting him, but his way of talking about it was. Even if your salary isn't $80,000-plus-plus-plus, you can easily put off the hiring manager if she thinks your salary will be a problem. You have to give her a chance to find out about you, and you have to think about how you can create a job that is appropriate for your salary. You must tell her, "Salary will not be a problem"—*especially if you know it is a problem.* You have to think to yourself that it won't be a problem when she gets to know you better and understands what you will do for her. Otherwise, you will not get anywhere.

**Your position has to be that "salary won't be a problem." It is your job to reassure the hiring manager that you are both on the same team and can work this out. When they get to know you better—and what you have to offer—salary *won't* be a problem.**

If you are making more than the market rate, do your best to create a job that warrants the salary you want and defer the discussion of salary until you have the offer. When you're asked, "What are you making now?" use a response from the following list to reassure the hiring manager that you are both on the same team and can work this out. These responses are listed in sequence from easiest to most difficult. Try the easy response first. If the hiring manager persists, you may have to move on to one of the other responses. You are simply trying to postpone the discussion of salary until she knows you better and you have an offer.

The manager asks, "What are you making now?" You respond:

- "I'd prefer to postpone talking about the salary until I'm more clear about the job I'll be doing. When we come to some agreement on the job, I know that salary won't be a problem."
- "Salary won't be a problem. But I'm not exactly sure what the job is, so maybe we can talk more about that. I'm very flexible, and I'm sure that when we come to some agreement on the job, we can work out the salary."
- "Salary won't be a problem. I know that you do not want to bring someone in at a salary that makes you resentful, and I'm sure you do not want me to be resentful either. I know that we'll come to a happy agreement."
- "I'm making very good money right now, and I deserve it. But I'd hate to tell you what it is because I'm afraid it will put you off. I know that salary will not be a problem. I'm a fair person and I'm sure you are, too. I know we'll come to an agreement."

## How to Answer: If You are Making below Market Rates

Again, you have a few options. For example, if a manager asks what you are making, you could answer instead with what you are looking for.

Manager: "What are you making right now?"
You: "I understand the market is paying in the $45,000 to $55,000 range."
Manager: "That's outrageous. We can't pay that."
You: "What range are you thinking of for this position?"

Note: You haven't revealed either what you are making or what you want—but you've still tested the hiring manager's expectations. The person who states a number first is at a negotiation disadvantage.

Or you could say, "My current salary is $32,000. I know the marketplace today is closer to $45,000. I have been willing to trade off the salary in order to build my skills [or whatever]. But now I am in a position where I don't need to trade off money, and I'm ready to take a position at market rates."

*Take calculated risks. That is quite different from being rash.*

George S. Patton

## If You Are Pushed to Name Your Salary

Don't simply state your salary—develop a line of patter to soften it. Simply stating a number can be very confrontational, as with the $80,000-plus-plus-plus job hunter. If you have exhausted all the responses and the hiring manager throws you up against the wall and shouts, "I want to know what you are making!" you can still soften your answer by saying, for example:

- "I'm earning very good money right now—in the $65,000 to $75,000 range, depending on bonus. And I'm certainly worth it. But I'm very interested in your company, and I know we can work something out."
- "My salary is very low—only $20,000—and I know that's dramatically below market rates. But I was willing to do that as an investment in my future. Now, however, I expect to make market rates."

You should name your salary only as a last resort. Managers want to know your last salary as a way of determining your worth to them, but it is certainly not the most reasonable way to decide what you are worth. For example, you would want to be paid more if the job requires 70 hours a week and lots of travel, versus one that requires only 35 hours a week. How do you know how much you want unless you know what the job entails? You are being sensible to talk about the job first and the salary later.

Some managers cannot deal that way, so you have to be prepared in case you are forced to discuss salary prematurely. And even if you do name your salary, there are different ways you can couch it. For example:

- "My current salary is $32,500."
- "I make in the high 40s."
- "My base is around $25,000 and my bonus [commissions] is usually around $15,000, which brings my total package to $40,000."
- "I make in the range of $40,000 to $70,000, depending on my bonus." (This, of course, tells them very little.)

Remember to soften your mention of your salary with a line of patter or your response will sound too confrontational and too much like a demand: "I make . . . but salary won't be a problem because. . . ."

**You are trying to postpone the discussion of salary until after you have an offer, but in real life that is not always possible. Therefore, postpone it if you can. And if you can't, be sure you *know* how you want to answer the questions:**

- **"What are you making now?" and**
- **"What are you looking for?"**

## No Absolute One Way

Salary negotiation is the most nerve-racking part of the job hunting process. At the beginning of your job hunt you are at loose ends—not knowing where you are going and feeling like you will never get there. But salary negotiation is the part people fear the most. It is a surprise monster at the end of your search.

**You're in a great negotiating position if you can walk away from the deal. Therefore, make sure you have 6 to 10 things in the works. If this deal is the only thing you have going, see how quickly you can get something else going.**

## Search Firms

Search firms must know the *range* of salary you are making or the amount you are looking for. They do not need an exact amount.

## Ads

In answering ads, you will rarely give your salary requirements. The trend at the moment is for many ads to read, "Please state salary requirements." Most job hunters do not, and the hiring company does *not* exclude them. Stating your salary or requirements not only puts you at a negotiating disadvantage but also allows you to be eliminated from consideration because you are too high or too low.

On the other hand, some ads state, "You will absolutely not be considered unless you state your salary requirements." Then, you should state them.

## What Is Negotiable?

Everything's negotiable. That doesn't mean you'll *get* it, but it is negotiable. First, think of what is important to you. Make a personal list of what you must have versus what you want. Decide where you can be flexible, but also know the issues that are deal breakers for you.

Think of your musts versus your wants. If you get everything you *must* have, then perhaps you won't even mention items on your *want* list. Go in knowing your bottom-line requirements, what you would be willing to trade off, and what benefits/perks could compensate you if you hit a salary snag. Have your own goals in the negotiation clearly in mind.

Salary is not the only form of compensation that might be negotiated. Other items might include:

- the timing of the first review
- reimbursements for education (if you are working full-time as a regular employee, large employers may pay for your tuition so you can complete your degree or even pay for graduate school)
- association or club memberships
- closing costs on a new home or a relocation package
- use of a company car
- bonus

Which is the most meaningful or valuable to you?

### Get Salary Information on the Web

Want to see what others make in your field? Want to see what you should expect? Check out these sites. But remember that the salaries can be slightly overstated because those polled may slightly exaggerate how much they are making.

- *www.salary.com*
- *www.compensation.com*
- *www.jobstar.org* (Go to *Salary Information.*)
- *www.homefair.com* (for cost-of-living comparisons if you are moving to another state)

# How to Gain Negotiating Leverage

*Great is the art of beginning,*
*but greater the art of ending.*
Henry Wadsworth Longfellow

**The most important negotiating leverage you have is being in demand elsewhere. Develop other options. Be able to walk away from the deal. You can create this situation without much difficulty.**

Most job hunters say to themselves, "I'm so far along with this one possibility, I'll just ride it out and see what happens. If I don't get an offer from them, then I'll think of what else I should do."

Bad move. Have at least a tentative answer to the question of what you would do if this doesn't work. Having an alternative:

- helps you to be more relaxed in your discussions
- increases your chances of having this possibility work out
- puts you in a better position to negotiate this position wisely
- helps you to tolerate the months that may go by before it comes to closure
- gives you something with which to compare this offer so you can make a more objective decision

As one Five O'Clock Clubber said during her *graduation speech* after accepting a new position, "When you are going after only one job, you think that, if it falls through, you will lose a few weeks in your search. Instead of losing a few weeks, you lose a few months. First, you have to recover from the disappointment. Then you have to gear yourself up and decide where to look next. Then you have to get your entire search going again. Take it from me, it's better to never lose that momentum at all."

## CASE STUDY *Gregory*
## Skipping a Step

When I met Gregory, he had three job possibilities in the works and wanted to bring them to closure. After all, he said, he had a family to support.

It seemed to me that Gregory's prospects were not a good match for him. After much discussion, Gregory agreed to contact additional prospective employers: This would not slow down his current negotiations and may even make things move faster.

To develop more appropriate targets, Gregory had to complete the assessment process (the Seven Stories and other exercises), which he had skipped. Perhaps Gregory could find work that he would enjoy doing and also meet his family responsibilities.

Gregory received six job offers. The three new companies offered him appropriate positions *before* the first three companies made him any offers at all.

Do not skip the assessment part of your search. The results help you to target correctly from the start, give you something against which to compare your offers, and help you be more objective about which job you should take next.

## CASE STUDY *Carolina*

### Self-Discipline to Do the Right Thing

Carolina had only one job prospect and was anxious about whether she would get an offer. Her most important meeting with the company was scheduled for the following week, and she wanted to land that job. "Believe it or not," I told her, "you will do better in your upcoming round of interviews if we could first develop a strategy for getting more possibilities in the works."

That day, after Carolina prepared for the interview, she went to the library, researched 150 other companies in her target area, wrote a great cover letter, and sent it with a résumé to all of them.

By the time her important meeting came around, Carolina was so relaxed that she had almost forgotten about it. When the small things inevitably went wrong, she could say to herself, "At least I've got 150 letters in the mail working for me."

Three weeks later, Carolina got the offer she wanted. In addition, she received calls because of her mail campaign. She accepted the job with the company with whom she had been meeting but continued to speak with the other companies just to be sure she had made the right choice. For a few weeks after starting the new job, she still kept in touch with the other companies—until she was completely sure that she had made the correct decision.

## CASE STUDY *Sergio*

### Acting Like a Consultant

In search only two weeks, Sergio had no trouble getting interviews. However, he was having an important first interview the day after our Five O'Clock Club meeting. He was hyped up, stressed out, and breathlessly told the group, "This job pays a lot of money. I want to go in tomorrow and get them to hire me. I think they want someone who is more technical than I am, so I have to sell myself really hard. I've prepared a handout to give them at the end of the meeting. Take a look at it and see if she is likely to give me the job."

At first, the group was mildly confused. No one looked at the handout. They knew that was not the problem. Then people in the group commented:

"Do you really want this job, Sergio?"

"What other companies are you talking to? It's so easy for you to get interviews."

"You've got to slow down."

"If this job pays as much as you say it does, they're not going to make you an offer at the first meeting."

I built on the group's good comments: "Sergio, become this woman's friend. To help her, you need more information. Find out why she wants a person with strong technical experience. Find out more about her vision for the department. Help her decide what is really best for her—even if it seems, from time to time, as though you are putting yourself out of the running. Tell her that you will think about her situation and get back to her later. Then do some research. What you want from this first meeting is another meeting."

Sergio immediately calmed down. The group could hear it in his voice. In his panicky state, Sergio could not have done well in that interview. He was very grateful for the group's guidance.

Sergio met a few times with that company, kept his search going, and received four excellent offers from other companies. The one he had been so eager about faded from his interest.

## If You Are Currently Working

Employed people have the same leverage as those who have other possibilities in the works. If a hiring manager says to you, "Why are you leaving?" You can say, "I don't know that I am. I may stay right here." You don't know for sure *what* you are going to do. To be in a strong negotiating position—and an appealing candidate—you need options.

## Pretending to Have Other Offers

Why not say that you have other possibilities when, in fact, you have nothing else? Pretending you have other offers rarely works. The danger is not that you may be caught in a lie. The danger is that the company may say, "You should take the other offer," and three months later you still have no other alternatives, and you have also closed off this possibility. It's so easy to get other job possibilities in the works; focus on doing that.

## Win–Win

You want a win–win situation—one with which you can both live. After you have received a job offer, the situation is no longer adversarial. You and the company are both on the same side of the table, trying to make this deal work.

Actually, it is up to *you* to control this part of the process. You have the most at stake. The fact is, once a hiring manager has made an offer, he or she usually wants to close quickly. His or her job is done. Now your job begins.

Therefore, you must make sure you bring up everything you want in a way that is collaborative. Set a tone that reassures the hiring manager that you are thrilled to have the job, cannot wait to get started but have just a few details to work out. You can say, for example, "I really appreciate your spending this time. Some of these things may not mean much to you, but they mean a lot to me."

**Do not be swayed by the possibility of making $2,000 or $10,000 more. Select the job or assignment that positions you best for the long term. That is the most important criterion.**

*Human . . . life is a succession of choices, which every conscious human being has to make every moment. At times these choices are of decisive importance; and the very quality of these choices will often reveal that person's character and decide his fate. But that fate is by no means prescribed: for he may go beyond his inclinations, inherited as well as acquired ones. The decision and the responsibility is his: for he is a free moral agent, responsible for his actions.*

John Lukacs, *A History of the Cold War*

# Starting Out on the Right Foot in Your New Job

*Destiny is not a matter of chance, it is a matter of choice; it is not a thing to be waited for, it is a thing to be achieved.*

William Jennings Bryan

Starting out can be tricky: You are *on board* but the jury is still out on you. It is a time of trial. You are often being watched to see if you will work out. Here are some things you need to do to start out on the right foot and keep moving in the right direction.

## Before You Start

Say thank you. Contact all the people who helped you get the new position. Often people don't make this effort because they feel they'll be in the new job for a long time. But today, when the average American changes jobs every four years, the odds say you're going to change jobs again soon. You need to keep up those contacts.

Then think about ways to keep in touch with these contacts—if you read something that someone on your list would appreciate, clip it and send it.

## Right Away

- Don't fix things or do anything *big* for the first three months. That is one of the biggest mistakes people make. Take time to learn the system, the people, and the culture. You cannot possibly understand, in those first months, the implications of certain decisions you may make. You may be criticizing a project that was done by someone really important. Or you could be changing something that will affect someone on the staff in ways of which you aren't aware.
- Make yourself productive immediately. This does not contradict the point I just made. Do things that are safe. For example, install a new system where there has been none. This is *safe* because you aren't getting rid of some other system. What isn't safe? Firing half your staff the first week!
- Introduce yourself to everybody. Be visible: Walk around and meet people as soon as possible, including those who work for you. Meet everybody. Too many managers meet only the *important* people while ignoring those who actually do the day-to-day work.
- Don't make friends too fast. Someone who befriends you right away could also be on the way out. That doesn't mean you shouldn't be friendly, however. Go to lunch with several people rather than becoming known as someone who associates only with so-and-so. Get to know everybody, and then decide with whom to get closer.

**Try not to do anything too daring for the first three months. Take time to learn the system.**

*Know how to ask. There is nothing more difficult for some people. Nor for others, easier.*
Baltasar Gracian, *The Art of Worldly Wisdom*

## In the First Three Months

- Learn the corporate culture. People new to jobs lose those jobs often because of personality conflicts rather than a lack of competence.

Keep your head low until you learn how the company operates. Some companies have certain writing styles. Some expect you to speak a certain way. In certain companies, it's the way they hold parties. Do people work with their doors open or their doors shut?

All those things are part of the culture, and they are unwritten. To learn them, you have to pay attention.

Pay your dues before doing things at a variance with the corporate culture. After you build up some credits, you have more leeway. Let your personality emerge when you understand the company and after you have made some contribution.

- Learn the organizational structure—the real structure, not the one that is drawn on the charts. Ask your secretary to tell you who relates how with whom, who knows what, who thought of this project, who is important. You could be surprised.
- Find out what is important in your job. For example, when I counsel people for a corporation, counseling is not the only important thing in my job. The people who come to me are sent by personnel, and I must manage my relationship with the personnel people. It doesn't matter how good a counselor I am if I don't maintain a good relationship with personnel.
- Pay attention to your peers. Your peers can prove as valuable to you as your boss and subordinates. Do not try to impress them with your brilliance. That would be the kiss of death because you'd cause envy and have a very large reputation to live up to. Instead, encourage them to talk to you. They know more than you do. They also know your boss. Look to them to teach you and, in some cases, protect you.
- Don't set up competition. Everyone brings something to the party and should be respected for his or her talent, no matter what their level. Find ways to show your respect by asking for their input on projects that require their expertise.
- Set precedents you want to keep. If you start out working 12-hour days, people come to expect it of you—even if no one else is doing it. When you stop, people wonder what's wrong.

**Pay attention to your peers. Look to them to teach you and, in some cases, protect you.**

## Three Months and Beyond . . .

- Continue to develop contacts outside the company. If you need information for your job, sometimes the worst people to ask are your boss and people around you. A network is also a tremendous resource to fall back on when your boss is busy—and you will seem resourceful, smart, and connected.

**You'll be busy in your new job and may not keep up your outside contacts. In today's economy, that's a big mistake.**

- Keep a hero file for yourself, a hanging file where you place written descriptions of all your successes. If you have to job hunt in a hurry, you'll be able to recall what you've done.

You will also use it if you stay. If you want anything, whether it be a raise or a promotion, or the responsibility for a particular project, you can use the file to build a case for yourself.

- Keep managing your career. Don't think, "I'll just take this job and do what they tell me," because you might get off on some tangent. Remember where you were heading and make sure your career keeps going that way.

Be proactive in moving toward your goal. Take on lots of assignments. If a project comes up that fits into your long-term plan, do it. If one doesn't fit into your plan, you can do it or you can say, "Oh, I'd love to do that, but I'm really busy." Make those kinds of choices all the time.

*It is not the critic who counts; not the man who points out how the strong man stumbled or where the doer of deeds could have done better. The credit belongs to the man who is actually in the arena, whose face is marred by dust and sweat and blood; who strives valiently; who errs and comes short again and again; who knows the great enthusiasms, the great devotions; who spends himself in a worthy cause; who, at best, knows in the end the triumph of achievement, and who, at worst, if he fails, at least fails while daring greatly, so that his place shall never be with those timid souls who knew neither victory nor defeat.*

Theodore Roosevelt

**Someday soon, you'll be able to write one of these too.**

## Thank You Note after Getting a Job

Vivian Belen
400 First Avenue
Dayton, Ohio 22090

May 8, 20xx

Mr. Ellis Chase
3450 Garden Place
Des Moines, Iowa 44466

Dear Ellis:

The happy news is that I have accepted a position at Ohio State Trust as Controller for their Ohio branches. I'll be responsible for financial reporting and analysis, loans administration, budgeting and planning. I think it's a great match and will make good use of both my management skills and banking experience and the environment is congenial and professional.

I really appreciated your interest in my job search. I very much enjoyed speaking with people like you about your career and I appreciated your advice and encouragement. The fact that you so willingly gave of your time meant a great deal to me, and certainly was beneficial.

If I can reciprocate in some way, please feel free to be in touch with me. I will also probably be in contact with you in the months ahead. My new office is at 75 Rockfast Corner, Dayton 22091. You can reach me at 200-555-1212.

Sincerely,

Vivian Belen

# Epilogue

*. . . the country demands bold, persistent experimentation. It is common sense to take a method and try it. If it fails, admit it frankly and try another. But above all, try something.*

Franklin Delano Roosevelt Speech, Atlanta, 1932

There is no one way to job hunt; one neat solution to job hunting cannot answer it all. There are many ways.

The results of what you do in a job hunt are neither good nor bad; they are simply results to be observed and thought about. They are indicators of the correctness of the direction you are pursuing; they are not indictments. They are not personal; they are the world's feedback to what we are doing. These results can keep us on track, and if we look at them objectively, then they should not throw us offtrack.

Information is not good or bad; it is simply information. Things are changing so fast that we each need all the relevant information we can get. We may tend to block out information we find threatening—but that is precisely the information we need to get. Knowing the truth of what is happening around us may help us decide how to take care of ourselves. The information is not out to harm us—it is simply there.

---

*To view your life as blessed does not require you to deny your pain. It simply demands a more complicated vision, one in which a condition or event is not either good or bad but is, rather, both good and bad, not sequentially but simultaneously.*

Nancy Mairs (who has multiple sclerosis), *Carnal Acts*

*To be what we are, and to become what we are capable of becoming is the only end of life.*

Robert Louis Stevenson

There is a place for you, and you must look for it. Do not be stopped when others seem as though they are moving ahead. You, too, have a lot to offer if you would only think about yourself and not them. You are on your own track. Put your energy into discovering what is special about you, and then hold on to it.

You will be knocked down enough during your job hunting. Don't knock yourself; push back. Push past the people who offer you discouragement. Find those nurturing souls who recognize your worth and encourage you.

---

*. . . there are days when the result is so bad that no fewer than five revisions are required. In contrast, when I'm greatly inspired, only four revisions are needed.*

John Kenneth Galbraith

Don't tell me the facts about yourself; tell me who you really are. When you are writing to someone, ask yourself, What am I really trying to say to this person? What would I say if this person were right here? You are writing to a real person, and when your personality comes through and you say what you mean to say, then your note is unique.

Read your work out loud. It will give you a sense of the timing, the flow. You will find out if it is readable. You will notice where it stumbles.

Have someone else read it, too. Most people need an editor.

Take a few risks, but do it with some restraint. Don't be self-indulgent, but do let your personality seep through. You are not simply a *marketing professional with major banking experience*. You are *energetic with excellent training and a sense of stability*.

Pare down your writing. Get rid of the lines that have no energy. Think about getting rid of your first paragraph completely. Perhaps you wrote it just to warm up.

Write to make an impact, to influence the reader.

---

*It is impossible to enjoy idling thoroughly unless one has plenty of work to do.*

Jerome K. Jerome

Continue to job hunt, but be easy on yourself. I worked on this book whenever I could, but some days I didn't feel like thinking, so I researched quotes or made a chart or organized my material. All of these things later made my writing easier—so I was always making progress.

The same can be applied to your job hunt. Some days you may research an industry or a number of companies, or you may write a proposal or a follow-up note. But you have to spend most of your time interviewing—just as I had to spend most of my time writing.

Job hunting takes practice, just as writing takes practice. I am not a professional writer, and you are not a professional job hunter. Neither of us, you nor I, is perfect. But we are each trying to understand the process. This understanding will make us each less anxious and more patient about what we are doing.

Develop tricks to nudge yourself along. Find someone to report your progress to. If you cannot join our job-hunt group, then meet with a friend. Talking gives you perspective and the energy to keep on going.

Set goals for yourself. For example, aim at all times to be in contact, either in person or in writing, with six people who are in a position to hire you or recommend that you be hired. Keep in touch with these six people. Strive to add more people to your list, because others will drop off. Plan to continue to network even after you find a job. Make networking a part of your life.

Keep pushing even when you get afraid—especially when you get afraid. On the other hand, if you have been pushing nonstop for a while, take a break completely, relax, and then push again.

Get together with a friend and talk about your dreams. In talking about them, they seem possible. And in hearing yourself say them out loud, you can test how you really feel about them. Then you can discover the central dream—the one that will drive you.

---

*Where I was born and how I have lived is unimportant. It is what I have done with where I have been that should be of interest.*

Georgia O'Keeffe

You will find endless resources inside yourself. Get inside yourself and find out what the dream is, and then do it. Stir yourself up. Go for it.

The fact is, if you don't try, no one will care anyway. The only reason to do it is for yourself—so you can take your rightful place in the universe. The only reason to do it is because we each have our place, and it seems a shame to be born and then to die without doing our part.

---

*We are all controlled by the world in which we live. . . . The question is this: are we to be controlled by accidents, by tyrants, or by ourselves?*

B. F. Skinner

The world is big. There are many options; some job hunters try to investigate them all. Instead, begin with yourself. Understand that part. Then look at some options and test them against what you are. You can hold on to that as a sure thing. You can depend on what you are for stability.

A former client called me today. When I first met him, he had been out of work for a year. Now he was calling, a few years later, to say that he had received a big promotion at his company. He has found his niche and has never been happier. Everyone notices it. And he keeps on networking—keeps on enjoying the process.

The world keeps changing. It won't stop. We must change, too. We are the dreamers of dreams.

---

*I am larger, better than I thought,*
*I did not know I held so much goodness.*

Walt Whitman

*We are the music-makers,*
*And we are the dreamers of dreams . . .*
*Yet we are the movers and shakers*
*of the world for ever, it seems.*

Arthur O'Shaughnessy,
"Music and Moonlight"

*Far better it is to dare mighty things, to win glorious triumphs, even though checkered by failure, than to take rank with those poor spirits who neither enjoy much nor suffer much, because they live in the gray twilight that knows not victory nor defeat.*

Theodore Roosevelt

PART SIX

# What Is The Five O'Clock Club?

## AMERICA'S PREMIER CAREER-COACHING NETWORK

# How to Join the Club

***The Five O'Clock Club:
America's Premier
Career-Coaching
and
Outplacement Service***

*"One organization with a long record of success in helping people find jobs is The Five O'Clock Club."*

*Fortune*

- Job-Search Strategy Groups
- Private Coaching
- Books and Audio CDs
- Membership Information
- When Your Employer Pays

**THERE *IS* A FIVE O'CLOCK CLUB NEAR YOU!**

For more information on becoming a member, please fill out the Membership Application Form in this book, sign up on the web at: www.fiveoclockclub.com, or call: **1-800-575-3587** (or **212-286-4500** in New York)

## The Five O'Clock Club Search Process

The Five O'Clock Club process, as outlined in *The Five O'Clock Club* books, is a targeted, strategic approach to career development and job search. Five O'Clock Club members become proficient at skills that prove invaluable during their *entire working lives.*

## Career Management

We train our members to *manage their careers* and always look ahead to their next job search. Research shows that an average worker spends only four years in a job—and will have 12 jobs in as many as 5 career fields—during his or her working life.

## Getting Jobs . . . Faster

Five O'Clock Club members find *better jobs, faster.* The average professional, manager, or executive Five O'Clock Club member who regularly attends weekly sessions finds a job by his or her 10th session. Even the discouraged, long-term job searcher can find immediate help.

The keystone to The Five O'Clock Club process is teaching our members an understanding of the entire hiring process. A first interview is primarily a time for exchanging critical information. The real work starts *after* the interview. We teach our members *how to turn job interviews into offers* and to negotiate the best possible employment package.

## Setting Targets

The Five O'Clock Club is action oriented. *We'll help you decide what you should do this very next week to move your search along.* By their third session, our members have set definite job targets by industry or company size, position, and geographic area, and are out in the field gathering information and making contacts that will lead to interviews with hiring managers.

*Our approach evolves* with the changing job market. We're able to synthesize information from hundreds of Five O'Clock Club members and come up with new approaches for our members. For example, we now discuss temporary placement for executives, how to use voice mail and the Internet, and how to network when doors are slamming shut all over town.

## The Five O'Clock Club Strategy Program

The Five O'Clock Club meeting is a carefully planned *job-search strategy program*. We provide members with the tools and tricks necessary to get a good job fast—even in a tight market. Networking and emotional support are also included in the meeting.

Participate in 10 *consecutive* small-group strategy sessions to enable your group and career coach to get to know you and to develop momentum in your search.

## Weekly Presentations via Audio CDs

Prior to each week's teleconference, listen to the assigned audio presentation covering part of The Five O'Clock Club methodology. These are scheduled on a rotating basis so you may join the Club at any time. (In selected cities, presentations are given in person rather than via audio CDs.)

## Small-Group Strategy Sessions

During the first few minutes of the teleconference, your small group discusses the topic of the week and hears from people who have landed jobs. Then you have the chance to get feedback and advice on your own search strategy, listen to and learn from others, and build your network. All groups are led by trained career coaches with years of experience. The small group is generally no more than six to eight people, so everyone gets the chance to speak up.

---

*Let us consider how we may spur one another on toward love and good deeds. Let us not give up meeting together, as some are in the habit of doing, but let us encourage one another.*

Hebrews 10:24–25

## Private Coaching

You may meet with your small-group coach—or another coach—for private coaching by phone or in person. A coach helps you develop a career path, solve current job problems, prepare your résumé, or guide your search.

Many members develop long-term relationships with their coaches to get advice throughout their careers. If you are paying for the coaching yourself (as opposed to having your employer pay), please pay the coach directly (charges vary from $100 to $175 per hour). **Private coaching is *not* included in The Five O'Clock Club seminar or membership fee.** For coach matching, see our website or call **1-800-575-3587** (or **212-286-4500** in New York).

### From the Club History, Written in the 1890s

At The Five O'Clock Club, [people] of all shades of political belief—as might be said of all trades and creeds—have met together. . . . The variety continues almost to a monotony. . . . [The Club's] good fellowship and geniality—not to say hospitality—has reached them all.

It has been remarked of clubs that they serve to level rank. If that were possible in this country, it would probably be true, if leveling rank means the appreciation of people of equal abilities as equals; but in The Five O'Clock Club it has been a most gratifying and noteworthy fact that no lines have ever been drawn save those which are essential to the honor and good name of any association. Strangers are invited by the club or by any members, [as gentlepeople], irrespective of aristocracy, plutocracy or occupation, and are so treated always. Nor does the thought of a [person's] social position ever enter into the meetings. People of wealth and people of moderate means sit side by side, finding in each other much to praise and admire and little to justify snarlishness or adverse criticism. People meet as people—not as the representatives of a set—and having so met, dwell not in worlds of envy or distrust, but in union and collegiality, forming kindly thoughts of each other in their heart of hearts.

In its methods, The Five O'Clock Club is plain, easy-going and unconventional. It has its "isms" and some peculiarities of procedure, but simplicity characterizes them all. The sense of propriety, rather than rules of order, governs its meetings, and that informality which carries with it sincerity of motive and spontaneity of effort, prevails within it. Its very name indicates informality, and, indeed, one of the reasons said to have induced its adoption was the fact that members or guests need not don their dress suits to attend the meetings, if they so desired. This informality, however, must be distinguished from the informality of Bohemianism. For The Five O'Clock Club, informality, above convenience, means sobriety, refinement of thought and speech, good breeding and good order. To this sort of informality much of its success is due.

***Fortune, The New York Times, Black Enterprise, Business Week,* NPR, CNBC and ABC-TV are some of the places you've seen, heard, or read about us.**

## The Schedule

See our website for the specific dates for each topic. All groups use a similar schedule in each time zone.

Fee: $49 annual membership (includes Beginners Kit, subscription to *The Five O'Clock News,* and access to the Members Only section of our website), **plus** session fees based on member's income (price for the Insider Program includes audio-CD lectures, which retails for $150).

Reservations required for first session. Unused sessions are transferable to anyone you choose or can be donated to members attending more than 16 sessions who are having financial difficulty.

The Five O'Clock Club's programs are geared to recent graduates, professionals, managers, and executives from a wide variety of industries and professions. Most earn from $30,000 to $400,000 per year. Half the members are employed; half are unemployed. ***You will be in a group of your peers.***

**To register, please fill out form on the web (at www.fiveoclockclub.com) or call 1-800-575-3587**
(or **212-286-4500** in New York).

## Lecture Presentation Schedule

- History of the 5OCC
- The 5OCC Approach to Job Search
- Developing New Targets for Your Search
- Two-Minute Pitch: Keystone of Your Search

- Using Research and Internet for Your Search
- The Keys to Effective Networking
- Getting the Most Out of Your Contacts
- Getting Interviews: Direct/Targeted Mail
- Beat the Odds When Using Search Firms and Ads
- Developing New Momentum in Your Search
- The 5OCC Approach to Interviewing
- Advanced Interviewing Techniques
- How to Handle Difficult Interview Questions
- How to Turn Job Interviews into Offers
- Successful Job Hunter's Report
- Four-Step Salary-Negotiation Method

All groups run continuously. Dates are posted on our website. The textbooks used by all members of The Five O'Clock Club may be ordered on our website or purchased at major bookstores.

**The original Five O'Clock Club was formed in Philadelphia in 1883. It was made up of the leaders of the day who shared their experiences "in a spirit of fellowship and good humor."**

# Questions You May Have about the Weekly Job-Search Strategy Group

Job hunters are not always the best judges of what they need during a search. For example, most are interested in lectures on answering ads on the Internet or working with search firms. We cover those topics, but strategically they are relatively unimportant in an effective job search.

At The Five O'Clock Club, you get the information you really need in your search—*such as how to target more effectively, how to get more interviews, and how to turn job interviews into offers.*

What's more, you will work in a small group with the best coaches in the business. In these strategy sessions, your group will help you decide what to do, this week and every week, to move your search along. You will learn by being coached and by coaching others in your group.

---

*We find ourselves not independently of other people and institutions but through them. We never get to the bottom of our selves on our own. We discover who we are face to face and side by side with others in work, love, and learning.*

Robert N. Bellah, et al., *Habits of the Heart*

**Here are a few other points:**

- For best results, attend on a regular basis. Your group gets to know you and will coach you to eliminate whatever you may be doing wrong—or refine what you are doing right.
- The Five O'Clock Club is a members-only organization. To get started in the small-group teleconference sessions, you must purchase a minimum of 10 sessions.
- The teleconference sessions include the set of 16 audio-CD presentations on Five O'Clock Club methodology. In-person groups do not include CDs.
- After that, you may purchase blocks of 5 or 10 sessions.
- We sell multiple sessions to make administration easier.
- If you miss a session, you may make it up any time. You may even transfer unused time to a friend.
- Although many people find jobs quickly (even people who have been unemployed a long time), others have more difficult searches. Plan to be in it for the long haul and you'll do better.

Carefully read all of the material in this section. It will help you decide whether or not to attend.

- The first week, pay attention to the strategies used by the others in your group. Soak up all the information you can.
- Read the books before you come in the second week. They will help you move your search along.

**To register:**

1. Read this section and fill out the application.
2. After you become a member and get your Beginners Kit, call to reserve a space for the first time you attend.

To assign you to a career coach, we need to know:

- your current (or last) field or industry
- the kind of job you would like next (if you know)
- your desired salary range in general terms

For private coaching, we suggest you attend the small group and ask to see your group leader to give you continuity.

---

*The Five O'Clock Club is plain, easy-going and unconventional. . . . Members or guests need not don their dress suits to attend the meetings.*

(From the Club History, written in the 1890s)

## What Happens at the Meetings?

*Each week,* job searchers from various industries and professions meet in small groups. The groups specialize in professionals, managers, executives, or recent college graduates. Usually, half are employed and half are unemployed.

The weekly program is in two parts. First, there is a lecture on some aspect of The Five O'Clock Club methodology. Then, job hunters meet in small groups headed by senior full-time professional career coaches.

*The first week,* get the textbooks, listen to the lecture, and get assigned to your small group. During your first session, *listen* to the others in your group. You learn a lot by listening to how your peers are strategizing *their* searches.

*By the second week,* you will have read the materials. Now we can start to work on *your* search strategy and help *you* decide what to do next to move your search along. For example, we'll help you figure out how to get more interviews in your target area or how to turn interviews into job offers.

*In the third week,* you will see major progress made by other members of your group and you may notice major progress in your own search as well.

*By the third or fourth week,* most members are conducting full and effective searches. Over the remaining weeks, you will tend to keep up a full search rather than go after only one or two leads. You will regularly aim to have 6 to 10 things *in the works* at all times. These will generally be in specific target areas you have identified, will keep your search on target, and will increase your chances of getting multiple job offers from which to choose.

Those who stick with the process find it works.

Some people prefer to just listen for a few weeks before they start their job search and that's okay, too.

## How Much Does It Cost?

*It is against the policy of The Five O'Clock Club to charge individuals heavy up-front fees.* Our competitors charge $4,000 to $6,000 or more, up front. Our average fee is $360 for 10 sessions (which includes audio CDs of 16 presentations for those in the teleconference program). Those in the $100,000+ range pay an average of $540 for 10 sessions. For administrative reasons, we charge for 5 or 10 additional sessions at a time.

You must have the books so you can begin studying them before the second session. (You can purchase them on our website or at major bookstores.) If you don't do the homework, you will tend to waste the time of others in the group by asking questions covered in the texts.

## Is the Small Group Right for Me?

The Five O'Clock Club process is for you if:

- You are truly interested in job hunting.
- You have *some* idea of the kind of job you want.
- You are a professional, manager, or executive—or want to be.
- You want to participate in a group process on a regular basis.

- You realize that finding or changing jobs and careers is hard work, but you are absolutely willing and able to do it.

*If you have no idea about the kind of job you want next,* you may attend one or two group sessions to start. *Then* see a *coach privately* for one or two sessions, develop tentative job targets, and return to the group. You may work with your small-group coach or contact us through our website or by calling **1-800-575-3587** (or **212-286-4500** in New York) for referral to another coach.

## How Long Will It Take Me to Get a Job?

Although our members tend to be from fields or industries where they expect to have difficult searches, *the average person who attends regularly finds a new position within 10 sessions.* Some take less time and others take more.

One thing we know for sure: **Research shows that those who get *regular* coaching during their searches get jobs faster and at higher rates of pay than those who search on their own or simply take a course.** This makes sense. If a person comes only when they think they have a problem, they are usually wrong. They probably had a problem a few weeks ago but didn't realize it. Or the problem may be different from the one they thought they had. Those who come regularly benefit from the observations others make about their searches. Problems are solved before they become severe or are prevented altogether.

Those who attend regularly also learn a lot by paying attention and helping others in the group. This *secondhand* learning can shorten your search by weeks. When you hear the problems of others who are ahead of you in the search, you can avoid them completely. People in your group will come to know you and will point out subtleties you may not have noticed that interviewers will never tell you.

## Will I Be with Others from My Field/Industry?

Probably, but it's not that important. If you are a salesperson, for example, would you want to be with seven other salespeople? Probably not. You will learn a lot and have a much more creative search if you are in a group of people who are in your general salary range but not exactly like you. Our clients are from virtually every field and industry. The *process* is what will help you.

We've been doing this since 1978 and understand your needs. That's why the mix we provide is the best you can get.

## Career Coaching Firms Charge $4,000–$6,000 Up Front. How Can You Charge Such a Small Fee?

1. We have no advertising costs, because 90 percent of those who attend have been referred by other members.

   A hefty up-front fee would bind you to us, but we have been more successful by treating people ethically and having them pretty much *pay as they go.*

   We need a certain number of people to cover expenses. When lots of people get jobs quickly and leave us, we could go into the red. But as long as members refer others, we will continue to provide this service at a fair price.
2. We focus strictly on *job-search strategy,* and encourage our clients to attend free support groups if they need emotional support. We focus on getting *jobs,* which reduces the time clients spend with us and the amount they pay.
3. We attract the best coaches, and our clients make more progress per session than they would elsewhere, which also reduces their costs.
4. We have expert administrators and a sophisticated computer system that reduces our overhead and increases our ability to track your progress.

## May I Change Coaches?

Yes. Great care is taken in assigning you to your initial coach. However, if you want to change once for any reason, you may do it. We don't encourage group hopping: It is better for you to stick with a group so that everyone gets to know you. On the other hand, we want you to feel comfortable. So if you tell us you prefer a different group, you will be transferred immediately.

## What If I Have a Quick Question Outside of the Group Session?

Some people prefer to see their group coach privately. Others prefer to meet with a different coach to get another point of view. Whatever you decide, remember that the group fee does *not* cover coaching time outside the group session. Therefore, if you wanted to speak with a coach between sessions—even for *quick questions*—you would normally meet with the coach first for a private session so he or she can get to know you better. *Easy, quick questions* are usually more complicated than they appear. After your first private session, some coaches will allow you to pay in advance for one hour of coaching time, which you can then use for quick questions by phone (usually a 15-minute minimum is charged). Since each coach has an individual way of operating, find out how the coach arranges these things.

## What If I Want to Start My Own Business?

The process of becoming a consultant is essentially the same as job hunting and lots of consultants attend Five O'Clock Club meetings. However, if you want to buy a franchise or existing business or start a growth business, you should see a private coach.

## How Can I Be Sure That The Five O'Clock Club Small-Group Sessions Will Be Right for Me?

Before you actually participate in any of the small-group sessions, you can get an idea of the quality of our service by listening to all 16 audio CDs that you purchased. If you are dissatisfied with the CDs for any reason, return the package within 30 days for a full refund.

Whatever you decide, just remember: *It has been proven that those who receive regular help during their searches get jobs faster and at higher rates of pay than those who search on their own or simply attend a course.* If you get a job just one or two weeks faster because of this program, it will have more than paid for itself. And you may *transfer unused sessions to anyone you choose.* However, the person you choose must be or become a member.

# When Your Employer Pays

*Does your employer care about you and others whom they ask to leave the organization?* If so, ask them to consider The Five O'Clock Club for your outplacement help. The Five O'Clock Club puts you and your job search first, offering a career-coaching program of the highest quality at the lowest possible price to your employer.

## Over 25 Years of Research

The Five O'Clock Club was started in 1978 as a research-based organization. Job hunters tried various techniques and reported their results back to the group. We developed a variety of guidelines so job hunters could choose the techniques best for them.

The methodology was tested and refined on professionals, managers, and executives (and those aspiring to be) from all occupations. Annual salaries ranged from $30,000 to $400,000; 50 percent were employed and 50 percent were unemployed.

Since its beginning, The Five O'Clock Club has tracked trends. Over time, our advice has changed as the job market has changed. What worked in the past is insufficient for today's job market. Today's Five O'Clock Club promotes all our relevant original strategies—and so much more.

*As an employee-advocacy organization,* The Five O'Clock Club focuses on providing the services and information that the job hunter needs most.

## Get the Help You Need Most: 100 Percent Coaching

There's a myth in outplacement circles that a terminated employee just needs a desk, a phone, and minimal career coaching. **Our experience clearly shows that downsized workers need qualified, reliable coaching more than anything else.**

Most traditional outplacement packages last only 3 months. The average executive gets office space and only 5 hours of career coaching during this time. Yet the service job hunters need most is the career coaching itself—not a desk and a phone.

Most professionals, managers, and executives are right in the thick of negotiations with prospective employers at the 3-month mark. Yet that is precisely when traditional outplacement ends, leaving job hunters stranded and sometimes ruining deals.

It is astonishing how often job hunters and employers alike are impressed by the databases of *job postings* claimed by outplacement firms. Yet only 10 percent of all jobs are filled through ads and another 10 percent are filled through search firms. Instead, direct contact and networking—done The Five O'Clock Club way—are more effective for most searches.

## You Get a Safety Net

**Imagine getting a package that protects you for a full year.** Imagine knowing you can come back if your new job doesn't work out—even months later. Imagine trying consulting work if you like. If you later decide it's not for you, you can come back to The Five O'Clock Club.

We can offer you a safety net of one full year's career coaching because our method is so effective that few people actually need more than 10 weeks in our proven program. But you're protected for a year.

## You'll Job Search with Those Who Are Employed—How Novel!

Let's face it. It can be depressing to spend your days at an outplacement firm where everyone is unemployed. At The Five O'Clock Club, half the attendees are working, and this makes the atmosphere cheerier and helps to move your search along.

What's more, you'll be in a small group of your peers, all of whom are using The Five O'Clock Club method. Our research proves that those who attend the small group regularly and use The Five O'Clock Club methods get jobs faster and at higher rates of pay than those who only work privately with a career coach throughout their searches.

## So Many Poor Attempts

Nothing is sadder than meeting someone who has already been getting job-search *help,* but the wrong kind. They've learned the traditional techniques that are no longer effective. Most have poor résumés and inappropriate targets and don't know how to turn job interviews into offers.

## You'll Get Quite a Package

You'll get up to 14 hours of private coaching—well in excess of what you would get at a traditional outplacement firm. You may even want to use a few hours after you start your new job.

And you get up to one full year of small-group career coaching. In addition, you get books, audio CDs, and other helpful materials.

## To Get Started

The day your human resources manager calls us authorizing Five O'Clock Club outplacement, we will immediately ship you the books, CDs, and other materials and assign you to a private coach and a small group.

Then we'll monitor your search. Frankly, we care about you more than we care about your employer. And since your employer cares about you, they're glad we feel this way—because they know we'll take care of you.

**What They Say about Us**

*The Five O'Clock Club product is much better, far more useful than my outplacement package.*

Senior executive and Five O'Clock Club member

*The Club kept the juices flowing. You're told what to do, what not to do. There were fresh ideas. I went through an outplacement service that, frankly, did not help. If they had done as much as the Five O'Clock Club did, I would have landed sooner.*

Another member

**When Your *Employer* Pays for The Five O'Clock Club, *You* Get:**

- **Up to 14 hours of guaranteed private career coaching** to determine a career direction, develop a résumé, plan salary negotiations, and so on. In fact, if you need a second opinion during your search, we can arrange that too.
- Up to **ONE YEAR of small-group teleconference coaching** (average about 5 or 6 participants in a group) headed by a senior Five O'Clock Club career consultant. That way, if you lose your next job, you can come back. Or if you want to try consulting work and then decide you **don't like it, you can come back**.
- **Two-year membership** in The Five O'Clock Club: Beginners Kit and two-year subscription to *The Five O'Clock News*.
- **The complete set of our four books** for professionals, managers, and executives who are in job search.
- **A boxed set of 16 audio CDs** of Five O'Clock Club presentations.

## COMPARISON OF EMPLOYER-PAID PACKAGES

| Typical Package | Traditional Outplacement | The Five O'Clock Club |
|---|---|---|
| Who is the client? | The organization | Job hunters. We are employee advocates. We always do what is in the best interest of job hunters. |
| The clientele | All are unemployed | Half of our attendees are unemployed; half are employed. There is an upbeat atmosphere; networking is enhanced. |
| Length/type of service | 3 months, primarily office space | 1 year, exclusively career coaching |
| Service ends | After 3 months—or *before* if the client lands a job or consulting assignment | After 1 full year, no matter what.<br>You can return if you lose your next job, if your assignment ends, or if you need advice after starting your new job. |
| Small-group coaching | Sporadic for 3 months<br>Coach varies | Every week for up to 1 year; same coach |
| Private coaching | 5 hours on average | Up to 14 hours guaranteed (depending on level of service purchased) |
| Support materials | Generic manual | • 4 textbooks based on over 25 years of job-search research<br>• Sixteen 40-minute lectures on audio CDs<br>• Beginners Kit of search information<br>• 2-year subscription to the Five O'Clock Club magazine, devoted to career-management articles |
| Facilities | Cubicle, phone, computer access | None; use home phone and computer |

# The Way We Are

*The Five O'Clock Club means sobriety, refinement of thought and speech, good breeding and good order. To this, much of its success is due. The Five O'Clock Club is easy-going and unconventional. A sense of propriety, rather than rules of order, governs its meetings.*

J. Hampton Moore, *History of The Five O'Clock Club* (written in the 1890s)

Just like the members of the original Five O'Clock Club, today's members want an ongoing relationship. George Vaillant, in his seminal work on successful people, found that "what makes or breaks our luck seems to be . . . our sustained relationships with other people." (George E. Vaillant, *Adaptation to Life,* Harvard University Press, 1995)

Five O'Clock Club members know that much of the program's benefit comes from simply showing up. Showing up will encourage you to do what you need to do when you are not here. And over the course of several weeks, certain things will become evident that are not evident now.

Five O'Clock Club members learn from each other: The group leader is not the only one with answers. The leader brings factual information to the meetings and keeps the discussion in line. But the answers to some problems may lie within you or with others in the group.

Five O'Clock Club members encourage each other. They listen, see similarities with their own situations, and learn from that. And they listen to see how they may help others. You may come across information or a contact that could help someone else in the group. Passing on that information is what we're all about.

If you are a new member here, listen to others to learn the process. And read the books so you will know the basics that others already know. When everyone understands the basics, this keeps the meetings on a high level, interesting, and helpful to everyone.

Five O'Clock Club members are in this together, but they know that ultimately they are each responsible for solving their own problems with God's help. Take the time to learn the process, and you will become better at analyzing your own situation, as well as the situations of others. You will be learning a method that will serve you the rest of your life, and in areas of your life apart from your career.

Five O'Clock Club members are kind to each other. They control their frustrations because venting helps no one. Because many may be stressed, be kind and go the extra length to keep this place calm and happy. It is your respite from the world outside and a place for you to find comfort and FUN. Relax and enjoy yourself, learn what you can, and help where you can. And have a ball doing it.

---

*There arises from the hearts of busy [people] a love of variety, a yearning for relaxation of thought as well as of body, and a craving for a generous and spontaneous fraternity.*

J. Hampton Moore, *History of The Five O'Clock Club*

# Lexicon Used at The Five O'Clock Club

Use The Five O'Clock Club lexicon as a shorthand to express where you are in your job search. It will focus you and those in your group.

## I. Overview and Assessment

**How many hours a week are you spending on your search?**
Spend 35 hours on a full-time search, 15 hours on a part-time search.

**What are your job targets?**

Tell the group. A target includes industry or company size, position, and geographic area.

The group can help assess how good your targets are. Take a look at *Measuring Your Targets.*

**How does your résumé position you?**

The summary and body should make you look appropriate to your target.

**What are your backup targets?**

Decide at the beginning of the search before the first campaign. Then you won't get stuck.

**Have you done the Assessment?**

If your targets are wrong, everything is wrong. (Do the Assessment in *Targeting a Great Career.*) Or a counselor can help you privately to determine possible job targets.

## II. Getting Interviews

**How large is your target (e.g., 30 companies)? How many of them have you contacted?**
Contact them all.

**How can you get (more) leads?**

You will not get a job through search firms, ads, networking, or direct contact. Those are techniques for getting interviews—job leads. Use the right terminology, especially after a person gets a job. Do not say, "How did you get the job?" if you really want to know "Where did you get the lead for that job?"

**Do you have 6 to 10 things in the works?**

You may want the group to help you land one job. After they help you with your strategy, they should ask, "How many other things do you have in the works?" If *none,* the group can brainstorm how you can get more things going: through search firms, ads, networking, or direct contact. Then you are more likely to turn the job you want into an offer because you will seem more valuable. What's more, 5 will fall away through no fault of your own. Don't go after only 1 job.

**How's your Two-Minute Pitch?**

Practice a *tailored* Two-Minute Pitch. Tell the group the job title and industry of the hiring manager they should pretend they are for a role-playing exercise. You will be surprised how good the group is at critiquing pitches. (Practice a few weeks in a row.) Use your pitch to separate you from your competition.

**You seem to be in Stage One (or Stage Two or Stage Three) of your search.**

Know where you are. This is the key measure of your search.

**Are you seen as an insider or an outsider?**

See *How to Change Careers* for becoming an insider. If people are saying, "I wish I had an opening for someone like you," you are doing well in meetings. If the industry is strong, then it's only a matter of time before you get a job.

## III. Turning Interviews into Offers

**Do you want this job?**

If you do not want the job, perhaps you want an offer, if only for practice. If you are not willing to go for it, the group's suggestions will not work.

**Who are your likely competitors and how can you outshine and outlast them?**

You will not get a job simply because "they liked me." The issues are deeper. Ask the interviewer: "Where are you in the hiring process? What kind of person would be your ideal candidate? How do I stack up?"

**What are your next steps?**

What are *you* planning to do if the hiring manager doesn't call by a certain date or what are you planning to do to assure that the hiring manager *does* call you?

**Can you prove you can do the job?**

Don't just take the *trust me* approach. Consider your competition.

**Which job positions you best for the long run? Which job is the best fit?**

Don't decide only on the basis of salary. You will most likely have another job after this. See which job looks best on your résumé and will make you stronger for the next time. In addition, find a fit for your personality. If you don't *fit,* it is unlikely you will do well there. The group can help you turn interviews into offers and give you feedback on which job is best for you.

*"Believe me, with self-examination and a lot of hard work with our coaches, you can find the job . . . you can have the career . . . you can live the life you've always wanted!"*

Sincerely,
Kate Wendleton

## Membership

**As a member of The Five O'Clock Club, you get:**

- A year's subscription to *The Five O'Clock News*—10 issues filled with information on career development and job-search techniques, focusing on the experiences of real people.
- Access to *reasonably priced* weekly seminars featuring individualized attention to your specific needs in small groups supervised by our senior coaches.
- Access to one-on-one coaching to help you answer specific questions, solve current job problems, prepare your résumé, or take an in-depth look at your career path. You choose the coach and pay the coach directly.
- An attractive Beginners Kit containing information based on over 25 years of research on who gets jobs . . . and why . . . that will enable you to improve your job-search techniques—immediately!
- The opportunity to exchange ideas and experiences with other job searchers and career changers.

**All that access, all that information, all that expertise for the annual membership fee of only $49, plus seminar fees.**

### How to become a member—by mail or E-mail:

Send your name, address, phone number, how you heard about us, and your check for $49 (made payable to "The Five O'Clock Club") to The Five O'Clock Club, 300 East 40th Street - Suite 6L, New York, NY 10016, or sign up at www.fiveoclockclub.com.

We will immediately mail you a Five O'Clock Club Membership Card, the Beginners Kit, and information on our seminars followed by our magazine. Then, call **1-800-575-3587** (or **212-286-4500** in New York) or e-mail us (at info@fiveoclockclub.com) to:

- reserve a space for the first time you plan to attend, or
- be matched with a Five O'Clock Club coach.

# Membership Application

## The Five O'Clock Club

☐ **Yes! I want to become a member!**
I want access to the most effective methods for finding jobs, as well as for developing and managing my career.

I enclose my check for $49 for 1 year; $75 for 2 years—payable to *The Five O'Clock Club*. I will receive a Beginners Kit, a subscription to *The Five O'Clock News*, access to the Members Only area on our website, and a network of career coaches. Reasonably priced seminars are held across the country.

Name: ______________________________

Address: ______________________________

City: ____________________ State: ________ Zip: ____________

Work phone: ( ________ ) ______________________________

Home phone: ( ________ ) ______________________________

E-mail: ____________________

Date: ____________________

How I heard about the Club: ______________________________

**Launching the Right Career**
The following *optional* information is for statistical purposes. Thanks for your help.

Salary range:

☐ under $30,000 ☐ $30,000–$49,999 ☐ $50,000–$74,999

☐ $75,000–$99,999 ☐ $100,000–$125,000 ☐ over $125,000

Age: ☐ 20–29 ☐ 30–39 ☐ 40–49 ☐ 50+

Gender: ☐ Male ☐ Female

Current or most recent position/title: ______________________________

Please send to:
Membership Director, The Five O'Clock Club,
300 East 40th St.-Suite 6L, New York, NY 10016

*The original Five O'Clock Club® was formed in Philadelphia in 1893. It was made up of the leaders of the day who shared their experiences "in a setting of fellowship and good humor."*

# Index

## D



## E



## F

## G



## H



## I



## J



## K

## Q



## R



## S

## About the Author

Kate Wendleton is a nationally syndicated columnist and a respected authority and speaker on career development, having appeared on the *Today Show,* CNN, CNBC, *The Larry King Show,* National Public Radio, and CBS, and in *The Economist, The New York Times, The Chicago Tribune, The Wall Street Journal, Fortune* magazine, *Business Week,* and other national media.

She has been a career coach since 1978, when she founded The Five O'Clock Club and developed its methodology to help job hunters and career changers of all levels in job-search strategy groups. This methodology is now used by branches of The Five O'Clock Club that meet weekly in the United States and Canada.

Kate also founded Workforce America, a not-for-profit affiliate of The Five O'Clock Club that ran for 10 years. It served adults in Harlem who were not yet in the professional or managerial ranks. Workforce America helped adults in Harlem move into better-paying, higher-level positions as they improved their educational level and work experience.

Kate founded, and directed for seven years, The Career Center at The New School for Social Research in New York. She also advises major corporations about employee career-development programs and coaches senior executives.

A former CFO of two small companies, she has 20 years of business-management experience in both manufacturing and service businesses.

Kate attended Chestnut Hill College in Philadelphia and received her MBA from Drexel University. She is a popular speaker for associations, corporations, and colleges.

When she lived in Philadelphia, Kate did long-term volunteer work for the Philadelphia Museum of Art, the Walnut Street Theatre Art Gallery, United Way, and the YMCA. Kate currently lives in Manhattan with her husband.

Kate Wendleton is the author of The Five O'Clock Club's four-part career-development and job-hunting series, among other books.

## About The Five O'Clock Club and the "Fruytagie" Canvas

Five O'Clock Club members are special. We attract upbeat, ambitious, dynamic, intelligent people—and that makes it fun for all of us. Most of our members are professionals, managers, executives, consultants, and freelancers. We also include recent college graduates and those aiming to get into the professional ranks, as well as people in their 40s, 50s, and even 60s. Most members' salaries range from $30,000 to $400,000 (one-third of our members earn in excess of $100,000 a year). For those who cannot attend a Club, *The Five O'Clock Club Book Series* contains all of our methodologies—and our spirit.

### The Philosophy of The Five O'Clock Club

The "Fruytagie" Canvas by Patricia Kelly, depicted here, symbolizes our philosophy. The original, which is actually 52.5" by 69" inches, hangs in the offices of The Five O'Clock Club in Manhattan. It is reminiscent of popular 16th century Dutch "fruytagie," or fruit tapestries, which depicted abundance and prosperity.

I was attracted to this piece because it seemed to fit the spirit of our people at The Five O'Clock Club. This was confirmed when the artist, who was not aware of what I did for a living, added these words to the canvas: "The garden is abundant, prosperous and magical." Later, it took me only 10 minutes to write the blank verse "The Garden of Life," because it came from my heart. The verse reflects our philosophy and describes the kind of people who are members of the Club.

I'm always inspired by Five O'Clock Clubbers. They show others the way through their quiet behavior . . . their kindness . . . their generosity . . . their hard work . . . under God's care.

We share what we have with others. We are in this lush, exciting place together—with our brothers and sisters—and reach out for harmony. The garden is abundant. The job market is exciting. And Five O'Clock Clubbers believe that there is enough for everyone.

### About the Artist's Method

To create her tapestry-like art, Kelly developed a unique style of stenciling. She hand-draws and hand-cuts each stencil, both in the negative and positive for each image. Her elaborate technique also includes a lengthy multilayering process incorporating Dutch metal leaves and gilding, numerous transparent glazes, paints, and wax pencils.

Kelly also paints the back side of the canvas using multiple washes of reds, violets, and golds. She uses this technique to create a heavy vibration of color, which in turn reflects the color onto the surface of the wall against which the canvas hangs.

The canvas is suspended by a heavy braided silk cord threaded into large brass grommets inserted along the top. Like a tapestry, the hemmed canvas is attached to a gold-gilded dowel with finials. The entire work is hung from a sculpted wall ornament.

Our staff is inspired every day by the tapestry and by the members of The Five O'Clock Club. We all work hard—and have FUN! The garden *is* abundant—with enough for everyone.

We wish you lots of success in your career. We—and your fellow members of The Five O'Clock Club—will work with you on it.

—Kate Wendleton, President

---

*The original Five O'Clock Club was formed in Philadelphia in 1883.*
*It was made up of the leaders of the day, who shared their experiences*
*"in a spirit of fellowship and good humor."*

**THE GARDEN OF LIFE IS abundant, prosperous and magical. ❦ In this garden, there is enough for everyone. ❦ Share the fruit and the knowledge ❦ Our brothers and we are in this lush, exciting place together. ❦ Let's show others the way. ❦ Kindness. Generosity. ❦ Hard work. ❦ God's care.**

# Five O'Clock C...
## Professionals, Managers and Executi...

We'll take you through your entire career. 1. Start by understanding y... what you want in **Targeting a Great Career**. 2. ***Package Yourself with a Targeted Résumé*** done The Five O'Clock Club Way. 3. Then ***Shortcut Your Job Search*** by following our techniques for getting meetings. 4. Turn those interviews into offers with ***Mastering the Job Interview*** and ***Winning the Money Game***. 5. Finally, do well in your new job with ***Navigating Your Career***.

- Figure out what to do with your life and your career
- Develop a résumé that separates you from your competitors
- Shortcut your search by using the Internet and other techniques properly
- Learn how to turn those job interviews into job offers
- Use our Four-Step Salary Negotiation Method to get what you deserve

**In... job-sea... regularly and ... unemployed up to tw... new job within only ten w...**

Most people conduct a passive job sea... Their approach is ordinary, non-directed, fragmented, and ineffective.

The Five O'Clock Club was started in 1978 as a research-based organization. The methodology was tested and refined on professionals, managers, and executives (and those aspiring to be)–from all occupations and economic levels.

Ever since the beginning, The Five O'Clock Club has tracked trends at every meeting at every at every location. Over time, our advice has changed as the job market has changed. What worked in the past is not always sufficient for today's job market. Today's Five O'Clock Club Book Series contains all the relevant old strategies–and so much more. The Five O'Clock Clubbers who do best read and re-read the books, marking them up and taking notes. Do the same and you will do better in your search.

### Launching the Right Career

Now, students, recent grads, and those who want a career instead of a job can use the same techniques used by thousands of professionals, managers and executives. Get that internship, develop a resume that gets you interviews, and learn how to interview well.

Targeting a Great Career
ISBN: 1-4180-1504-0

Packaging Yourself: The Targeted Résumé
ISBN: 1-4180-1503-2

Shortcut Your Job Search: The Best Way to Get Meetings
ISBN: 1-4180-1502-4

Mastering the Job Interview and Winning the Money Game
ISBN: 1-4180-1500-8

Navigating Your Career: Develop Your Plan, Manage Your Boss, Get Another Job Inside
ISBN: 1-4180-1501-6

Launching the Right Career
ISBN: 1-4180-1505-9

258 pp., 7 3/8" x 9 1/4", softcover

## About the Author:

**Kate Wendleton** is a nationally syndicated careers columnist and recognized authority on career development, having appeared on *The Today Show*, CNN, CNBC, *Larry King Live*, National Public Radio, CBS, and in the *New York Times, Chicago Tribune, Wall Street Journal, Fortune, Business Week,* and other national media. She has been a career coach since 1978 when she founded The Five O' Clock Club and developed its methodology to help job hunters and career changers at all levels. A former CFO of two small companies, Kate has twenty years of business experience, as well as an MBA.

www.delmarlearning.com

**To place an order please call:** (800) 347-7707 or fax: (859) 647-5963
**Mailing Address:** Thomson Distribution Center, Attn: Order Fulfillment, 10650 Toebben Dr., Independence, KY 41051